D1831711

SOCIO-ECONOMIC AND POLITICAL DEVELOPMENT IN SOUTH ASIA

(In 3 Volumes)

POLITICAL DEVELOPMENT IN SOUTH ASIA

(Volume-3)

Editors

Dr. T.R. Sareen,

Dr. S.R. Bakshi

ISHA BOOKS

DELHI-110 033

Socio-Economic and Political Development in South Asia

Rs. 2500 (Set)
Rs. 835 (each volume)

ISBN: 81-8205-074-X (Set)
ISBN: 81-8205-077-4 (Vol. 3)

© Dr. T.R. Sareen, Dr. S.R. Bakshi

All rights reserved. No part of this book may be reproduced in any manner without written permission.

Published in 2004 in India by
Isha Books, D-43, Prithviraj Road,
Adarsh Nagar, Delhi-110 033

Laser Typesetting at : Shree Vaishnavi Creations, Delhi
Printed at : Chawla Offset Press, Delhi

Contents

Preface

The South Asian region is unique demographically, racially, religiously, economically, socio-culturally and politically. A large segment of world population inhabits in South Asia. Though grouped under 'developing countries' manifested by many problems—poverty, hunger, overpopulation, unemployment, political instability, insurgency and social turmoil, health hazards, etc. rich biodiversity, climatic variations, exotic fauna and flora, mineral and marine resources, abode of many autochthones, and a hot bed of world politics and economy are some of the salient features of the region.

South Asia is also confronting both the positive and negative economic and cultural dimensions of globalization while coping with gross inequities in the distribution of development's benefits within society. This poses severe challenges to the region's established, though still maturing, democratic institutions, which continue to evolve as models observed by the rest of the developing world.

The book presents an in-depth analysis of political development in South Asia with a view to gaining a better understanding of the strengths and weaknesses of democratic process. The growth of democratic development, security issues, regional and international relations, etc., are described in detail. It also highlights the policies and strategies that might strengthen the future of the political development. The wide yet panoramic coverage of political development in different countries of South Asia presented in this work will serve as a reliable reference tool for scholars, policy makers and laymen equally.

Editor

1

South Asian Development: Priorities and Challenges

US-South Asian Relations: Issues and Opportunities

In a landmark development in U.S.-South Asia relations, the United States and India are getting along better than at any time since India became independent in 1947. Over the medium term, the policy challenge through 2010 is to broaden and deepen the links that bind the two countries so that their relationship will mature into a genuine partnership.

Indo-US Relations

For the United States, India-with its billion-plus population, democratic institutions and values, steadily growing economy, and substantial defense establishment-represents a partner of great value. In a few years, India will become one of the world's largest economies, the principal security factor in the Indian Ocean region, and increasingly important in the overall and uncertain Asian power equation. India has become a partner in combating terrorism and, despite past differences on nuclear issues, shares U.S. concerns about preventing the further spread of weapons of mass destruction (WMD). On the economic side, the United States stands to gain from steadily expanding ties, especially in knowledge industries in which India possesses major strengths. More cooperative U.S.-India ties can also narrow the gap between industrialized and developing countries on global issues such as trade, the environment, AIDS, and poverty alleviation. New Delhi has an equal if not greater stake in transformed relations with Washington.

As India presses ahead with its economic development, it sees good relations with the world's largest economy as a spur to more foreign direct investment, to increased trade, and to easier access to advanced technology, in particular to what Indian leaders call "the trinity" of dual-use products, renewed cooperation in nonmilitary space activities, and civilian nuclear technology. India also hopes that closer ties will further increase American sensitivity to New Delhi's key security concerns, most of all those relating to Pakistan. In the broader Asian context, cooperative security ties would serve Indian interests-like those of the United States-as a hedge were China to become an aggressive threat.

Both New Delhi and Washington have learned from past problems in dealing with each other. The United States is paying more sustained high-level attention to India. New Delhi is handling its relations with Washington in a more pragmatic and self-assured fashion. When India disagrees with U.S. policy, it says so frankly but does not go out of its way to offer gratuitous public criticism, as was often the case in the past. The two countries have learned to disagree without being disagreeable. To consolidate the "transformed" relationship, a number of important steps are needed over the medium term.

During the Cold War, India's preachy neutralism and close security ties with the Soviet Union upset Americans. Close U.S.-Pakistan security ties and the U.S. tendency to lecture others upset the Indians. New Delhi's socialist economic policies, particularly the emphasis on import substitution and reluctance to accept foreign investment, were a further impediment. Although India and the United States shared the common values inherent in democracy, the two nations often found themselves not only geographically, but politically and economically on opposite sides of the globe. This began to change in the 1990s.

- — Came the end of the Cold War and the subsequent collapse of the Soviet Union. Although India has maintained close arms-supply relations with Russia, this no longer causes serious concerns in Washington.
- — U.S.-Pakistan security ties were ruptured after sanctions were imposed against Pakistan for its nuclear program in October 1990, suspending military and economic aid. The relationship remained in the doldrums until Pakistan joined the war on terrorism after September 11, 2001.
- — 1991, when forced by circumstances, India introduced major economic reforms to reduce government controls and restrictions in a shift from socialist toward free-market policies.

Despite these developments, U.S.-India relations did not get better immediately. Memories of past problems remained a burden. Indian economic reforms stirred considerable positive U.S. interest, but bilateral frictions, especially over nuclear nonproliferation issues, continued. After India conducted nuclear tests in May 1998, relations plummeted once again. A disappointed Clinton administration imposed an array of congressionally mandated sanctions. Paradoxically, relations then improved. Even though twelve rounds of talks between U.S. Deputy Secretary of State Strobe Talbott and Indian Minister of External Affairs Jaswant Singh failed to significantly narrow differences on nuclear issues, the discussions gave New Delhi and Washington a clearer understanding of each other's viewpoints and marked the most intensive high-level U.S.-India dialogue in decades. Washington's vigorous intervention in the 1999 Kargil crisis to pressure Pakistan to withdraw its forces from the Indian side of the Line of Control (LOC) in Kashmir had a further positive impact. In 2000, President Bill Clinton's highly successful five-day visit to India and Prime Minister Vajpayee's more subdued but successful visit to the United States signaled a new, positive chapter in relations.

Soon after George W. Bush took office in 2001, he made clear his interest in continuing and intensifying the Clinton opening to India. New Delhi quickly showed interest in reciprocating. The Vajpayee government muted criticism of U.S. opposition to the Kyoto Protocol on global climate change and reacted positively to President Bush's controversial missile-defense initiative. When al-Qaeda terrorists struck on September 11, 2001, India promptly offered its full cooperation in the war on terrorism. After Pakistan joined the antiterrorist coalition and turned on its former Afghan Taliban allies, New Delhi feared that Washington would again "tilt" toward Islamabad. Even though the United States has only partially allayed these concerns, the improved relationship has not been derailed.

In response to major terrorist attacks by Pakistan-based groups between October 2001 and May 2002, India threatened military retaliation. After the United States extracted a pledge from Pakistani President Pervez Musharraf to permanently stop infiltration across the LOC, New Delhi refrained from hitting back. Washington, however, lost credibility when it failed to react strongly to Musharraf 's failure to deliver. Many Indians concluded that the Bush administration has a double standard on terrorism: one when America is the target and another when India is the victim. Although disappointed, Indian authorities have continued to pursue stronger ties with the United States. Still, Pakistan will remain a highly sensitive issue in the U.S.-India bilateral equation as long as Islamabad and New Delhi continue to be hostile neighbours.

India's handling of Iraq also reflects the desire for better relations. Although the U.S.-U.K. military action was widely unpopular in India and condemned by both houses of Parliament, the Vajpayee government muted official criticism and was careful not to align India with outspoken critics such as France, Germany, and Russia. Similarly, the government tried to avoid an outright rejection of the U.S. request for peacekeeping troops by finding a variety of diplomatic excuses not to agree-e.g., lack of an adequate UN mandate, absence of a domestic political consensus, and need for the troops in combating insurgencies within India.

India's Foreign Policy

Since the end of the Cold War, India's foreign policy has substantially evolved. Long-standing support for nonalignment and intimate security ties with the Soviet Union have lost much of their relevance. In the altered global landscape, New Delhi has sought to improve and broaden relations with as many major power centers as possible, especially, but not exclusively, with the United States. In the hopes of enlarging its room for maneuver, India has launched strategic dialogues and undertaken other initiatives with the European Union (EU) and the major nations of western Europe, with Southeast Asian countries, and with Iran and Israel. Even though India greatly values improved relations with Washington, it remains uncomfortable with the idea of a single dominant superpower. New Delhi prefers a multipolar world in which India will, in time, become a pole. Even though Indians realize that substantially more economic growth is needed to achieve great power status, they would like a permanent seat on the UN Security Council but are not currently pressing the issue. If and when there is a comprehensive restructuring of the Security Council, the United States should be prepared to give serious consideration to India's membership. New Delhi's primary foreign policy concern remains its neighbour Pakistan.

Suffice it to say here that chronic tensions, in addition to triggering three wars and periodic crises, have diminished the political role that India can play on the global stage. Until India finds a way to work out a modus vivendi with Pakistan, it is likely to face continuing difficulties in achieving international status commensurate with its aspirations.

Relations with the other nations of South Asia-Bangladesh, Nepal, Sri Lanka, the Maldives, and Bhutan-are also of key importance to New Delhi policymakers. In dealing with these countries, India has swung between acting as the regional hegemony, putting pressure on smaller capitals when they refuse to follow its lead, and at times following a "good neighbour" policy. The latter approach-known as the "Gujral Doctrine" after the policy adopted by Foreign Minister and then Prime Minister Inder K. Gujral in the mid-1990s-enabled India and Bangladesh to resolve a dispute over the Farakka Barrage that had damaged relations for several decades.

After the disintegration of the Soviet Union led to the establishment of five independent Central Asian republics, India had high hopes for closer trade and political relations with the new states. While frustrated by tensions in Afghanistan and troubles with Pakistan, these hopes have been revived since the fall of the Taliban in November 2001.

Their realization will depend on establishing viable overland transit links so that commerce in bulk can move freely between India and Central Asia. In turn, this will require a thaw in India-Pakistan economic relations and a stable Afghanistan. New Delhi has established close and friendly ties with the post-Taliban Afghan regime.India had previously provided assistance to the Northern Alliance, and many current Afghan leaders, including President Hamid Karzai, have lived in India. In addition to providing a substantial assistance program, New Delhi has established consulates in several Afghan cities, a step that dismayed Islamabad. The United States and India share common goals in a stable Afghanistan and have cooperated toward this end. It is important that they continue to do so.

Relations between India and China-the world's most populous countries share a two-thousand-kilometer border in the Himalayas—have strategic significance well beyond South Asia. As India's defeat in the 1962 border war with China has slowly receded from memory, Beijing and New Delhi have gradually improved their bilateral relations. Trade has expanded substantially. There has been a series of high-level goodwill visits, the latest by Prime Minister Vajpayee this past summer. Even though India and China have yet to settle the frontier dispute that triggered the 1962 clash, they have gradually improved other facets of their relations.

Indeed, the manner in which New Delhi and Beijing have handled their ties provides a model that India and Pakistan could usefully adopt in their bilateral dealings. India has been deeply impressed by China's dynamism and the rapid development of the Chinese economy over the past two decades. At the same time, Indians are proud of democracy and the political freedoms that are absent in China.

Strategically, New Delhi continues to regard its northern neighbour warily. Beijing's traditionally close security ties with Pakistan remain a matter of concern. Chinese assistance for Pakistan's nuclear weapons and missile programs has not been forgotten. In large part, India justified its own nuclear tests in 1998 as a response to the Chinese nuclear threat rather than the one from Pakistan. Clearly, how these two giant nations manage their relations will have a major impact on the future balance of power not only in the subcontinent but also throughout Asia and on the global scene.

Economic Development

The Indian economy can be viewed as a glass "half full" or "half empty." Despite the hesitant pursuit of reform in recent years, India's gross domestic product (GDP) has grown at a respectable 6 percent annually over the past decade. Even though India's 2002 growth of 5.8 percent remains below the peak achieved in the mid-1990s-when the country's GDP increased by more than 7 percent for three years in a row-the Indian economy is moving ahead.

Among the larger Asian economies, India's overall performance has been second only to China's. Still, India could advance significantly faster and achieve an 8-9 percent annual growth rate were the government more vigorous in introducing and implementing necessary policy and administrative reforms. Indian authorities have repeatedly spoken of the need to rationalize bankrupt state electricity boards, to reduce nonproductive subsidies, to ease restrictive labour laws, to lower bars to mass production of low-technology manufactures (where China has excelled), to accelerate the privatization of money-losing public sector enterprises, and to reduce the combined federal-state fiscal deficit (now 11 percent of GDP). In the face of opposition from special interests, the bureaucracy, and anti-foreign- and pro-public-sector sentiment from the extreme ends of the political spectrum, action on economic reforms by the ruling National Democratic Alliance (NDA) coalition, which is led by the Hindu-nationalist Bharatiya Janata Party (BJP), has fallen short of rhetoric.

The budgets for fiscal years (FYs) 2002 and 2003 took some modest steps to advance the reform agenda but represented less than a full-fledged commitment. A recent disappointment was the decision to defer introducing a national value-added sales tax in the face of opposition from the trading community. Information technology (IT) has been the bright star of the Indian economy. Even though the global computer industry remains depressed, Indian IT continues to grow at a brisk pace and now accounts for more than 3 percent of India's GDP and 16 percent of its exports. Industry turnover passed the $15 billion level in 2002, including $7.5 billion in exports. More than two-thirds of foreign sales were to the United States. Earnings abroad come mainly from software programming for the U.S. market, but computer related services-call offices and help lines, medical transcriptions, and back-office operations for financial institutions, airlines, and other large enterprises-have been booming of late. Indeed, The Economist has predicted that this sector will develop into a $17 billion industry and employ more than 1 million people by 2010. A number of factors explain this success.

— Thanks to India's first prime minister, Jawaharlal Nehru, and his emphasis on science and technology education, India has a large pool of well-trained, English-speaking computer engineers and specialists.

— Because of its relatively low wage rates, India has comparative advantage over the United States and other industrial countries in providing qualified computer engineers.

— Satellite communications directly link Indian and U.S. companies, bypassing India's poor telecommunications system.

— The IT sector had the good luck to mature in the postreform environment and has been able to operate largely free of government regulation and control.

— The presence in the United States of so many Indian-American computer specialists has aided the outsourcing of software programming and research activities to India.

Today, Microsoft, Intel, IBM, Sun Microsystems, Adobe, Oracle, Texas Instruments, and other major U.S. computer firms have significant and growing operations in India. In what is becoming an annual affair, Bill Gates paid his third visit to India in November 2002. During the trip, Gates announced a further $400 million investment by Microsoft in India.

Nuclear Issue

Nuclear nonproliferation-a decade ago the key problem in bilateral relations-has moved off center stage. Although the 1998-99 Talbott-Singh talks failed to obtain agreement on India's freezing production of fissile material, signing the Comprehensive Test Ban Treaty (CTBT), or adopting other nuclear restraints, the Bush administration has not pressed on this front except to urge stricter Indian controls over exports of materials and technology that could be used for WMD.

New Delhi agrees in principle, and talks are under way about ways to tighten India's export controls. On the CTBT, the two countries appear to be on the same page given the Bush administration's opposition to the treaty. Both continue to maintain respective moratoria on testing, but U.S. decisions on developing new types of nuclear weapons (e.g., bunker busters) could have an impact on Indian thinking. Soon after assuming office, the Bush administration upended traditional nonproliferation policy by abrogating the antiballistic missile treaty in order to develop a missile defense system. To Washington's surprise, New Delhi did not respond negatively when the president publicly unveiled the controversial concept in May 2001.

Since then, there have been periodic bilateral discussions on missile defense. In operational terms, however, the immediate issue that the Bush administration faces is Indian interest in technical discussions about the joint U.S.-Israeli Arrow missile defense system or about the U.S. Patriot system. Regarding India's own nuclear weapons, New Delhi seems set on following the recommendations of its Nuclear Security Advisory Board to develop "a minimum credible deterrent" force to meet the nuclear threat perceived from China and from Pakistan. India has not yet specified how large a force constitutes a minimum deterrent and is unlikely to do so.

In terms of nuclear doctrine, unlike Islamabad, New Delhi has declared that it will not be the first to use nuclear weapons but will employ them only in response to a nuclear attack. Barring some sort of South Asian arms agreement, India and Pakistan are almost certain to continue expanding their nuclear weapon capabilities in response to what each perceives the other is doing. This is similarly true with regard to missile-delivery systems. Thus, especially in the absence of India-Pakistan nuclear discussions and confidence-building measures (CBMs), the threat of any major conflict's going nuclear remains real.

At present, India can deliver its nuclear weapons against targets in Pakistan via French Mirage and Soviet SU-30 fighter-bombers or indigenous Agni medium-range missiles. India is working on a longer-range missile, the Agni plus, capable of striking major urban centers in eastern China. India also hopes to develop a submarine-based delivery system in order to have the third leg of a nuclear triad. Based on past experience, if India persists in the exercise, it will eventually succeed in developing a submarine-based launch capability. Funding constraints and technical difficulties, however, will surely make the process a long and drawn-out affair.

Democratic Values

India has succeeded where most developing countries have failed: in establishing and maintaining an open political system. Like that of the United States, India's democracy is based on constitutional norms, representative government, free speech, and free elections. Although pursuit of national interests remains the principal foreign and security policy driver, shared political values matter and have become an increasingly important, if intangible, component of the U.S.-India relationship. In recent years, the two countries have begun to cooperate in promoting democracy elsewhere. There is much for other nations to learn from America's and India's democratic experiences-similar in the fundamentals, but radically different in the societal and historical settings.

Domestically, major changes in the Indian political landscape during the past decade have seen the replacement of the Indian National Congress, the party that ruled the country for forty-five years, as the leading political force by the Hindu-nationalist BJP. Regional parties limited to a single state now also play a much larger role than they did previously. As neither of the major parties seems likely to win a national majority, coalition governments will probably continue in New Delhi. Apart from a promise of less corrupt and more effective governance than was the norm under the Congress Party, the BJP's principal and emotionally charged electoral plank has been its desire to promote Hindutva, or Hindu values, as the country's political and social leitmotif.

The BJP wants to substitute Hindutva for the "secular values" stressed by India's founders, especially Jawaharlal Nehru, who emphasized the importance of respect and tolerance for all religions and communities in India's pluralistic society.

How the campaign for Hindutva plays out in upcoming state and national elections and in the years beyond will have a vital impact on India's social peace and communal equilibrium-already badly shaken by the violence against Muslims in Gujarat last year. If extremists in the BJP prevail, strident Hindu chauvinism could well undermine India's cultural and political pluralism and severely impair the human rights of its 150 million Muslims, 20 million Christians, and other, smaller, minorities.

Recurrence of large-scale communal violence, such as that which followed the destruction of a mosque in Ayodhya in northern India in 1992 and savaged the state of Gujarat in 2002, could tear apart the country's fragile social fabric. Over the years, India has demonstrated enormous resiliency in containing social unrest and integrating diverse religious, ethnic, and social groups; this has been one of the greatest strengths of India's democracy. The Task Force is hopeful that Prime Minister Vajpayee and other moderates will prevail over BJP extremists.

People-to-People Ties

U.S.-India people-to-people ties have expanded tremendously in recent years. When the United States liberalised immigration laws in 1965, there were only 25,000 Indian Americans. The 2000 census counted some 1.7 million. In 2003, the total is about 2 million. Indians are by far the largest recipients of work visas: in 2002 they accounted for 43 percent of all H1-B visas issued. In academic year 2001-2002, 66,836 Indian students attended U.S. colleges and universities and India moved past China as the largest source of foreign students. The Indian-American community is extremely well educated. Eighty-seven percent have finished high school and 58 percent of those over the age of twenty-five have at least a bachelor's degree. They have been extraordinarily successful economically. In medicine, in the business world, and especially in computers and information technology, Indian Americans have excelled. Their median family income of $60,093 is the highest of any ethnic group and well above the U.S. national median of $38,885.

In many ways, Indian Americans have become an increasingly sturdy and significant bridge between the two countries, greatly enlarging U.S. understanding of India and Indian understanding of the United States. The community's success in the computer, medical, and scientific areas has also markedly improved the Indian image in this country. The image has received a further boost from the contribution of Indian authors to contemporary English literature. At the time of Indian independence in 1947, few Americans would have been able to name a single Indian author. With the exception of Nobel Prize winner Rabindranath Tagore and author

R. K. Narayan, virtually no Indian had works generally available in U.S. bookstores. Today, a host of writers from India and the diaspora (V. S.Naipaul, Anita Desai, Jhumpa Lahiri, Arundhati Roy, Amitav Ghosh, Rohinton Mistry, Salman Rushdie,Vikram Seth, and Shashi Tharoor are among the better known) have gained best seller status and many prizes for their literary achievements.

Another area where India looms much larger in the United States is on Capitol Hill. Familiar with the give-and-take of democratic politics, Indian Americans have become active participants in U.S. political life and significant financial contributors to election campaigns. Ten years ago, Representative Frank Pallone (D-NJ) took the initiative to organize a bipartisan India caucus in the House of Representatives. Reflecting the growing significance of the community, membership in the caucus has risen rapidly and, in 2003, numbers some 163-more than a third of the House of Representatives. In 2002, India's Parliament organized a parallel group, now some 80 strong, that is called the Indo-U.S. Parliamentary Forum. Delegations from the forum have twice visited Washington to meet with their counterparts, most recently in June 2003, and many India caucus members have travelled to India. In addition to having a positive influence on bilateral relations, the two parliamentary groups provide an important vehicle for Indian and U.S. politicians to gain greater understanding about each other's political process. American academic programs on India flourished in the 1950s and 1960s, but then fell off sharply during the next three decades. In part, this reflected the view that India had become relatively marginal for U.S. political and economic interests. Policy restrictions imposed by India on foreign scholars also reduced interest, and India programs and courses decreased in number and scope. In the past few years, the study of India has enjoyed a considerable revival. The desire of young Indian Americans to learn more about their heritage has been one reason.

Think tanks and research centers in Washington and elsewhere have also been showing substantially greater interest in South Asia. In the 1990s, few had regional specialists and their focus was almost entirely on nuclear nonproliferation and the threat of India-Pakistan conflict. Today, more than half a dozen of the leading centers have programs on India and South Asia that consider a broad range of political and economic as well as strategic issues. Hardly a week goes by without several South Asia programs on the Washington think-tank or public-interest circuit. Here too, Indian Americans have become an important source of financial backing. Despite the overall warming in relations, however, India's approach to academic exchanges still leaves much to be desired. Although there has been improvement, the government of India continues to pose difficulties for those interested in pursuing academic exchanges and research. Restrictive policies and the slowmoving and cumbersome administrative approval process make India a more difficult place for scholars to work than almost any other democratic country.

The result often puts off the very people who want to learn more about India and over time would bring increased understanding of India to the higher reaches of U.S. government, business, and academe. As part of the mutual effort to broaden and deepen relations, it is in India's interest to make American (and other foreign) academics and researchers more welcome by a vigorous attack on policy barriers and bureaucratic red tape. In the days of large bilateral U.S. aid programs during the 1950s and 1960s, many social and economic development activities received generous funding. As official aid tapered off to its current modest levels, the Ford Foundation became the major U.S. sponsor of these programs in India. Other U.S. foundations could do much more, especially in social-sector and health areas.

Exploring ways to use modern technology to bridge the economic and social barriers that keep so many Indians in poverty should be an exciting area for corporate cooperation and foundation efforts. In the 1960s, research funded by the Rockefeller Foundation paved the way for the "green revolution" that has enabled India to increase dramatically its food-grain production. In recent years, wealthy Indian Americans have begun to provide financial support for health, social, and antipoverty programs in their country of origin. As the community prospers in the United States, its help for cooperative programs should provide an important bilateral link. Here too, with regard to private cooperative activities, the Indian government should be making a greater effort to reduce policy and administrative roadblocks.

Pakistan represents one of the toughest and most complex policy challenges that the United States faces anywhere in the world. The record of bilateral relations of the past fifty years has been checkered and volatile and the United States has been unable on a sustained basis to accomplish its key objective: a stable Pakistan at peace with itself and its neighbours.

The challenge for U.S. policy over the medium term is to develop and maintain a positive relationship that helps Pakistan become "a modern, progressive, and dynamic" nation, as President Pervez Musharraf put it in January 2002. The United States must have clear objectives and policies, be willing to use its influence, and devote substantial assistance resources in improving the prospects for Pakistan's success. Its national failure would have enormous costs for the entire region and the Muslim world at large and put at risk vital U.S. stakes in a stable and peaceful Afghanistan, in the developing partnership with India, and in winning the war on terrorism. The United States needs to take a fresh look at its approach to Pakistan.

This almost entirely Muslim country of 145 million people-a population the size of Russia's-has been plagued by chronic political instability, lack of a clear sense of national identity, sub-par economic performance, and deteriorating institutions. Even though the economy has recently improved, severe educational, health, and unemployment challenges remain. Enmity with neighbouring (and seven times more populous) India dominates national security policy and has spurred extremely high spending on conventional military forces and the development of nuclear weapons.

Pakistan's support for a violent insurgency in the disputed territory of Kashmir has brought the foes to the edge of a war that could involve nuclear weapons, notwithstanding the stated policies of the two countries. Domestically, radical Islamist political parties have gained substantial ground, especially in the strategic Northwest Frontier Province (NWFP) and Baluchistan, both of which share a border with Afghanistan. Since President Musharraf joined the war on terrorism after September 11, 2001, official U.S.-Pakistan relations have dramatically improved. As in the 1980s, geography has made Pakistan a critical staging area for the pursuit of America's foes in Afghanistan. Washington has a vital interest in ensuring Islamabad's cooperation in rooting out terrorist remnants that have fled to Pakistan.

Yet, as in the past, U.S. and Pakistani interests and policies only partially coincide and in some important respects conflict. In the war on terrorism, Pakistan provides valuable help against al-Qaeda but has been less aggressive in pursuing Taliban supporters. It has also continued to back " *jihadi*" groups, labelled terrorists by the United States and freedom fighters by Pakistan, that are active in India-administered Kashmir.

While Washington has been striving for more cooperative relations with New Delhi, Pakistan continues to regard India as the major and active threat to its national security. For the United States, preventing the further spread of nuclear weapons has the highest priority, yet Pakistan's record of nuclear and ballistic-missile transactions with North Korea suggests a willingness to become involved in the most dangerous kinds of nuclear proliferation.

Encouraging Pakistan to advance toward becoming "a modern, progressive, and dynamic state" should be the principal aim of U.S. policy over the medium term. The task will not be easy. Pakistan's unstable polity, weak human and institutional infrastructure, and increasing support for Islamist extremism, and the depth and intensity of anti-U.S. sentiments pose formidable obstacles. Moreover, the sincerity of the Pakistan army, the ultimate arbiter of power, in carrying through fundamental reform remains uncertain.

US-Pakistan Relations

Despite the flowery rhetoric during Musharraf 's June 2003 state visit to Washington, interaction between the United States and Pakistan is handicapped by a half-century of relations that have been like a roller-coaster ride. Driven by a Cold War search for alliances, the United States made Pakistan a military ally against communism in 1954. Later, Islamabad served as the bridge for President Richard Nixon's dramatic opening to China in 1971 and was the key partner in the struggle against the Soviet occupation of Afghanistan in the 1980s. Today, the Bush administration talks of Pakistan as an "indispensable ally" in the war against terrorism. Yet, during the 1960s, Pakistan's burgeoning friendship with then enemy China angered Washington. In the late 1970s and again in the 1990s, Pakistan's search for nuclear weapons triggered the suspension of American military and economic help.

As the new century began, Islamabad's support for the Taliban and for the insurgency in Kashmir, its nuclear weapons tests, and the army's ouster of the elected civilian government further strained ties. The extraordinary volatility of past relations, especially the U.S. refusal to back then-ally Pakistan during its 1965 war with India and Washington's imposition of nuclear sanctions in 1990 after the Soviet military withdrew from Afghanistan, has convinced many Pakistanis that the United States is a fickle and unreliable friend. Deep opposition to U.S. actions in the Israeli-Palestinian dispute, and in Iraq and Afghanistan, has intensified anti-American sentiments. There is also resentment about the treatment of Pakistanis in the United States since September 11, 2001; new visa procedures are regarded by many as onerous, humiliating, and contradictory to U.S. assertions that it regards Pakistan as a good friend.

Since Islamabad joined the war on terrorism, Washington has waived sanctions and other restrictions to provide substantial amounts of economic assistance, debt relief, and security aid. Close military, intelligence, and law-enforcement ties have been re-established. Although the ISI's intimate links with Islamist extremists helped fuel global terrorism, Pakistan's strategic location and Musharraf 's decision to turn against the Taliban have made it part of the solution. Islamabad cooperated with U.S. forces during Operation Enduring Freedom and has continued to do so in pursuing the remnants of al-Qaeda. Islamabad has been less vigorous in pursuing Taliban supporters that have found refuge in the Pashtun tribal areas bordering Afghanistan, particularly after pro-Taliban Islamist parties won provincial elections in the NWFP and joined the ruling coalition in Baluchistan.

A previous U.S.-Pakistan balancing act in the 1980s (a period in which Islamabad's pursuit of nuclear weapons was deemed less important by Washington than its cooperation in evicting Soviet forces from Afghanistan) ended in a painful divorce. The current balancing act (in which Washington regards Islamabad's continued cooperation against al-Qaeda as more important than its nuclear and missile activities and halfhearted actions against Taliban remnants and Kashmir-oriented "jihadis") could end in another painful U.S.-Pakistan separation. The U.S. government would do well to recall the lessons of the Afghan war years of the 1980s, when it handsomely supported President Mohammed Zia ul-Haq and ignored his domestic Islamization agenda, which had long-lasting and harmful consequences for Pakistan, Afghanistan, and the United

States. America has a strong interest in friendly, stable, and long-term ties with Pakistan. Such a relationship, however, will be difficult to sustain unless Islamabad firmly turns its back on terrorist groups, plays fully by nonproliferation rules, and genuinely seeks to live at peace with its neighbours.

In the fifty-six years since Pakistan became an independent state, it has not been able to achieve a stable political system; instead it has careened between periods of civilian and military rule. Pakistan had the bad luck of losing its two most capable leaders, Mohammed Ali Jinnah and Liaquat Ali Khan, in its formative years. Their successors lacked the ability to dominate senior army and civil service officers who, believing that Pakistan was not ready for democracy, seized power in 1958. By then, the Muslim League, the umbrella movement that had spearheaded the drive for Pakistan, had splintered as a national political party after achieving its goal of the partition of India into two countries. Neither Pakistan's soldiers nor its politicians have offered honest or competent leadership for any extended period and the country has failed to develop a clear sense of national identity. No elected government has yet completed its term in office.

Civil service and judicial standards have eroded. Only the Pakistani military has been able to maintain its institutional cohesion. But the price has been the military's entrenchment as the country's dominant political force and very high outlays on defense to the detriment of the country's economic and social development. During the three years after the army seized power in October 1999, Musharraf 's regime-a mix of technocrats and military officers-emphasized curbing corruption (selective progress was made), devolving significant powers to locally elected bodies (uncertain that the sweeping changes will work), and putting Pakistan's battered economy back on track (substantial progress has been made at the macroeconomic level).

On the positive side, Musharraf did not appreciably tamper with the free press that had developed over the previous decade. Far less creditable were his "confirmation" as president in a dubious referendum in April 2002 and his altering of the 1973 Constitution by fiat so that he (rather than the civilian prime minister) would retain the substance of power. In the October 2002 national elections, the ISI blatantly interfered to promote a pro-Musharraf faction of the Pakistan Muslim League, the PML-Quaid-i-Azam (PML-Q), and to weaken Benazir Bhutto's Pakistan Peoples Party (PPP) and Nawaz Sharif 's faction of the Muslim League (PML-N).

The PML-Q ultimately emerged as the largest party in the National Assembly and was able to cobble together a bare majority government led by a little-known Baluchi politician, Mir Zafrullah Khan Jamali. Both Bhutto and Sharif, each a former prime minister, were barred from taking part in the elections and remained in exile. Despite official harassment, the PPP gained more votes than the PML-Q but won fewer seats thanks to Pakistan's first-past-the-post voting system. The biggest surprise of the elections was the unexpectedly strong showing of the Muttahida Majlis-e-Amal (MMA), a coalition of religious parties that gained nearly one-fifth of the National Assembly seats, won a landslide victory in NWFP provincial elections, and formed a coalition government in Baluchistan.

An unlikely assemblage of formerly squabbling Islamist parties, including some that are vehemently pro-

Taliban, the groups in the MMA share several common positions: strong anti-American views, opposition to Pakistan's role in the U.S.-led war on terrorism, and a desire to impose an Islamist state on Pakistani society. Nationally, the MMA won only 11 percent of the vote, roughly equal to the previous best showing of the religious parties. The unaccustomed unity, however, gained the MMA an unprecedented 18 percent of National Assembly seats.

Because Pakistan was created as political homeland for the Muslims of British India, there has been a rhetorical emphasis on Islamic principles from the country's earliest days. Islamist political parties, however, made few inroads and had little impact during the first two decades of independence. Founder Mohammed Ali Jinnah was a strong secularist, as was Mohammed Ayub Khan, Pakistan's first military dictator and the country's president from 1958 to 1969. Moreover, the major Islamist party, the Jamaat-e-Islami, and its influential leader, Maulana Maududi, actually opposed the creation of Pakistan. The religious parties began to acquire legitimacy only in the late 1970s thanks largely to the promotion of Islamization by Zia ul-Haq after he seized power in a military coup. Their legitimacy and organizational strength grew in the 1980s as a result of ties established with the ISI to wage "jihad" against the Soviets in Afghanistan. The Islamist parties were further helped in the 1990s by their support, again in league with the ISI, for the Taliban in Afghanistan and the anti-India insurgency in Kashmir. Militant offshoots of different religious parties provided many of the foot soldiers for the anti-Soviet and anti-India insurgencies and for the Taliban.

As to the future, some observers doubt that the MMA's success in the 2002 elections will be repeated, judging this largely to have been a consequence of strong anti-U.S. sentiments among Pashtuns and of the ISI efforts to weaken the PPP and split the PML. Others, however, believe that the Islamists are likely to register further gains in view of the unpopularity of Musharraf's pro-U.S. policy, the unchecked spread of Islamist propaganda, and the disarray of the mainstream political parties. Unlike the PPP and different Muslim League factions, the MMA has a political message: to impose Islamist values as the answer to Pakistan's ills. Although the MMA speaks a good democratic game, the ultimate aim is more likely to be the imposition of an authoritarian state. This was the political model promoted by Jamaat-e-Islami founder Maulana Maududi, who saw democracy as a means to this end. After Musharraf joined the war on terrorism, his government at first cracked down on extremist groups.

The most radical, including the Jaish-e-Mohammed and Lashkar-e-Taiba (both designated as terrorist organizations by the U.S. government), were banned. Their leaders and many followers were arrested. The pressure on these extremists has since eased, however. All but a handful of detainees have been released, including Jaish-e-Mohammed leader Mazood Azhar and Lashkar-e-Taiba head Hafiz Saeed. The banned groups have resurfaced under different names, have been able to agitate openly for violent action, and are accused of supporting continued terrorist attacks in Indian-controlled territory. Even though Musharraf strongly opposes Islamist extremism, he and his Pakistan army colleagues favor a hard-line policy on Kashmir and believe that they need the militants to maintain pressure on India. Musharraf has thus been unwilling (or unable) to rein in "jihadis" despite his promise to stop infiltration across the Line of Control (LOC) in Kashmir permanently. Moreover, the people and terrorist groups active in Kashmir have substantial links with al-Qaeda and the Taliban, and it is not easy to maintain distinctions between them.

Although the Bush administration has intermittently pressed Musharraf to deliver on his pledge, it has been unwilling to push the Pakistani leader too hard for fear that this would result in reduced cooperation against al-Qaeda. Washington, however, should be raising the issue in a more explicit and persistent fashion. What is being asked of Pakistan—to end support for terrorists, as promised by Musharraf-is consistent with Islamabad's participation in the war on terrorism and is in Pakistan's own interest in reducing the threat to itself from Islamist extremism.

Political Reforms in Pakistan

It remains to be seen whether Musharraf's political dispensation will prove any more durable than those of Pakistan's earlier army rulers. In addition to sharp political differences with the Islamist parties, Musharraf has managed to alienate many "mainstream" Pakistani politicians who back the PPP or the PML-N. His base of support, the PML-Q, is narrow and opportunistic; ultimately, Musharraf depends on the continued backing of his fellow generals to stay in power. Since his unwise referendum in April 2002 and his manipulation of the October 2002 national elections, Musharraf has not shown a sure political touch. His thinking continues to reflect the traditional antipathy of the senior military toward civilian politicians and the messiness of Pakistani politics. Partly as a result of his disdain for mainstream politicians and his reluctance to deal with them, Musharraf currently faces a deadlock in the National Assembly and a potential crisis over his desire to change the constitution by fiat and to stay on as army chief while serving as president.

Even though the record of Pakistan's civilian politicians is hardly inspiring, over the long run democracy must be given a chance if Pakistan is truly going to implement the reform agenda. With this in mind, the United States should be giving priority to assistance projects that will strengthen civil society, governmental institutions, and the mainstream parties. By themselves, these activities will not bring about fundamental change, but they can help improve Pakistan's weak civilian institutions. They will also underscore that the United States is interested in promoting long-term reform that benefits all Pakistanis, not just in rewarding Musharraf 's cooperation against al-Qaeda in the war on terrorism.

Pakistan's economic and social problems

In the mid-1960s, Pakistan boasted one of the most promising economies in the developing world. At the time, it had the highest growth rate in South Asia and exported more manufactured goods than did Indonesia, Malaysia, the Philippines, and Thailand combined. A textile industry based on indigenous cotton evolved from scratch in 1947 to become an important global producer of cotton yarn and gray goods. In recent years, Pakistan has not only been left behind by the East Asian "tigers," but its growth rate has fallen below those of India and even Bangladesh. Political instability, poor quality of governance, bad economic policy choices, and chronic tension and conflict with India have been the main causes of Pakistan's sub-par economic performance.

The 1965 war with India over Kashmir had heavy costs, including the loss of U.S. military aid and reduced economic assistance. In the 1970s, Prime Minister Zulfikar Ali Bhutto's nationalization of major industries, commercial banks, and insurance companies burdened Pakistan with an inefficient and corrupt public sector. In the 1980s, a surge of foreign assistance from the Afghan war and a substantial rise in remittances from Pakistani workers in the Persian Gulf boosted growth of the country's gross domestic product (GDP) to 6 percent a year. Even though poverty declined significantly, President Zia ul-Haq failed to address underlying weaknesses, especially inadequate schools and health care, and did not dismantle the money-losing public sector.

Foreign assistance dropped precipitously after the Soviet military withdrew from Afghanistan and the United States, in October 1990, barred new economic and military aid because of Pakistan's nuclear program. Under Prime Ministers Bhutto and Sharif, the economy deteriorated because of heavy foreign borrowing, frequent policy shifts with changes of government, rampant corruption, and growing physical insecurity caused by increased lawlessness and surging sectarian violence between Sunni and Shiite extremists. Over the past decade, violence in Karachi, the country's commercial and manufacturing hub and its sole seaport, has badly damaged the economy and had a chilling impact on foreign investment. Sometimes the bloodshed has been due to Karachi's brutal ethnic politics, sometimes to sectarian rivalries, sometimes to a political banditry, and sometimes to attacks by terrorists. When Musharraf took power in October 1999, Pakistan was nearly bankrupt and in danger of defaulting on service of its foreign debt. Although the economic situation has much improved since then, the underlying statistics remain troubling and point to Pakistan's past failure to meet basic needs.

Average GDP growth dropped to only 0.6 percent per annum between 1996 and 2000, far less than either Bangladesh or India during the same period. The Pakistani government's economic survey reported that those living in poverty (defined as earning less than $1 a day) soared from 18 percent of the population in 1987-88 to 32 percent in 1998-99. Limited educational opportunities for girls and the lack of a strong family planning program have helped keep Pakistan's population growth rate well ahead of those of India and Bangladesh: in 2000, Pakistan's population rose at 2.4 percent a year, India's at 1.8 percent, and Bangladesh's at 1.6 percent.

Education and the Madrassas

Depressing literacy figures reflect the dismal state of education: only 43.2 percent of adult Pakistanis could read and write in 2000-57.5 percent of males and a shockingly low 28.9 percent of females. The minority of young Pakistanis who belong to the middle and upper economic classes has access to reasonably good education through an extensive private-school system that now includes some 36,000 institutions and teaches six million students. For the poor majority, however, the choice lies between crumbling government schools and bare-bones madrassas (Islamic schools). Enrollment in government schools actually declined in the 1990s owing to rising poverty and lower educational standards. Public expenditure on education dropped from 2.7 percent of GDP in 1996-97 to 2.1 percent in 2000-2001. Zia ul-Haq began promoting the madrassas in the late 1970s as part of his support for Islamization. Since then, they have mushroomed and now are estimated to be educating more than a million students. Funding for the madrassas comes from private Pakistani donations and from abroad, especially from Saudi Arabia.

For many of the rural and urban poor, the religious schools offer the only possibility of education. The traditional function of preparing students for the clergy by teaching them to recite the Qur'an by rote is hardly sufficient to ready youngsters for the challenges of modern life and society. Even though many madrassas are apolitical, their graduates are narrowly trained to become clerics and lack broader skills. More radical madrassas, sponsored by Islamist extremists, however, imbue their students with hatred of alleged enemies of Islam (the United States, India, the West, etc.). It is these madrassas that served as incubators for the Taliban and that continue to graduate fanatic foot soldiers ready to give their lives for *"jihad."*

Musharraf has declared publicly that he wants to reform the madrassas by bringing their finances under government control and by broadening their academic curricula. In effect, he has proposed to transform them into a Pakistani version of the parochial school. His words, however, have not been followed by actions.

Musharraf and his army colleagues have either lacked the political will or felt unable to implement proposed reforms in the face of opposition from Islamist organizations. The army has been reluctant to take on the very groups on whose "*jihadi*" offshoots it depends to implement the country's hawkish Kashmir policy. The political success of the MMA has made the task of madrassa reform harder. Yet unless Pakistan modernizes its Islamic schools and makes a far larger investment in public education, most of its youth will continue to be woefully unprepared for the challenges of the twenty-first century and will be even more susceptible to the call of Islamist extremism.

Economic reforms

To his credit, Musharraf has made economic reform a top priority and has developed a program (in close cooperation with international financial institutions) to:

— reform the system of tax collection and expand the government's revenue base;

— restructure and privatize public-sector companies, including state-run commercial banks;

— reduce the country's heavy debt-service burden; and

— implement a comprehensive poverty-reduction program designed to improve education, health care, and economic opportunities.

Substantial progress has been registered in government finance and in the balance of payments. Foreign-exchange reserves have risen from almost nothing when Musharraf took over to more than $10 billion, nearly equal to a year's imports. The trade picture has also much improved. Reflecting better economic performance, GDP rose 4.5 percent in 2002, the best showing in many years. If current budget projections are realized, the coming years will show a considerable increase in social-sector expenditures, notably for education and health. These areas have been starved for funds for more than a decade, contributing to the disastrous increase in poverty and the disturbingly low literacy and health performance.

Even though the International Monetary Fund (IMF) and the World Bank have given Pakistan good marks for its economic performance, it remains premature to conclude that the corner has been turned definitively. Much of the improvement has been due to increased foreign aid and debt relief since September 11, 2001. There has not yet been a significant increase in domestic investment nor has foreign investment substantially picked up. While both are essential for job creation, foreign investment has particular importance in view of Pakistan's low level of domestic savings. In short, Islamabad has only begun to tackle the country's deep-seated social and economic ailments. Economic and social reform will have to remain a top priority for many years. To achieve sustained growth and a reduction in poverty, Pakistan needs a solid stretch of domestic political stability and peace with its neighbours.

U.S. Assistance to Pakistan

After Pakistan joined the war on terrorism, the United States lifted or waived various sanctions and has since provided substantial economic and military aid. In fiscal year (FY) 2002, $626 million of economic aid was made available, of which $600 million went directly into the Pakistani treasury to help reduce the debt burden and offset costs of the war in Afghanistan, and $26 million was allocated for economic development projects. For FY 2003, the total amount was a bit over $500 million, with some $188 million appropriated to buy back $1 billion worth of debt owed to the United States. The remainder was divided between project assistance and security-related aid. The FY 2004 request is for approximately $400 million, with about half for debt reduction, $75 million for economic assistance, and $125 million for security related help. During Musharraf 's June 2003 visit to Washington, President Bush proposed that Congress authorize a five-year, $3 billion assistance program for FYs 2005 through 2009, to be divided equally between economic and military aid (i.e., roughly $300 million of each annually). The administration's decision to seek a multiyear assistance authorization is welcomed as a tangible sign of the U.S. commitment to help Pakistan over the longer term.

Strengthen Civil Society and Government Institutions: Along with education and support for the Pashtun areas, a third major focus of U.S. economic assistance should be to promote democracy by strengthening Pakistan's weak civil society and its political and governmental institutions. One priority should be to help the mainstream political parties become more accountable, professional, and issue-oriented organizations. Regrettably, the MMA was the only party to issue a political program during the 2002 elections. Although the PPP and the PML, in the Pakistani context, are considered to be center-left and center-right groups, respectively, neither is internally democratic and both have suffered badly after the exile of their respective leaders, Benazir Bhutto and Nawaz Sharif. A related priority should be to help improve Pakistan's system of justice and law enforcement. The court system and the police suffer from lack of professionalism, political interference (as much during the Bhutto-Sharif era as under Musharraf), poor salaries, and related endemic corruption. With the possibility of long-term funding, a multi year program should be developed that aims at better training and stronger professionalism.

Strengthen NGOs: Wherever possible, assistance should be given to strengthen Pakistan's nongovernmental organizations. Many of these groups are visionary yet weak, especially those that emphasize education and access to financial assets for women, rural development, and the promotion of human rights. In Bangladesh (the former East Pakistan), local NGOs have registered extraordinary achievements in promoting economic, educational, and social progress in areas such as female education, family planning, small industry growth, and microfinance. Bangladesh provides a model of how dramatic progress can be achieved by involving people at the grassroots level in the development process. U.S. assistance should be used to help Pakistan try to replicate the Bangladesh success story.

Buy Back Official Debt: To date, the Bush administration has been especially helpful in providing debt relief and should continue this as part of the multiyear assistance program. During FY 2003, the United States wrote off $1 billion worth of debt after Congress appropriated $188 million for this purpose. Washington also rescheduled another $3 billion of debt and supported the IMF's rescheduling of $9 billion of Pakistan's total external debt of $38.5 billion. Reduction in the debt-service burden has been a key factor in enabling Pakistan to increase its spending on the social sector, so essential in the reform process. Provided

Pakistan continues to allocate additional budgetary resources to implement social sector programs, the United States should buy back the remaining official debt, appropriating the funds necessary for this purpose. Ease Import Restrictions on Pakistani Textiles. Increased foreign trade provides more immediate and significant economic benefits than aid, but regrettably the Bush administration has been unwilling to accede to Islamabad's request for an easing of import barriers for textiles, Pakistan's major export to the United States.

In 2001-2002, textile sales accounted for some two-thirds of total Pakistani exports of $9.2 billion and were nearly 90 percent of its $2.2 billion in sales to the United States. Even though U.S. quotas will end when the international multifiber agreement to eliminate these barriers comes into force in 2005, greater access to the American market during the coming two years would provide a quick and helpful boost to economic activity and employment, especially in the hard-hit but critical city of Karachi. Given the U.S. stake in Pakistan's "getting it right," the Bush administration should be willing to bear the political criticism from domestic producers by making it easier for Pakistan to sell its major export product in the United States. Since the Bush administration is urging Musharraf to take steps that are politically difficult in the Pakistani context, it should not shrink from taking some politically difficult steps itself by widening market access for Pakistani textile products.

Provide security assistance: On the security side, military-to military relations that atrophied after 1990 have resumed. Substantial transfers of defense equipment, barred since 1990, have begun. The executive branch has called for a major boost in security assistance to Pakistan-$300 million annually from FY 2005 through

2009-as part of the multiyear aid commitment. Pakistani military officers are again receiving military training in the United States under the International Military Education and Training Program (IMET). The Task Force urges that this program be fully funded and supported. Sustained training links are an invaluable way to give foreign military officers the opportunity to gain a firsthand understanding of the United States. Maintaining the IMET program is particularly important given the key role that the military plays and current strong anti-American sentiments in Pakistan.

National Security Policy

The driver for national security policy has been and remains India and Pakistan's related dissatisfaction with the status quo. The two neighbours have fought three and a half wars since they gained independence from the United Kingdom (the 1999 Kargil episode is the "half " war). The world fears that the *"jihad"* that Pakistan has been supporting in Kashmir could trigger a fourth conflict. Under pressure from the United States and others after New Delhi threatened war in December 2001 and again in May 2002, Musharraf promised to take steps to stop infiltration permanently across the LOC. He has done so only partly, however, presumably calculating that the U.S. need for Pakistani cooperation against al-Qaeda is such that Washington will not press too hard on this issue. Musharraf and his fellow generals want to keep the pressure on India. But as the Bush administration has repeatedly stated, there are no good or bad terrorists, just bad ones. Pakistan should thus be pressed harder to prevent its territory's being used by *"jihadi"* terrorists to mount attacks against Kashmir.

Even though there are few direct financial costs to Pakistan from supporting *"jihad"* in Kashmir, the indirect costs have been substantial. Apart from periodically threatening war and serving as the main cause of regional instability, chronic tension with India has provided the rationale for Pakistan's extremely high defense expenditures-roughly a quarter of its national budget and 5-6 percent of GDP. With the Indian economy growing at about 6 percent per annum and its defense spending not more than 3 percent of GDP, New Delhi can absorb the additional costs of dealing with the Kashmir insurgency without greatly impairing its overall economic prospects. Pakistan, however, is too poor to opt for both "guns and butter." Continuing the hawkish approach toward India, in effect, is a decision to opt for "guns". Indeed, ever since the army regained effective control of national security policy after the ouster of Zulfikar Ali Bhutto in 1977, Pakistan has underfunded the social sector with devastating impact on the country's social and human development. A change in the military's mindset on Kashmir and its India-centric outlook is an essential step if Pakistan is to find the resources needed to implement the domestic economic and social reform agenda.

Security Challenges

Pakistan recognized and supported the Taliban regime until Musharraf reversed course after September 11, 2001. Abandoning the Taliban marked a defeat for Islamabad's "forward" policy of trying to transform Afghanistan into a client state to provide "strategic depth" against India. Even though Islamabad is not happy with the strong Tajik position in the Karzai government, it has desisted from officially sponsoring disgruntled Afghan Pashtuns. Yet, in the border areas of the NWFP and in FATA, where the central government's control is weak, pro-Taliban elements have been able to find sanctuary and have used FATA as a base to stir trouble in the Pashtun-dominated southern and eastern parts of Afghanistan.

The situation has substantially worsened since the MMA with its ties to the Taliban came to power in the NWFP. The surge in attacks from Pakistan's tribal areas has caused a serious deterioration in security, set back reconstruction, and weakened the position of the Karzai government even further in the Pashtun areas of Afghanistan. For their part, the Afghan authorities have blamed Pakistan for failing to prevent the use of its territory by pro-Taliban elements. Relations were further shaken when an angry mob attacked the Pakistani embassy in Kabul. In an effort to prevent additional trouble, the United States, Pakistan, and Afghanistan have recently established a commission to address security issues. For its part, the United States should make crystal clear to Musharraf that ISI support for cross-border attacks against Afghanistan is unacceptable. Washington should emphasize that this support is not only inconsistent with Pakistan's role in the war on terrorism, but will have serious negative consequences for U.S.-Pakistan relations, including the amount of assistance to be made available.

Nuclear Weapons

In acquiring nuclear weapons, Pakistan's goal was to match the capability that India had demonstrated in 1974 and to provide a deterrent against its neighbour's conventional military superiority. Possession of nuclear weapons has taken the edge off India's conventional arms advantage by raising the stakes any time New Delhi considers military action against Islamabad. Even though Pakistan has achieved its deterrent, recent near-war crises underscore that it has not yet become secure. As discussed in the section on India, there may well be a continuing nuclear arms race and mounting proliferation dangers in South Asia.

Although the Bush administration has so far avoided this issue, which admittedly presents difficult and complex policy choices, the Task Force believes that Washington should seriously and comprehensively explore ways to fit Pakistan and India into the global nonproliferation system. The most immediate proliferation concerns relate to the leakage of sensitive nuclear technology and to command-and-control and security over weapons. When U.S. officials learned of North Pakistan Korean help to Pakistan's missile programme in 1998, they questioned top leaders in Islamabad as to whether Pakistan was providing uranium-enrichment technology in return.

Pakistani officials responded that they would stop such activity if, in fact, it was occurring. Despite these assurances, it has been reported that transfers of technology to North Korea took place subsequently and that these may have continued after September 11, 2001. After firmly avoiding comment on the issue, the executive branch asserted in March 2003 that it had insufficient cause to impose sanctions on Pakistan for helping North Korea. At the same time, because of confirmation that Pakistan was continuing to receive missile assistance from North Korea (first announced in 1998), Washington barred the Khan Research

Laboratories, a key part of Pakistan's nuclear weapons program, from any dealings with the United States. The whole episode seems murky at best; at worst it suggests that the executive branch overlooked a major breach of nonproliferation rules and ignored a transfer of sensitive nuclear technology that poses the gravest possible threat to U.S. and international security concerns. If the reports are correct-and Secretary of State Colin Powell's refusal to "talk about the past" whenever questioned on the subject suggests that they are-President Bush would have been far wiser to have used the authority that the law gives him to waive sanctions in the national interest. The danger to U.S. and international security posed by North Korea's uranium-enrichment program is too serious for Pakistan's involvement to be swept under the rug.

The Kashmir Issue

When the British folded their imperial tents in August 1947, they left the future of Jammu and Kashmir unresolved. Within months, India and Pakistan, the two successors to the Raj, were fighting over the princely state. After a UN-sponsored ceasefire came into force more than a year later, on January 1, 1949, India controlled the southern two-thirds of the state, including the Kashmir valley, the core of the dispute and the home to most speakers of the Kashmiri language. Pakistan possessed the northern one-third. Nearly fifty-five years later, the ceasefire line, since renamed the Line of Control (LOC), continues to separate the territory held by India and Pakistan, and differences over Kashmir remain at the heart of their rivalry. If the two countries are to live amicably with one another, they will have to address the Kashmir issue, contain the dangers, and one day achieve a settlement. Their festering hostility remains the greatest single threat to regional stability.

Given that India and Pakistan are now armed with nuclear weapons, the possibility that another conflict might involve the first use of atomic weapons since Hiroshima and Nagasaki in 1945 is all too real. Frictions over Kashmir have fueled religious extremism in both India and Pakistan and will continue to do so unless tensions are better managed. Political cultures in the two states have evolved in a way that makes the Kashmir question highly emotional and renders it extremely difficult for the national leadership of either country to put forward ideas for its resolution that the other side is likely to find palatable.

The gap between the Indian and Pakistani positions remains too wide to be easily bridged. Yet until the problem of Kashmir is settled or in some fashion mitigated, it will remain a major barrier to India's aspirations for great power status, Pakistan's hopes for achieving fundamental reform, and American interests in a peaceful and stable South Asia. In recent years, U.S. policy toward Kashmir has been one of crisis management. Washington has sprung into action to prevent crises from getting out of hand-in June-July 1999 after Pakistan crossed the LOC near Kargil, in December 2001 after terrorists attacked the Indian Parliament, and in May 2002 when several dozen women and children were killed at an Indian army camp in Kashmir. At other times, the United States has limited itself to hortatory calls for the two protagonists to try to solve their problems through peaceful dialogue. After considerable deliberation, the Task Force consensus concludes that such a reactive approach is inadequate given the inherent danger that an India-Pakistan crisis will one day spiral into a broader conflict, conceivably one involving use of nuclear weapons. New Delhi and Islamabad have a poor record of managing their differences, and the present pause, like past respites, is likely to be the lull before the next storm. The Task Force therefore proposes more forward-leaning U.S. diplomacy that would facilitate-not arbitrate or mediate-Indian and Pakistani efforts to manage their tensions and to create an improved environment that eventually will permit a solution of the Kashmir dispute. To this end, a special working group should be established among those dealing with South Asian affairs in Washington. Its purpose should be to:

1) track Kashmir developments and discussions between New Delhi, Srinagar, and Islamabad; and
2) provide ideas, guidance, and instructions to U.S. chiefs of mission in India and Pakistan and senior visitors to the region on how progress can best be achieved.

In the short term, the goal for U.S. diplomacy should be to help start a bilateral process of India-Pakistan negotiation. Pakistan should be pressed more vigorously to make good on Pakistani President Pervez Musharraf 's pledge to stop infiltration across the LOC. India should be urged to lighten the pressure on Kashmiris from security forces as militancy declines. Pakistan should alter its negotiating strategy of holding all bilateral differences hostage to progress toward a Kashmir settlement. India should strive harder to reach an understanding with the elected Jammu and Kashmir State government to permit greater political autonomy and spur economic development. A plausible place to start India-Pakistan discussions would be working out a comprehensive ceasefire along the LOC, the most likely flash point of wider conflict.

Other issues that should be addressed include steps to reduce the risk of nuclear war, to resolve the Siachen glacier dispute, to promote bilateral trade, to ease restrictions on the movement of people, and to reduce hate propaganda. Despite the recent thaw in relations, neither New Delhi nor Islamabad at this time seems inclined to move purposefully toward a final Kashmir settlement-except on its own terms. Given this fact and the depth of mutual mistrust, it would be counterproductive at this point for the United States to put on the table ideas about an ultimate settlement and how to get there. Instead, Washington should focus on lending behind-the-scenes and sustained help so that New Delhi and Islamabad can start and maintain a process that, over time, moves the two antagonists onto a more positive bilateral path. Even if the near-term outlook for progress is cloudy, a constructive and long-term U.S. effort could fuel new thinking about a way forward, help lessen tensions between India and Pakistan, reduce the risk of war, and improve prospects for an eventual Kashmir accord.

The official Indian position on Kashmir has long been that: The entire former princely state of Jammu and Kashmir has been an integral part of India since its accession by Maharajah Hari Singh to India on October 26, 1947. Nothing in UN Security Council resolutions in any way modifies Indian sovereignty over the territory of the entire pre-independence princely state. In keeping with UN resolutions, the only legally admissible issue on the table is the need for Pakistan to "vacate" the Kashmir territory it occupies. The future status of the state is an exclusively Indian domestic matter to be settled "within the four corners of the Indian constitution." Talks on Kashmir should be conducted bilaterally in conformity with the agreement India and Pakistan reached at Simla in July 1972.

Notwithstanding the official position and periodic rhetoric claiming the entire state, India has long been willing to settle on the basis of the status quo, converting the LOC into an international border. Prime Minister Jawaharlal Nehru suggested this to Secretary of State John Foster Dulles as long ago as May 1953. Except for the extreme right wing, the entire Indian political spectrum could support such a settlement. There is firm opposition, however, to any arrangement or process that would result in a loss of territory to Pakistan, an independent Kashmir, or a diminution of Indian sovereignty.

Although the official Pakistani position has not changed over the years, the unofficial stance has evolved. Today, Pakistan would be willing to accept something less than a statewide plebiscite, such as one along district lines. It would also probably be prepared to agree to an independent status for the Kashmiri-speaking areas or some special arrangement for the Kashmir valley as long as this no longer remains totally subject to Indian sovereignty. Few Pakistanis, however, are willing to accept the status quo as the basis for a settlement. There is some support for putting Kashmir "on the back burner" while trying to improve other facets of India-Pakistan relations, but the Pakistan army, which effectively determines policy, shows little sign of a significant shift on the issue.

In 1947-48, Pakistan tried to seize Kashmir by force. In the fall of 1947, irregulars took physical control of the area now called Azad (Free) Kashmir (or, in India, POK or Pakistan-Occupied Kashmir). After the maharajah of Jammu and Kashmir acceded to India, Indian forces and Pakistani troops and irregulars battled during 1948 before the two sides accepted a UN-sponsored ceasefire that came into effect on January 1, 1949. From 1948 through 1961, Pakistan pressed its case through diplomacy mainly at the UN.A series of UN (and also three U.S.) mediation efforts foundered largely on Indian unwillingness to proceed. After Pakistan became a military ally of the United States in 1954, New Delhi hardened its stance on the plebiscite, asserting that the 1952 elections for a constituent assembly showed that Kashmiris wanted to be part of India and no further vote was needed.

In 1962 and 1963, India and Pakistan tried direct negotiations. Six rounds of bilateral India-Pakistan talks-initiated under pressure from London and Washington after the Sino-Indian border conflict-failed to advance a settlement but marked the last sustained bilateral effort to resolve the dispute. During the discussions, both countries rejected a U.S.-U.K. proposal to partition the Kashmir valley as a basis for an accord. In 1965, Pakistan's effort to seize Kashmir by force ended in fullscale war. India won the seventeen-day conflict by not losing. After accepting a UN-proposed ceasefire, India and Pakistan agreed in the Soviet-brokered Tashkent Agreement to return to the status quo ante in Jammu and Kashmir. The dispute did not play a significant role in the 1971 India-Pakistan war that resulted in the emergence of an independent Bangladesh.

In July 1972, the two sides agreed at Simla to settle Kashmir and other disputes bilaterally but without prejudice to each other's principles. The ceasefire line was renamed the Line of Control and physically demarcated on the ground. A decade and a half of relative calm followed. Kashmir remained an issue but did not cause intense India-Pakistan tensions. Indian mismanagement and election-rigging helped spark the trouble. Subsequently, Pakistan's Inter-Services Intelligence Directorate (ISI), drawing on its experience in fighting a guerilla war against the Soviets in Afghanistan, has helped train, equip, and provide tactical guidance to Islamist extremists who infiltrate across the LOC.

Despite frosty relations, India and Pakistan have taken three major but unsuccessful initiatives toward better relations in recent years.

In 1997, Prime Ministers Nawaz Sharif and Inder K.Gujral began wide-ranging talks on bilateral problems, including Kashmir. The discussions petered out when the weak Gujral government collapsed. In February 1999, after the two countries conducted nuclear weapons tests, Indian Prime Minister Atal Behari Vajpayee visited Lahore, where he and Nawaz Sharif agreed on a comprehensive agenda that included talks on Kashmir; this effort began what came to be known as the "Lahore process." Several months later, Pakistan's effort to occupy strategic heights on the Indian side of the LOC near Kargil scuttled the Lahore process and triggered a new crisis, which was resolved only after Pakistan, under U.S. pressure and in the face of a strong Indian military response, agreed to withdraw its forces across the LOC.

In July 2001, Vajpayee invited Pakistan's president and army chief, Pervez Musharraf, who had by then taken power from Nawaz Sharif, to India. Their unscripted summit at Agra failed, however, when they were unable to agree on a communiqu. After the U.S. war on terrorism began, India-Pakistan bilateral relations badly deteriorated. The two countries came close to war following major terrorist actions against India by groups linked to Pakistan. High-level intervention by the United States and others helped avert Indian military retaliation in December 2001 after an assault on the Indian Parliament and in May 2002 following the killing of many women and children in an Indian army camp in Kashmir. For nearly a year, more than a million troops were massed along the border and the LOC. Virtually all ties between India and Pakistan were cut.

In October 2002, the situation on the ground in India's part of Kashmir significantly changed after elections for the Kashmir State Assembly. Despite a boycott by separatists and a wave of terrorist attacks, 44 percent of those eligible voted to defeat the long ruling but unpopular National Conference. The victors were the opposition Indian National Congress Party and the Peoples Democratic Party (PDP), whose leader, Mufti Mohammed Sayeed, became Kashmir's chief minister. A regional party, the PDP supports a peace platform and has promised to bring a "healing touch" to long-suffering Kashmiris. The new government in Srinagar has made moves to ease tensions by releasing some political prisoners and abolishing the Special Operations Group, a local police force notorious for human rights abuses. The elections have given India a fresh opportunity to seek an accommodation with its Kashmiris, presumably by agreeing to greater autonomy in line with the 1952 agreement between Nehru and then-Kashmiri leader and National Conference founder Sheikh Mohammed Abdullah, by doing more to boost economic development, and by reducing the heavy hand of Indian security forces. A successful negotiation with the state government would weaken the basis for an insurgency rooted in Kashmiri unhappiness with New Delhi's manipulation of the state's internal affairs and the erosion of the autonomy promised in the 1952 agreement.

Afghan Issue

After three years of the defeat of the Taliban and their terrorist al-Qaeda allies, Afghanistan is still a long way from the U.S. goal of a stable self-governing state that no longer provides a haven for terrorists. In recent months, the country has become increasingly insecure outside the capital city of Kabul, where the International Security Assistance Force (ISAF) maintains order. In much of Afghanistan, political power remains in the hands of semiautonomous regional leaders and warlords. Progress in economic reconstruction has been slow. Public discontent has been rising. The political process calling for a constitution and national elections by June 2004 remains shaky. Unless the situation improves, Afghanistan risks sliding back into the anarchy and warlordism that prevailed in the 1990s and helped give rise to the Taliban. Such a reversion would have disastrous consequences for Afghanistan and would be a profound setback for the U.S. war on terrorism. To prevent this from happening, the United States must provide more effective security, diplomatic, and economic support to the transitional government of President Hamid Karzai. Current security policy, as articulated by Secretary of Defense Donald Rumsfeld during his May 1, 2003, visit to Kabul, does not include peacekeeping responsibilities for U.S. forces.

In the Afghan setting, where the United States has the primary military power, this approach fails to address the growing security challenge that the Karzai government faces. Until the authorities in Kabul develop greater capability to maintain the peace, the United States should be prepared to help, especially in dealing with recalcitrant regional leaders and warlords. Specifically, Washington should:

— make peacekeeping outside of Kabul part of the mandate for the 11,000 U.S. and coalition forces or, alternatively, support an enlarged ISAF with an expanded role;

— actively participate in the planned effort to demobilize, demilitarize, and reintegrate (DDR) local militias; and

— dramatically accelerate the training and development of the Afghan National Army (ANA).

The current target of 9,000 troops for the summer of 2004, when a permanent Afghan government is slated to assume office, is painfully inadequate. To give the central government a more credible peacekeeping capability, the United States should be targeting a force of approximately 27,000 men, including integrated militias. The Ministry of Defense also needs to be reformed into a more nationally representative organization. Given the extent of Afghanistan's physical and human damage, a long-term assistance effort, stretching at least until 2010, will be required before the country can get back on its feet. There should be no illusions on this score. Although successful reconstruction depends on whether Afghanistan can achieve political stability and physical security, an adequate flow of foreign assistance is also vital.

The United States should also do more diplomatically to bolster the Afghan government by taking stronger steps to deter neighbours from interfering in Afghanistan. In this area, Washington should:

— urge Iran and Russia to avoid undercutting the Karzai government by supporting different Afghan factions, and press Pakistan to work harder at preventing pro-Taliban elements from using Pakistani tribal territory for attacks across the border; and

— launch a major diplomatic initiative to obtain a broad international agreement among all of Afghanistan's neighbours and other interested powers not to interfere in Afghan affairs, to bar arms supplies to warlords, and to recognize Afghanistan's frontiers.

Despite the fact that Secretary Rumsfeld has proclaimed an end to combat operations in Afghanistan, the victory in Operation Enduring Freedom will be jeopardized unless the United States helps provide the transitional government more effective tools to assert its authority and to promote economic reconstruction. The world thinks of Afghanistan as America's war. Losing the peace through inadequate support for the Karzai government would gravely erode U.S. credibility around the globe and make it far more difficult to obtain international support in dealing with similar crises in the future.

Unlike in Iraq, the process of political and economic reconstruction in Afghanistan has involved a broad multinational coalition coordinated by the UN and supported by donor agencies and many nations. After the fall of the Taliban, the United States and the international community developed the following common goals for Afghanistan:

— re-establish a viable self-governing state structure reflecting the will of the Afghan people;

— secure its national borders, maintain domestic peace, and deprive terrorists of a haven;

— stand on its feet economically and resume its traditional role as an interregional trade corridor;

— protect the rights of women and minorities and eschew religious extremism; and

— control narcotics production.

The rapid defeat of the Taliban during Operation Enduring Freedom caught the world unprepáred to tackle the daunting political and economic challenges that Afghanistan posed. Fortunately, at the December 2001 Bonn conference, the major Afghan groups reached a broad agreement to establish an interim government led by Hamid Karzai, a Pashtun opponent of the Taliban.

The Bonn accords also established a timetable for a political process leading to the formation of a permanent Afghan government within three years. In June 2002, a major milestone was successfully passed when a loya jirga (grand national assembly) elected Karzai to lead a transitional Afghan government. The Bonn conference also called for a draft constitution and a second loya jirgato consider the basic law by December 2003, and national elections conducted by the transitional administration to select a permanent government under the new constitution by June 2004. Under the direction of the UN secretary-general's special representative, Lakhdar Brahimi, the UN has been leading the coordination of political and economic assistance.

In a division of labour among the major external players in the security area, the United States is principally training the new Afghan army; Germany has assumed responsibility for training the national police force; Italy is focusing on legal reform; Japan is funding the effort to demobilize, demilitarize, and reintegrate the militias; and the United Kingdom has agreed to head the narcotics control effort. To provide security in the capital city of Kabul, ISAF has been established. U.S. forces continue the military effort against al-Qaeda and Taliban remnants but do not have a mandate for enhancing security.

A year and a half after the defeat of the Taliban, Afghanistan has become an increasingly insecure country. In recent months, the situation has worsened in the Pashtun-populated areas of the south and east, especially near the borders with Pakistan. Taliban elements and their allies, often operating out of Pakistan's tribal belt, have been responsible for attacks against Karzai supporters, foreign aid officials, and the U.S. military. Elsewhere in the country, an uneasy calm, punctured by sporadic violence, prevails. Strife between rival commanders (for example, in the Herat and Mazar-e-Sharif areas) or just plain banditry and lawlessness are the main sources of trouble, rather than incidents by pro-Taliban elements. In Kabul itself, ISAF, a 4,800-strong international peacekeeping force, has had a positive impact. Led for rotating six-month periods by the British, the Turks, and the Germans and the Dutch, ISAF will come under the leadership of the North Atlantic Treaty Organization (NATO) in August 2003. The force has been successful in ensuring reasonable security and deterrence in the capital city.

During the winter of 2002, there was discussion of expanding ISAF to five cities outside of Kabul and of establishing a "flying brigade" to provide a rapid-reaction capability elsewhere in the country. After the United States refused to provide airlift, intelligence, and extraction support, however, the proposal died. One of ISAF's major weaknesses-rotating leadership every six months-should be solved when NATO assumes permanent charge this summer. The possibility of expanding ISAF's charter to include security-enhancement functions outside the capital city should be revisited on an urgent basis, especially if the United States continues to be unwilling to accept these responsibilities. This time around, Washington should be forthcoming in providing necessary support to ISAF.

Reducing the political and military strength of semiautonomous regional leaders and commanders has now become an urgent need. American military cooperation with, and dependence on, local warlords and their militias during Operation Enduring Freedom has made it harder now for the central government to assert its authority. Although the mere presence of U.S. and coalition troops has provided a measure of stability in areas where they are located, the Pentagon has unwisely excluded from their mandate either security enhancement or support for the central government's efforts to bring unruly warlords under its sway. Over the long term, the presence of large armed militias-estimated at as many as 100,000 fighters-controlled by local leaders, instead of Kabul, is incompatible with a viable national government. Even though Afghanistan has a history of local tribal levees, these were traditionally integrated into the national military.

U.S. strategy has been to allow regional forces and militias to remain intact while the new Afghan National Army and other institutions, especially the national police, take shape and ultimately provide the security underpinning for the Kabul government. Although the concept is laudable, the pace of establishing, training, and equipping the ANA has been painfully slow and the force targets grossly inadequate. To date, just eight battalions have completed their ten-week basic training cycle. At the current rate, the ANA will have only 9,000 soldiers when the new government takes office a year from now. At the present schedule, under which a new battalion begins training every five weeks, only 6,000 troops will be added annually. The projected ANA force is far too small to deal with the security problems that the post-June 2004 government of Afghanistan will face. A 9,000-man force cannot be widely used around the country and will be too inexperienced to maneuver as a unit against regional militias.

The United States should drastically increase the pace of developing the ANA in order to give the post-2004 government a reasonable peacekeeping capability. Instead of 9,000, the United States should be targeting a force of around 27,000, including troops from militias integrated into the ANA. In addition to boosting the numbers of those passing through basic training, more attention also needs to be paid to the functioning and training of the ANA beyond the initial ten-week cycle. Salaries are too low for the common soldier to live in inflation ridden Kabul. Inadequate pay has been a factor in the poor quality of recruits, a high dropout rate, and a lack of professionalism.

On the positive side, initial reports indicate that the ANA battalions have received good support in areas of continued training and have done well in their temporary employment in stability operations. There has also been a considerable effort to make sure the soldiers in the ANA battalions represent a reasonable mix of Afghanistan's major ethnic groups. Given Afghanistan's strong ethnic sentiments, it is essential that the ANA be a truly national force. It is similarly important that there be a nationally representative officer corps, not a factional one. In many respects, the development and training of a national police force is as important as building the ANA. Police functions will include not only usual law-and-order responsibilities but also the control of Afghanistan's borders and the collection of customs duties. The latter is of great importance economically, since customs will provide the major source of revenue for the central government. As in the case of the ANA, progress toward training the new national police has been far too slow. Germany and others involved in the process need to accelerate their efforts to provide an adequate, professional force. Recently, the United States decided to deploy eight provincial reconstruction teams (PRTs), each of which includes fifty to seventy U.S. military personnel along with diplomatic-and, in principle, economic-assistance specialists.

To date, PRTs have been established in Kunduz, Bamian, and Gardez. The concept is controversial; aid officials and many nongovernmental organizations (NGOs) worry about blurring the distinction between security and reconstruction and between military and civilian purposes. The PRTs' main purpose is to help in reconstruction by "winning hearts and minds through small projects."

In June 2003, the transitional Afghan government remains in the early stages of extending its authority beyond Kabul's city limits. Governance outside the capital is shared between autonomous local leaders-the most prominent of which are Ismail Khan in Herat, Abdurrashid Dostum and his rival Atta Muhammad around Mazar-e-Sharif, and Gul Agha in Kandahar-and functionaries that work for the transitional administration. Some local leaders are responsible, but most are old-fashioned warlords—in many cases the very same warlords whose depredations, including toward women, paved the way for the rise of the Taliban. In the Pashtun areas in southern and eastern Afghanistan, political authority remains highly fractured. Karzai is often viewed as a token Pashtun and front man for Panjsheri and American interests. In the absence of effective security forces of the central government, private armies and militias continue to hold sway over most of the countryside. The immediate political tasks spelled out by the Bonn agreement are to complete work on a new constitution and to hold national elections. Significant constitutional and legal questions need to be resolved before convening a loya jirgato consider the draft constitution.

Modern Afghanistan has a history of centralized governance in nearly permanent tension with semiautonomous local and regional tribal rule. The challenge for the constitution makers is to find a legal formula that captures this continuing reality. The constitution must also define the role of Islam in the new state. This calls for balancing traditional Islamic legal values with the legal system that the monarchy established in the 1920s.

Although religious conservatives continue to have a strong voice, life under the Taliban provided Afghans with a cautionary example that may serve as a brake on the revival of the harshest forms of Islamist rule and of the related persecution of women. The task of organizing and conducting national elections by June 2004 poses complex challenges. Election and political party laws need to be adopted .Voters have to be registered. Some sort of census must be conducted to ensure the fair allocation of parliamentary seats. This is a daunting task in a country with such poor communications and administrative infrastructures. In determining the representation of different regions and ethnic groups, the census count and subsequent allocation of seats will raise extremely delicate political issues. To date, little if any progress has been made in these tasks. Time is running short.

Although the timetable for drafting the constitution and holding a loya jirga still seems feasible, there are growing doubts that national elections can be organized in an orderly and fair manner before June 2004. One way to address this problem would be to separate presidential and parliamentary polls, holding the voting for the head of state in line with the Bonn timetable but putting off the parliamentary elections until later. This would provide the additional time needed for the complex and highly sensitive task of conducting the census and demarcating electoral districts that accurately reflect the population's distribution. Such a procedure would be far preferable to a disorganized electoral process that fails to gain acceptance as free and fair and impairs the legitimacy of the future Afghan government.

The Afghan people badly want to get on with the job of building a new state structure after two decades of destruction and despair. Despite increased ethnic, regional, and sectarian rivalries, Afghans retain a strong sense of nationhood. Although politically weak, President

Karzai has gained legitimacy and far greater nationwide popularity than any other Afghan figure. Even if their cooperation is often halfhearted, regional and local leaders are willing, rhetorically at least, to acknowledge Karzai's pre-eminence and leadership. During the past two decades, Afghanistan's neighbours have actively interfered in the country's internal affairs, supporting ethnic and tribal brethren and local favorites. Breaking this habit will be difficult, but the United States must make this a major policy objective in the effort to bolster the stability of the new Afghan government. The recent upsurge in attacks by Taliban supporters, often mounted from Pakistan's tribal areas, has once more brought this issue to the fore. The porous frontier and the history of recent years make clear that elements in Pakistan can interfere in Afghanistan any time they choose to do so. Hence the deep concern caused by the electoral success of pro-Taliban Islamist parties in the October 2002 Pakistani elections.

The Pakistani Inter-Services Intelligence Directorate (ISI) is widely assumed to have maintained operational contacts with Taliban remnants, who have sought refuge in Pakistan's border areas, as well as with Gulbuddin Hekmatyar, a renegade former mujahideen commander. Whether these links are the result of lower-level rogue operatives or have the tacit support of upper echelons of the ISI remains an open question.

The United States should press Pakistan to do a better job of controlling the border areas and make emphatically clear that any official or unofficial support for interference in Afghanistan would be inconsistent with Pakistan's role in the war against terrorism and with improved U.S.-Pakistan relations. Iran can also disturb the fragile situation in Afghanistan by intensifying military and political support in certain areas, especially Herat and the Hazarajat. Even though the United States has no diplomatic relations with Iran, the two countries have had ongoing discussions, including Afghan-specific talks. Tehran may also listen to others, in particular, Europe and Russia, concerning Afghanistan. Moreover, the United States has considerable leverage, in terms of both military and financial carrots and sticks, with Herat's governor, Ismail Khan, who has close ties with Iran. Russia's providing military equipment to warlord Abdurrashid Dostum's forces and maintaining a separate, direct relationship with Marshall Fahim, while keeping cordial relations with the transitional government, are also disturbing and need to be addressed.

In the new strategic environment, Afghanistan's neighbours stand to benefit from its stability. The country's poverty and enormous reconstruction requirements ensure that no government in Kabul will be able to threaten regional stability or peace for the foreseeable future. But Afghanistan's neighbours can aggravate existing instability if they once more actively interfere in Afghanistan's internal affairs. Their governments all say that they are not interfering and in fact desire friendly relations with the Karzai government. The aim of U.S. diplomacy should be to see that reality corresponds with stated policy. In trying to deter outside meddling in Afghanistan, the United States should undertake a major diplomatic initiative to follow up the December 2002 effort of the Karzai government that obtained noninterference pledges from Afghanistan's neighbours.

This was a useful step but should be buttressed by a far broader and more ambitious international undertaking, the purpose of which would be to reaffirm and strengthen the pledge of noninterference in Afghanistan's internal affairs, to agree on banning the supply of arms and other military equipment to local Afghan groups, and to accept current Afghan borders, including the Durand Line frontier with Pakistan.

The U.S.-sponsored initiative should also promote regional agreements between Afghanistan and its neighbours to improve customs collection, transit trade, and border control. To be effective, the initiative must involve Afghanistan, all its immediate neighbours-Pakistan, Iran, Turkmenistan, Uzbekistan, Tajikistan, and China-and other interested powers, including the United States, Russia, Saudi Arabia, India, the European Union, and Japan. Although such a major international accord could not on its own end cross-border interference, it would create a barrier to this highly destabilizing conduct and strengthen the position of the new Afghan state. It would also provide a politically palatable vehicle to resolve the long-standing and still potentially troublesome frontier dispute with Pakistan. For the agreement to have maximum impact, its signing should coincide with the assumption of power by the new Afghan government in 2004.

Two decades of conflict-during which Afghanistan experienced Soviet occupation, jihad, civil war, Taliban rule, and Operation Enduring Freedom-have left the country a wasteland. Never well developed, the country's infrastructure lay in ruins when the Taliban were ousted in November 2001. Roads, electric power plants, hospitals, schools, and irrigation and telecommunications facilities were heavily damaged. The capital city of Kabul was in shambles. Afghanistan's administrative structure had collapsed. The process of developing a blueprint for rebuilding Afghanistan, deciding on a division of labour among aid donors, and establishing a coordinating mechanism has required time. The Karzai government started from scratch. In the beginning, there were ministers but no ministries. The assistance effort was at first predictably beset by confusion, differing and often conflicting procedures and priorities among donors, and inadequate donor coordination. Although the aid machinery has begun to function more efficiently, significant problems remain in the areas of donor coordination, high administrative costs, and ensuring the flow of adequate resources for reconstruction.

Understandably, the initial focus of assistance lay on meeting immediate humanitarian needs. The impact of several years of drought and an unexpectedly large inflow of returning refugees (in itself a positive sign) required a massive effort to prevent starvation and provide shelter from the winter's bitter cold. The transitional government has slowly gained capacity, even if it remains a work in progress.

One important achievement was the successful introduction of a new currency in the fall of 2002, a symbolically important assertion of sovereignty and authority. As summer 2003 begins, emphasis is shifting from providing short-term relief and humanitarian assistance to the longer-term task of national reconstruction. To its credit, the Karzai government has developed rational operational and development priorities and incorporated these into a consolidated national budget for 2003. In meetings in Kabul and in Brussels during March 2003, the foreign donor community accepted the Afghan budget as the basis for moving ahead. It agreed in principle to funnel assistance through the central government and to ensure that donor priorities match those that the Afghans themselves have established. It is essential that the United States and other donors implement these undertakings; failure to do so will seriously undercut the credibility of the central government and the reconstruction effort.

The 2003 budget calls for a total expenditure of $2.25 billion $550 million for salaries and government operations and $1.7 billion for development. Donor pledges cover 88 percent, leaving a gap of $276 million. Of the uncovered amount, $200 million is slated to cover salaries and government operations, a highly sensitive area. The transitional government, at this juncture, collects few taxes or customs revenues and has to rely on the uncertain largesse of foreign aid donors to pay civil servants and meet other basic administrative expenses. In order to strengthen the central government, it is vital that control of customs collection at the major border crossing points passes from regional leaders to the authorities in Kabul. Ismail Khan in Herat took in $100 million in custom duties last year, a sum larger than the $80 million that the transitional government was able to collect nationwide. He turned over only $10 million to the central government.

During fiscal year (FY) 2002, the United States contributed $928 million and has said that it intends to meet or exceed this amount in 2003. It is essential that the United States and other donors deliver fully on their aid pledges, that contributions are made in a timely manner, and that they address needs that the transitional authorities have identified. It is also important that foreign donors, including the United States, work through and not bypass the central government in developing and implementing their assistance projects. One of Hamid Karzai's major political strengths has been his ability to secure substantial amounts of foreign assistance. His capability to direct aid activities to different parts of the country-in effect the power of patronage-gives him a potent tool in enlarging the authority of the central government and valuable leverage in the process of incorporating regional leaders into the national administrative structure. A key element of the demobilization process will be Kabul's ability to provide alternative employment for former militia fighters. Economic development is also vital in stopping the resurgence of poppy production. Unfortunately, Afghanistan has once more become the world's largest producer of opium. In 2002, according to the UN, Afghanistan produced 3,400 tons of the drug.

New Priorities in South Asia more than eighteen times the amount produced during the last year of Taliban rule. The estimated value of this harvest to producers and traffickers (mostly the latter) was $2.5 billion-twice the total aid Afghanistan received from all donors in 2002. The British have taken lead responsibility in dealing with the narcotics problem but, absent alternative sources of income for the farmers, have made little progress.

Despite significant achievements since the defeat of the Taliban, Afghans feel frustrated and disappointed by the slow pace of economic reconstruction. Reality has fallen far short of public hopes and expectations. In part to provide more tangible signs of progress, the donor community agreed to rebuild the major roads between Kabul and the other principal Afghan cities: Mazar-e-Sharif in the north, Jalalabad in the east, Kandahar in the south, and Herat in the west. After two decades of conflict and neglect, these transportation links-mostly constructed by the United States or the Soviet Union during the Cold War competition-are in terrible condition. Their ruts and potholes represent a serious barrier to the resumption of more normal life and economic recovery. The United States has assumed responsibility for the stretch of road between Kabul and Kandahar. Saudi Arabia, Iran, Japan, and the Asian Development Bank have agreed to undertake other parts of the project. To bolster the overall credibility of the United States and the international assistance effort, it is essential that the U.S. Agency for International Development (USAID) complete the American portion by the end of 2003, as promised by President Bush, and that other donors move expeditiously in their sectors. The road projects have enormous symbolic value but will also have a great and positive economic impact.

2

South Asian Development: Paradigm Shift

While the United States and the world continue to debate whether the events of September 11, 2001, transformed world politics, the resulting U.S. war on terrorism clearly marks a critical shift in South Asian international relations. Although the Bush administration might have believed its initial involvement in South Asia after the attacks to be merely instrumental in the pursuit of larger U.S. aims, U.S. policy toward the region since September 11 has signaled a fundamental change in both the intensity and the quality of U.S. involvement in South Asia. Looking beyond the immediate objectives of the war on terrorism, the United States has begun to focus on the deeper conflicts that have long troubled the region. For its part, the region itself has been more receptive than ever before to the new U.S. engagement.

The result is a potential reorientation of the subcontinent. If the Bush administration can sustain the level of involvement it has demonstrated since September 11, the prospect of reordering both the subcontinent's interstate relations and its intrastate dynamics is real. And at the same time, South Asia might even prove an immediate, visible success of the Bush administration's expansive war against terrorism. Unlike elsewhere in the world, where criticism of the U.S. war on terrorism has been trenchant even among U.S. allies, key sections of the region's political class have seen the U.S. effort as an opportunity. Few areas in the world have experienced the ravages of international terrorism like the subcontinent, where terrorism has really become part of everyday life.

As the United States began to demonstrate greater interest in the region, South Asian leaders eagerly moved to draw Washington into their regional and internal disputes by offering military cooperation in the war on terror. Although unstated, the new welcoming attitude toward the U.S. military presence and an enhanced U.S. security role in the region reflect a recognition that South Asian security has become a global issue and that the region's problems now are no longer manageable within the confines of either domestic political or bilateral frameworks.

The return of the United States to the subcontinent at a deeper level of engagement than in the past can be considered poetic justice. After all, the successful U.S. strategy against the Soviet Union in the final phase of the Cold War set the stage for the rise of religious extremism and international terrorism in South Asia by pitting the jihadis against godless Communists in Afghanistan during the Reagan administration. After triumph over the Soviet Union, the United States turned its back on Afghanistan, and the region saw the rise of the bastard children born from such U.S. strategy-Osama bin Laden and the Taliban. The northwestern part of the subcontinent-where the

United States trapped the Soviet bear and bled it to death-became the new epicenter of international terrorism against the West. Although those jihadis were anticommunist, they were even more fundamentally anti-Western and opposed to the core values of the Enlightenment and modernity. It might take the full might of the world's sole superpower, drawn to the region by the drastic events of September 11, to begin to undo the unintended consequences of U.S. strategy in the last lap of the Cold War.

The United States attempted to deal with a broad spectrum of issues bedevilling the region-not merely religious extremism and international terrorism - throughout the 1990s, but the attacks in New York City and Washington, D.C., brought a new energy and purpose to U.S. engagement. In addition, for the first time in years, finding final solutions, or at least initiating processes to deal with long-standing regional conflicts, have won political attention in Washington. Although doubts remain in the region as well as in Washington about the U.S. ability to stay with South Asian problems in the coming years, U.S. involvement to this point has already begun to shape a new potential for South Asian security.

With the subcontinent more willing than ever to see the United States play a larger role, change is likely. This paradigm shift in U.S. policy toward the region since September 11 can be gleaned from heightened U.S. interest in balanced relations with India and with Pakistan, U.S. efforts to manage the nuclear flash point in Kashmir, and the conscious U.S. promotion of wider regional stability and economic integration.

The most significant discontinuity in South Asia since September 11 has been the development of sound bilateral relations between the United States and both India and

Pakistan. One year after the attacks, the Bush administration can rightfully boast of strong equities and unprecedented good relations with New Delhi and Islamabad.

Throughout the Cold War, U.S. policy toward India and Pakistan inevitably took shape in a zero-sum game. The critical nature of Pakistan in U.S. Cold War alliances coupled with India's drift toward the Soviet Union and its emphasis on nonalignment reinforced a special bond in Washington's ties with Islamabad as it slowly eviscerated U.S. relations with India. After the Cold War, Washington tried to build relations with both capitals on a different basis, but the excessive U.S. focus on nonproliferation limited prospects for closer ties.

Worse still, U.S. pressure to limit formally the two countries' nuclear programs eventually led to the overt nuclearization of the subcontinent in May 1998. The imposition of mandatory nuclear sanctions against India and Pakistan following the nuclear tests seemed to further undermine U.S. relations with both. U.S. engagement with postnuclear South Asia, however, produced unexpected and somewhat counter intuitive results-a significant improvement in U.S.-Indian relations and the perceptible stagnation if not deterioration of U.S.-Pakistani relations, as reflected in President Bill Clinton's tour of the subcontinent in 2000. He spent five days in India and barely a few hours in Pakistan, where he fit in a public broadcast to warn the Pakistani people that, if their nation did not change course, it would become isolated in the international arena.

Months before, in the Kargil conflict between India and Pakistan, the Clinton administration acted decisively in India's favor by pressuring Pakistan to end its aggression across the line of control unconditionally and unambiguously. This U.S. intervention was the very first in New Delhi's favor in the unending sequence of Indo-Pakistani conflicts.

Clinton's distinct approaches and emphases in dealing with India and Pakistan reflected the new sense in Washington that India was an emerging power in the global arena and a potential U.S. partner. In contrast, Pakistan was seen as a failing state headed further in the wrong direction. Perspectives on the subcontinent diverged as well. India saw the U.S. agenda as positive and covering a wide spectrum of issues while Pakistan viewed U.S. policy objectives negatively for the most part and directed toward ending Pakistani support of the Taliban, narcotics trafficking, and religious extremism.

President George W. Bush and his administration conveyed even more vigorously the U.S. distinction between India and Pakistan and the new, positive U.S. attitude toward New Delhi. India's quick and enthusiastic support of the U.S. missile defense initiative in May 2001-so dear to the administration's ideologues-first drew India closer to the Republican White House.

As the Bush administration sought to add a new strategic component to the U.S.-Indian relationship, it ultimately saw India as a potential counterweight to China, which until September 11 ranked high on the list of newly designated possible enemies of the United States. U.S.-Indian relations just before the attacks, therefore, were marked by expectations of a new journey about to begin. Pakistan, on the other hand, which had returned to military rule in October 1999, was increasingly isolated internationally and virtually off the radar screen for the United States. India appeared close to achieving its long-sought objective of marginalizing Pakistani relations with the United States. In Islamabad, fears grew that the Bush administration was leaning toward India. September 11 changed all that, and the new U.S. war against the Taliban and Al Qaeda brought Pakistan center stage. In the immediate aftermath of the attacks, India was quick to offer full military cooperation in the unfolding U.S. war against terrorism.

New Delhi's decision was widely unexpected and new for Indian foreign policy, which had been shaped for decades by the principles of nonalignment. India's offer was based on New Delhi's assessment that a decisive moment in world affairs had arrived and should be seized firmly. India also believed that supporting the U.S. war on terrorism would go a long way in dealing with its own security threats from Pakistan's support of terrorism in Kashmir and beyond. New Delhi calculated that the events of September 11 would finally clinch the much-vaunted natural alliance, which India had hoped to build since the late 1990s, and take it to new levels. Nevertheless, while India enthusiastically courted Washington after September 11, the United States chose reluctant Pakistan as its partner against the Taliban.

New Instincts and Strategies

Geographic access to the main theatre of war in Afghanistan as well as the Pakistani army's intimate knowledge of the Taliban were, of course, decisive in Washington's choice to invite Pakistani Gen. Pervez Musharraf's support for the new war. For Musharraf, the choice was not quite so easy. On one hand, the opportunity to renew a strategic relationship with the

United States at a critical moment for Washington might be too valuable for Pakistan to pass up. On the other hand, working with the United States would mean sacrificing two decades of Pakistan's political and emotional investment in Afghanistan.

Establishing a friendly, if not pliable, regime in Kabul, which traditionally had been closer to New Delhi than to Islamabad, had been a long-standing political objective for Pakistan. Moreover, powerful sections of the army had helped to nurture the very Islamic extremist groups in Afghanistan that the United States planned to confront. India's eagerness to offer all operational support to U.S. forces also severely constrained Musharraf's ability to negotiate the terms and conditions of Pakistani support with Washington.

Yet, the pros of working with the United States outweighed the cons for Musharraf, and he made the fateful choice to support the U.S. war on terror against the Taliban. Musharraf hoped that, by offering military bases and other support to the United States, he could salvage some gains from the old Afghan policy and retain a little political leverage in Kabul; end Pakistan's political isolation; prevent U.S targeting of his nuclear assets; and gain U.S. economic as well as political support for Pakistan's Kashmir policy vis-à-vis India.

Pakistan's secular elite, frustrated by the domestic consequences of the nation's Afghan policy and support for jihad, welcomed the renewed embrace of the United States as a way to end Pakistan's isolation and modify its alliance with Afghanistan's extremist forces. In India, however, renewed U.S. economic assistance to Pakistan and U.S. lionization of Musharraf for his contributions to the war against terrorism caused deep disappointment among those who hoped that the events of September 11 would solidify and heighten U.S.-Indian relations. Those Indians skeptical of New Delhi's extraordinary political investment in improving relations with the United States since the late 1990s now argued with some credibility that India had been barking up the wrong tree and that Washington had never been thinking about giving up its special relationship with Islamabad. This quick shift in U.S. affections on the subcontinent at such a crucial moment in international affairs seemed to bring the triangular relationship among New Delhi, Islamabad, and Washington back to an all too familiar and frustrating square one.

At the official level, India expressed a number of concerns about the unexpected turn of events. Perhaps the least important of New Delhi's concerns was that U.S. dependence on Pakistan to prosecute the war against the Taliban might mean retaining elements of the so-called moderate Taliban in the power structure in Kabul even after the war. Of greater concern was the possibility that Pakistan would be able to insulate its own support of terrorism in Kashmir from the more broadly declared objectives of the U.S. war on terrorism. In other words, New Delhi officials were fairly unanimous in their certainty that the United States, to keep Musharraf on its side, would employ double standards in its pursuit-pursuing those terrorists threatening its own security and not those tormenting India. And because groups in Pakistan were the source of Indian threats, the United States would be unwilling to counter them.

Finally, and most crucial to New Delhi, pessimism began to cloud public thinking on the future of U.S.-Indian relations based on the feeling that post-September 11 developments had swept away more than a decade of political efforts to restructure the relationship with the United States. The apparent undercutting of Indian expectations of a new relationship-the centrepiece of the foreign policy transition underway in New Delhi throughout the 1990s-made temptations to return to old ways of thinking irresistible. To its credit, the Bush administration managed the new challenge exceptionally well. Whether it had a conscious strategy or not, it displayed a rare U.S. sensitivity in not undermining its new relationship with India even as it reached out to Pakistan.

The Northern Alliance's rapid advance following weeks of U.S. bombing in Afghanistan and the Taliban's subsequent swift collapse, calmed Indian fears about retaining moderate elements in the regime. Furthermore, from India's point of view, the U.S. refusal to accept some of the conditions that Pakistan had made regarding preventing the Northern Alliance's entry into Kabul, for example, suggested that Washington would follow its own counsel rather than give weight to Pakistan's interests in the U.S. war in Afghanistan. Moreover, the Bush administration consistently sought to assure India that the war on terror would have no double standards.

The United States insisted that it would have to set priorities in confronting the challenge but also hinted that, once the immediate threat in Afghanistan was tackled, India's terrorist concerns would also be addressed. On their own, these assurances had limited credibility, but U.S. assurances gained legitimacy in New Delhi from Washington's response to a series of major terrorist incidents in India after September 11. On October 1, 2001, in Srinagar; on December 13, 2001, at the Parliament House in New Delhi; and on May 14, 2002, at Kaluchak in Jammu and Kashmir-as well as when India threatened to go to war against Pakistan in the summer of 2002-the United States moved to restrain Pakistan from supporting terrorist acts in India. As part of this activism, the United States formally acknowledged the link between Kashmiri terrorist groups operating in Pakistan and the Pakistani state itself for the first time. This act pressured Musharraf to proclaim in an important address to the nation on January 12, 2002, that Pakistani soil would not be used to export terror to any part of the world, resulting in formal commitments from Pakistan to end all cross-border infiltration and not to disrupt the fall elections for the Jammu and Kashmir Assembly in Kashmir.

Despite Pakistan's demands that India engage in talks on Kashmir immediately, the Bush administration backed India's broad negotiating position that the creation of an appropriate environment free of violence must precede negotiations. The U.S. decision to confront Pakistan about its support of Kashmiri terrorism marked a big gain for India, despite Indian doubts about Musharraf's ability and willingness to honour his commitments to end cross-border terrorism. Both Washington and New Delhi have become increasingly aware, however, that their intense interaction since September 11 has focused more on terrorism issues and management of the crisis between India and Pakistan than in the past. Unfortunately, the rapid, grand advancement in bilateral relations that would include stronger economic ties and U.S. liberalization of high-technology transfer, among other things, has not materialized.

Bilateral defense cooperation has resumed, and for the first time in decades, the United States is considering transferring weapons systems to India. Nevertheless, if the United States were to resume major arms sales to Pakistan, the incipient defense engagement between the United States and India could once again be pushed off the rails. More fundamentally, the perception that the Bush administration no longer feels an urgency to build a strategic partnership with India is gaining ground in New Delhi.

Senior officials in the Bush administration have reaffirmed that India matters, but reassurance has not reversed the growing sense in New Delhi that, despite India's break from the past in supporting the United States in several controversial arenas such as missile defense, the International Criminal Court, and environmental issues, Washington is holding back support on issues of importance to India, particularly high technology cooperation. The Bush administration appears committed to laying the foundation for a robust long-term relationship with India, but the realization of that foundation seems to remain some distance away.

Despite some disappointment in New Delhi about the U.S. ability to develop stronger bilateral ties with India or sufficiently influence Pakistan on terrorism, within the year following September 11, the United States without question has created the basis for a different kind of engagement in South Asia. Unlike in the early 1980s, when the renewed U.S.-Pakistani partnership pushed U.S.-Indian relations into the wilderness, Washington has managed today to sustain broad-based engagement with both Islamabad and New Delhi. The U.S. development of equities on both sides, however, is entirely different from the application of those equities to such practical purposes as assisting India and Pakistan to resolve the Kashmir dispute and normalize bilateral relations. Yet, the intense U.S. effort to defuse tensions between India and Pakistan in the summer of 2002 has in fact opened up the political space for the United States to move from crisis management to conflict resolution in South Asia. The Bush administration has rhetorically expressed reluctance to devote political energy to finding solutions to regional conflicts but has moved certainly-albeit slowly-toward attempting a potentially historic reconciliation between India and Pakistan.

Peace Initiatives

Fear that war between India and Pakistan over Kashmir could escalate to the nuclear level has been at the heart of U.S. foreign policy concerns in South Asia since the late 1980s. The notion of a nuclear flash point fused two separate issues at play between India and Pakistan. One was their continuing dispute over Jammu and Kashmir, which has acquired a new edge since the late 1980s, while the other was the U.S. objective to limit the proliferation of weapons of mass destruction (WMD) on the subcontinent. Since the 1990s, the United States has devoted considerable energy to dealing with these two separate challenges without much success. U.S. pressures on the nonproliferation front backfired with the Indian decision to go nuclear in May 1998 and Pakistan's move to follow suit. In addition, the Clinton administration's attempts to bring the Kashmir question to the center of its South Asian policy were strongly supported by Pakistan but vehemently rejected by India, leaving its Kashmir initiative in limbo. The Bush administration took office with less of an ideological commitment to nonproliferation and even less of an interest in getting embroiled in settling the Kashmir dispute. The United States hoped to build distinct relationships with India and Pakistan, with a special emphasis on the former. September 11 not only shifted U.S attention to Pakistan but also added new gravity to the need to diffuse recurring nuclear crises between India and Pakistan as well as the underlying causes for the enduring tension between the two.

Prior to September 11, 2001, the Bush administration seemed ready to lift the sanctions imposed against India after the May 1998 tests. Unlike the Clinton administration, which made progress on the nonproliferation front central to the normalization of bilateral relations with India, the Bush administration was prepared to move forward without even referring to nonproliferation.

Among the benchmarks set by the Clinton administration, India's ratification of the Comprehensive Test Ban Treaty (CTBT) was critical. The Bush administration rejected the CTBT and other multilateral arms control arrangements; it was not going to tie its relations with India to the fate of one treaty. Unlike the nonproliferation zealots of the prior administration, the new leadership in Washington seemed prepared to think out of the box about the subcontinent's nonproliferation problem-to live and deal with the reality of nuclear weapons rather than set unrealistic objectives for U.S. policy in the region.

Even prior to September 11, the Bush administration faced stiff bureaucratic resistance to unconventional proposals such as giving nuclear safety assistance to India and Pakistan to ensure stable deterrence or rethinking the value of denying advanced technologies to India in the name of nonproliferation. The administration, which has enforced new thinking on global arms control and deterrence in Washington and beyond, has yet to come up with different answers to the nuclear problem on the subcontinent. Observers believe that the administration is in the middle of a comprehensive review of U.S. nonproliferation objectives on the subcontinent. New regional concerns post-September 11 necessitate that this review deal with new challenges including New Delhi's quest for missile defenses, its desire for greater access to advanced U.S. technologies, the danger of Pakistani nuclear weapons falling into the hands of jihadis or a renegade section of the armed forces, and the destabilizing impact of cross-border terrorism on nuclear stability.

The administration must also consider that a technology denial regime against India makes little sense because it ignores recent technological developments in India; disregards New Delhi's emerging capability to export sensitive technologies, even while it remains outside the international architecture constructed to manage WMD proliferation; and belies U.S. proclamations of a strategic partnership with New Delhi. The Bush administration's efforts to prevent nuclear war between India and Pakistan mark the one consistency in U.S. nonproliferation policy.

As New Delhi and Islamabad moved toward acquiring nuclear capabilities in the late 1980s, the United States moved repeatedly to defuse military crises between the two rivals: the crisis over the Brass Tacks military exercises launched by India in the winter of 1986-1987; tensions between India and Pakistan in the summer of 1990; the 1999 Kargil conflict; and the Indian military mobilization after the attack on parliament on December 13, 2001. This last crisis, however, was more severe than the others, given the intensity and credibility of the Indian war threat if Pakistan did not put an end to cross-border terrorism. India's threat not only promptly drew the Bush administration into the crisis but also forced Washington to look at the political sources of the conflict and at finding ways to alleviate them.

The high-level political intervention of the United States in South Asia during May and June 2002 succeeded in that it ended, at least temporarily, the threat of imminent war. At the heart of the U.S. crisis-management strategy was the acquisition of a commitment from Pakistan to end cross-border infiltration permanently and a promise from India that it would engage in substantive dialogue on all bilateral issues, particularly the Kashmir dispute, when violence ceased. Although these reciprocal promises appeared to have staved off the immediate threat of war, that threat has not completely receded.

Washington learned that it cannot intervene every few years to defuse a nuclear crisis between India and Pakistan; instead, it must find a way to reduce the enduring hostility between the two nations. While defusing the 2002 crisis, the Bush administration stumbled upon three realizations that could provide the framework for a genuine peace process on the subcontinent:

— Pakistan's sponsorship of cross-border terrorism can no longer be ignored or condoned.

— Conflict resolution efforts are critical to end recurrent crises between India and Pakistan.

— Free, fair, inclusive, and nonviolent elections to the state assembly on the Indian side of Kashmir could be the starting point of a peace process on the subcontinent.

In the summer of 2002, U.S. crisis management anticipated that a credible election in Kashmir could pave the way for talks between New Delhi and Srinagar (the capital of the Indian state of Jammu and Kashmir) to deal with the internal dimensions of the Kashmir question. Negotiations between New Delhi and Islamabad to resolve the external dimensions of the Kashmir issue and normalize bilateral relations were also expected to follow elections, which have been widely seen as free and fair. Implementing this new framework requires that the Bush administration take an active role to promote the peace process between India and Pakistan.

The traditionally stated position that India and Pakistan should bilaterally resolve the Kashmir conflict while taking the wishes of the Kashmiri people into account is no longer sufficient. A significant change in Indian attitudes about U.S. involvement in the dispute has facilitated U.S. intervention in the Kashmir conflict and U.S. efforts to promote a peace process. For decades, India has emphasized bilateralism and fiercely opposed both U.S. intervention in its disputes with Pakistan and the internationalization of the conflict, but the Clinton administration's response to the Kargil experience in 1999 demonstrated that U.S. intervention need not be against Indian interests.

A new trust in U.S.-Indian relations, hopes for a more substantive relationship with Washington, U.S. efforts to press Pakistan to end cross-border terrorism, and the new political recognition of the importance of finding a final solution to the Kashmir dispute in both Washington and New Delhi have allowed India to contemplate an increased role for the United States in subcontinental relations. Although India is not likely to accept formal third-party mediation, if the United States can deliver the conditions for a serious peace process that could lead to a reasonable final solution to the Kashmir dispute, India is likely to welcome some form of discrete U.S. facilitation. On the Kashmir question and its broader relationship with Pakistan, however, India continues to insist that at the table there is only room for two-New Delhi and Islamabad. India will never accept direct third party mediation in its negotiations with Pakistan, where concessions and compromise might be determined and communicated through any actor other than itself and Pakistan. Even an overt U.S. enthusiasm-in the form of declaring an intent to mediate the dispute or appointing special envoys on Kashmir-could lead to political backlash in New Delhi and an eventual rejection of a third-party role all together. But unlike in the past, New Delhi does appear ready to accept a behind-the-scenes, low-key U.S. role in nudging the peace process along.

The Bush administration has demonstrated more subtlety in its diplomatic activism in Kashmir than its predecessor. It has established positive relations with both New Delhi and Islamabad, engineered a productive triangular diplomatic process, and is currently in a rare position to impart momentum to a resolution of the Indo-Pakistani conflict. It must acknowledge that Kashmir has a long history of failed international diplomatic efforts and should not underestimate the potential pitfalls of the present situation. A sustained effort by extremist groups as well as sections of the Pakistani armed forces to execute large-scale terrorist acts, leading to renewed military tensions between India and Pakistan, could undermine the delicate triangular diplomacy currently in play. Still, the prospect of fostering a changed relationship between India and Pakistan through U.S. diplomacy has never, in the last few decades, looked as real as it does now.

The events of September 11 not only lent a new urgency to U.S. involvement in India's and Pakistan's problems-historically on the U.S. radar screen, if not a pressing concern-but also catalyzed a new focus on other conflicts on the subcontinent, particularly in Sri Lanka and Nepal. The last years of the Clinton administration brought some new attention to Bangladesh as the discovery of large natural gas reserves, rising U.S. investments in the energy sector, improved economic and social indicators, and the sense that Bangladesh could emerge as a new symbol of successful democratic experimentation among Islamic nations collectively spurred some interest in Washington in developing relations with Dhaka.

For the most part, though, U.S. attention during the Clinton administration was motivated by these economic and political objectives. As part of the U.S. strategy to root out the forces of extremism and to encourage the resolution of conflicts that breed terrorism, the United States became more directly involved in the long-running civil war in Sri Lanka and the more recent but equally virulent Maoist insurgency threat in Nepal. High-level political contacts between Washington and Colombo have been more frequent in the year after September 11 than in recent decades; Washington also lent strong political support to international initiatives aimed at countering terrorism and promoting peace within each country.

The new realization in Washington that defeating terrorism meant dealing with failing states pushed the Bush administration to recognize that this kind of threat on the subcontinent was real in regions in addition to Kashmir and to build its political contacts with the leaders of Nepal and Sri Lanka by receiving them in Washington and dispatching senior leaders to these countries. U.S.

interest in finding ways to address the two-decades-old civil war in Sri Lanka, where nearly 60,000 lives have been lost in the ethnic conflict between the Singhalese majority and the Tamil minority, predates September 11.

Because the activity of the Liberation Tigers of Tamil Eelam (LTTE) had strong financing sources in the United States, the terrorist organization was technically under the ambit of U.S. law and was therefore designated a foreign terrorist organization in the late 1990s. The Clinton administration backed Norway's political initiative to facilitate a dialogue between the Sri Lankan government and the LTTE at the turn of the decade, which proved extremely valuable as it helped to broker a ceasefire at the end of 2001. The Norwegian initiative's success, however, also depended on the decisive warning from the United States to the LTTE in early 2002 not to use the peace talks to regroup, rearm, and provoke another round of confrontation, as it had done in the past.

Veiled in the warning was the suggestion that the LTTE could become a target of the U.S. war on terrorism, driving home an understanding among Tamil extremists that they would need to rethink their strategy. India's own strong support of the peace process in Sri Lanka and its refusal to allow the LTTE any leeway contributed to a new set of external circumstances, which helped to provide the opportunity to end civil war and move toward political settlement. In Nepal, there is less optimism about the prospects for ending the ongoing Nepali civil war between the government and the Maoist rebels, which has entered its sixth year. Deep divisions within the Nepali political class and within the ruling party have made it that much more difficult to deal with the greatest challenge in Nepali history. Along with Great Britain, the United States unveiled an international initiative in June 2002 to provide Kathmandu with military support to deal with the Maoist insurgency and with badly needed economic relief in a country where the principal source of income-tourism-has been badly damaged by terrorist threats. That this international initiative also seeks good governance reforms within Nepal can be interpreted as a direct reflection of the post-September 11 U.S. foreign policy tenet that failing and corrupt states tend to breed and condone terrorism. India, which historically has had a special relationship with Kathmandu and was suspicious of third-party meddling in the internal affairs of Nepal, now appears ready to work with the international community to address the challenges faced by Nepal. Its new positive relationship with the United States allowed New Delhi to join the international initiative to coordinate external military and economic assistance to Nepal.

Prospects for Partnership

The globalization of South Asian security promulgated by the events of September 11 brought an increase in U.S.-Indian consultation on subcontinental security issues. In the past, a desire to preserve India's exclusive role in managing conflicts and to prevent other great powers from infringing on what India considered its sphere of influence directed Indian policy toward its smaller neighbours. Although New Delhi could not fully stop China and Pakistan from penetrating this zone, protecting the sphere of influence remained a dominant national security imperative for New Delhi. Initially, India was deeply skeptical of the Norwegian initiative in Sri Lanka and even suspected that it might be the wedge for an Anglo-American foray into the subcontinent. Nevertheless, the broader context of improved U.S.-Indian relations, Norwegian efforts to keep India informed about the Sri Lankan peace process, and the shared Indian and Western interests in preserving Sri Lanka's territorial integrity and defeating the forces of terrorism and extremism in the region especially after September 11-collectively eased Indian concerns about U.S. involvement in its sphere.

Even when New Delhi sought and expected improved U.S.-Indian relations just prior to September 11, India would have opposed an increased U.S. military and diplomatic presence in its immediate neighborhood. In the current state of international affairs, however, India recognizes the U.S. potential to act as a stabilizing force and understands that its own regional interests are commensurate with, not opposed to, current U.S. priorities. Now, the challenge facing New Delhi and Washington is to transform a consultative process into more substantive political and security cooperation to address failing states, promote political moderation, resolve regional conflicts, and defeat regional extremism.

This cooperation should also extend to working together to nudge Pakistan in a more positive direction politically. Such a proposal might seem strange given the history of the triangular relationship among New Delhi, Islamabad, and Washington, but both India and the United States should have an interest in moving Pakistan toward political modernization and social stability. Although there is no concrete evidence that New Delhi and Washington could accomplish this task together, it is even less likely that either could on its own.

If the globalization of security post-September 11 has helped pave new paths for political cooperation between New Delhi and Washington, then economic change in the region during the 1990s laid the foundation for U.S.-Indian cooperation to promote rapid regional economic development through integration. Under the pressure of the Washington Consensus for globalization and privatization, all nations of the subcontinent adopted liberal economic policies during the 1990s. As they open their markets to the world, South Asian states are discovering that they cannot keep them closed to each other. While Islamabad continues to resist normal trade relations with New Delhi, the region's smaller countries are realizing that, like it or not, their economic futures are now intertwined with India.

Meanwhile, proposals for mega-projects such as pipelines and transportation corridors, straddling across borders in South Asia, promise to deepen economic integration on the subcontinent further. Whatever its other negative consequences might be, the relentless pressures of globalization are helping to break down the subcontinents' economic walls. Although entirely in India's favor at the moment, trade volumes within South Asia have begun to surge.

Bangladesh and Sri Lanka are among the top ten export destinations for Indian goods. Nothing less than a reversal of the economic partition of the subcontinent is now in the cards. After partition divided British India into separate states in 1947, insular economic policies and political differences preserved borders as high-security barriers. Globalization offers the prospect of transforming these borders into zones of cooperation to reconnect regions that were once part of the same economic and cultural space. One year after September 11, South Asia is at the cusp of a historic transformation. India has begun to shed the accumulated mistrust of Washington, is seeking stronger bilateral ties, and is ready to work with the United States to promote peace and prosperity in the region. Washington will have to overcome its tendency to obsess over single issues in the region -nonproliferation in the past and the war on terrorism now-but U.S. diplomacy since September 11 has set the stage for a more broadly based U.S. policy toward the subcontinent. New Indian receptivity to U.S. involvement in the region has opened doors for real progress. If the United States does not look beyond the immediate objective of pursuing Al Qaeda groups in the region, however, it risks missing this opportunity for expansive bilateral cooperation with India-in high-technology areas, in coordinating approaches to resolving regional conflicts, and in integrating the South Asian market-that can help reduce the kind of despair that threatens to serve as a breeding ground for violence and terror across the subcontinent.

Bringing Balance in South Asia

U.S. security interests in South Asia concentrate on weapons proliferation, strategies to reduce tensions, antiterrorism, and regional stability. The role of missiles in South Asian security because of their potential use as delivery vehicles for nuclear weapons. As such, the proliferation of missiles in the region is considered to be a central variable in calculations gauging regional stability. During the 1990s, the U.S. security focus in South Asia sought to minimize damage to the nonproliferation regime, prevent escalation of a nuclear arms and missile race, and promote Indo-Pakistani bilateral dialogue, especially on the sovereignty dispute over Kashmir. In light of these goals, the Clinton Administration established five "benchmarks" for India and Pakistan based on the contents of UN

Security Council Res. 1172, which condemned the two countries' nuclear tests of May 1998. These were:

— signing and ratifying the Comprehensive Nuclear Test Ban Treaty (CTBT);

— halting all further production of fissile material and participating in Fissile Material Cutoff Treaty (FMCT) negotiations;

— limiting development and deployment of WMD delivery vehicles;

— implementing strict export controls on WMD materials and technologies; and

— establishing bilateral dialogue between New Delhi and Islamabad.

Progress in each of these areas has been limited, and the Bush Administration makes no reference to the benchmark framework. Neither India nor Pakistan has signed the CTBT, and both appear to be continuing their production of weapons grade fissile materials. The status of weaponization and deployment is unclear, though there are indications that this is occurring at a slow, but more or less steady pace. Earlier optimism in the area of export controls waned as fears have gained credence that these countries, especially Pakistan, might seek to export WMD materials and/or technologies. Finally, while there has been no repeat of the intense 1999 military clashes in Kashmir - and a ten-month-long military standoff in 2002 ended without large-scale fighting—bilateral tensions remain significant, and no substantive dialogue between New Delhi and Islamabad is underway.

Upon taking office, the Bush Administration set out substantively to build upon an initial improvement in U.S.

relations with New Delhi begun by President Clinton, while also shifting U.S. nonproliferation policy from seeking to prevent South Asian nuclearization to encouraging India and Pakistan to be "more responsible nuclear powers." Some analysts have argued that, by moving the U.S. focus away from international nonproliferation treaties such as the CTBT and withdrawing from the Anti-Ballistic Missile Treaty, the Bush Administration's de-emphasis of "vertical proliferation" issues has contributed to legitimizing South Asia's strategic arsenals. In the face of congressional questioning about seeming "contradictions" in U.S.policy, Assistant Secretary of State for South Asia Christina Rocca stated in March 2003 that the United States is taking a "pragmatic approach" that seeks to have India and Pakistan "exercise restraint" with regard to the proliferation of strategic arsenals.

The September 2001 terrorist attacks on the United States and ensuing U.S.-led antiterrorism efforts transformed U.S. relations with India and, especially Pakistan, which again became a "front-line" ally and beneficiary of significant U.S. foreign assistance. India's swift offer of full support for U.S. antiterrorism efforts was widely viewed as reflective of much improved U.S.-India relations. In 2003, and for perhaps the first period in history, the United States simultaneously enjoys positive relations with both countries. This circumstance may mean that the ability of the United States to influence South Asian security dynamics is at an all-time high.

At the same time, differences with Pakistan (over issues of terrorism, proliferation, and democratization) and with India continue to cloud forecasts of future U.S. engagement with South Asia's two largest and nuclear-armed countries. The key issues for Congress addressed here are whether missile proliferation in South Asia enhances or detracts from regional stability and the role of U.S. policy in promoting such stability, as well as in tension reduction and nonproliferation. Levels of U.S. foreign assistance to India and Pakistan, the establishment of aid restrictions, the transfer of conventional weapons platforms (possibly including missile defense systems), the setting of export control parameters and nonproliferation goals, and the maintenance of policy and intelligence oversight of U.S. relations with India and Pakistan all have a vital congressional facet. Pending and future legislation could influence levels of stability in South Asia.

Regional Conflict and the U.S. Role

Understanding present-day missile proliferation in South Asia and relevant U.S. policy options is aided by a review of the historical setting. Three wars - in 1947- 48, 1965, and 1971 - and a constant state of military preparedness on both sides of their shared border have marked the half-century of bitter rivalry between India and Pakistan. A bloody battle in the Kashmiri mountains near Kargil in 1999 cost thousands of lives and marked history's first significant direct clash between the forces of two nuclear-armed countries. Most recently, a 10-month-long military standoff in 2002 involving up to one million Indian and Pakistani soldiers was viewed as the closest the two countries had been to full-scale war since 1971, and caused the U.S. government to become "deeply concerned ... that a conventional war ... could escalate into a nuclear confrontation. "A persistent and often times perplexing aspect of U.S. engagement in the region has been the difficulty of maintaining a more-or-less balanced approach toward two antagonistic countries while simultaneously promoting perceived U.S. interests in South Asia.

India has seven times the population and four times the land area of Pakistan. In 2002, the Indian GDP was more than eight times that of Pakistan, and the Indian military enjoys a 2:1 or 3:1 advantage in numbers of soldiers and conventional arms. Yet, despite India's clearly greater status in these concrete terms, the United States has for the past half-century found itself much more closely engaged with Pakistan, in particular during the 1950s, when Pakistan was part of the U.S.-led alliance system to contain the Soviet Union; the 1980s, when Pakistan was a front-line ally in U.S.-supported efforts to defeat the Soviet Army in Afghanistan; and today, when Pakistan is again a front-line ally, this time in U.S.-led efforts to defeat Islamic militancy.

India and Pakistan were established in August 1947 from what had been British India. Some 500,000 people died during the Partition, and by October the two countries were fighting a war over the disputed Kashmir region. Even before the onset of the U.S.-Soviet Cold War, there existed a "strategic divergence" between the United States and Indian nationalists that "set habits and patterns on both sides" which persisted for many decades. Over the course of the Cold War, U.S. interest in South Asia was inconsistent and almost wholly subordinated to efforts at containing Soviet and Chinese communist expansion. A perceived absence of compelling geostrategic or economic stakes limited the extent of U.S. involvement in South Asian affairs.

During the 1950s, Pakistan became embedded in U.S.-led treaty organizations that sought to encircle and contain communist expansion. Two key results were the institutionalization of close U.S.-Pakistan ties and the provision to Islamabad of large assistance packages. While this U.S.-Pakistan security relationship developed, Indian leaders concentrated on nation-building and followed a policy of what became known as nonalignment. By the mid-1950s, Washington's differences with New Delhi gave rise to what a top U.S. diplomat characterized as correct but rather chilly exchanges that would last for several decades. After a brief 1962 border war with China exposed serious weaknesses in the Indian Army, the United States initiated military assistance programs for New Delhi that totaled about $150 million by 1966. However, the second India-Pakistan war over Kashmir in 1965 spurred the United States to end military assistance to both countries. Given Pakistan's 10 years of close cooperation with the United States, some in Islamabad felt betrayed by this move.

However, when East Pakistan (now Bangladesh) fell into turmoil in 1971, leading to the forced partition of Pakistan after its defeat in a third war with India, President Nixon elected to "tilt" U.S. support toward Pakistan and, in so doing, brought U.S.-India relations to a nadir. India's "peaceful nuclear explosion" of 1974 made South Asian weapons proliferation a toptier U.S. concern for the remainder of the Cold War. The Soviet invasion of Afghanistan of 1979 transformed U.S.-Pakistan relations virtually overnight, and during the 1980s Pakistan became regarded as a front-line U.S. ally in the struggle against Soviet expansion.

The September 2001 terrorist attacks on the United States suddenly transformed U.S. relations with Pakistan, which again became a front-line U.S. ally, this time against radical Islamic terrorists and their supporters. India also joined the U.S.-led antiterrorism coalition, and remaining aid restrictions on both India and Pakistan were quickly lifted by Congress and President Bush. However, while the Bush Administration has moved to bolster U.S.-India relations on a broad front -including regular and unprecedented joint military exercises and potentially major arms sales to New Delhi - the U.S.-Pakistan relationship has continued to be constrained by U.S. concerns regarding Islamabad's possible role in WMD proliferation, terrorist infiltration into both Indian Kashmir and across the Durand Line separating Pakistan and Afghanistan, and perceived anti-democratic practices by President Gen. Pervez Musharraf. Despite these concerns, Islamabad again became a leading recipient of U.S. foreign assistance funds.

Indian and Pakistani government officials express a desire to avoid engaging in. a costly and potentially disastrous arms race, while also asserting that no such race is afoot. Yet a 2001 Defense Department review of proliferation threats indicated that, "Indian and Pakistani strategic programs continue to be driven by the perception of the other's effort," and that the two countries "are in a period of accelerated nuclear weapons and missile development" that may be termed a "slow-speed" arms race. In 2002, Director of Central Intelligence Tenet told the Senate Select Committee on Intelligence that, Apparent tit-for-tat ballistic missile tests in April 1999 and again in March 2003 have been viewed as evidence that an action-reaction dynamic is indeed at work. Many analysts argue that overt nuclear weaponization by either side—most especially of their ballistic missiles—could be highly destabilizing, especially if significant nuclear missile forces are deployed in the absence of secure command and control structures. If these forces are perceived as being vulnerable to attack, one or both sides might adopt a launch-on-warning status, making conflict escalation even more difficult to govern. Ever since the 1998 nuclear tests in South Asia, it has appeared that India's strategic decision-making is a key factor in shaping regional stability. One of the more dangerous scenarios is one in which India actively seeks to gain nuclear parity with China by building a larger nuclear arsenal and long-range delivery force. In the middle-term, the deployment of Agni missiles capable of striking China's eastern population centers could spur Beijing to re-target more nuclear forces to the south and likewise move Islamabad to seek some form of parity in this arena, thus potentially setting in motion a full-blown arms race on the Asian Subcontinent. Moreover, some observers suggest that U.S. sales of theatre missile defense systems in Asia - or the deployment of a national system covering U.S. territory - could spur further ballistic missile proliferation in South Asia.

India and Pakistan have the ability to strike and destroy military and civilian targets outside of their respective countries by means of nuclear weapons, ballistic missiles, and aircraft. These forces, associated readiness postures, command and control, and missile defense constitute a strategic capability on a regional scale. The capabilities and their impact on regional security.

In June of 1998, as required by the Chemical Weapons Convention (CWC), India declared that it possessed chemical weapons; it is now reportedly in the process of destroying its chemical weapons stockpile. India, a 1973 signatory of the Biological Weapons Convention (BWC), is believed to have an active biological defense research program as well as the necessary infrastructure to develop a variety of biological agents. Estimates on India's nuclear weapons arsenal vary but a number of analysts believes that, as of 2002, India had between 30 to 35 nuclear weapons with yields varying between 5 to 25 kilotons (Kts) (despite an Indian claim that it had detonated a nuclear device on May 11, 2002 with a 43 KT yield).

These devices are likely configured as aerial bombs or missile warheads. While a precise breakdown of number of bombs versus missile warheads is unknown, a senior Pakistani military official that the majority of India's nuclear weapons were configured as aerial bombs. While India has a number of different types of aircraft, some analysts believe that it would use 1970s- and 1980s-vintage Soviet-built MiG-27 Flogger aircraft, with a range of 800 km, and the Anglo-French Jaguar aircraft with a 1,600 km range to deliver nuclear aerial bombs. The Sukhoi-30 MKI aircraft purchased from Russia with capacity to carry an 8,000 kg payload, and with a normal range of 3,200 km and an air-to-air refueling range of about 7,000 km, gives India a nuclear deep strike capability and some experts believe that India acquired the Sukhoi to counter China's deep-strike capability.

India is suspected of having successfully flight tested an Agni II missile (range 3,000 - 3,500 km) carrying a nuclear warhead assembly without its plutonium core in 1999 and again in 2001. While such tests are considered crucial for warhead development by some experts, some nuclear scientists believe that additional flight testing to adequately test the weapon's fuze and trigger will be required before India could deploy nuclear-armed missiles operationally.

India's Defense Minister, George Fernandez, reported to the Indian Parliament on July 29, 2003 that India had conducted 20 tests of seven different types of missiles, including two Agni variants, during the first half of 2003. While not a weapon or delivery system, India's satellites contribute to its strategic capabilities. Some analysts believe that India's network of communication satellites and its Technology Experiment Satellite, which reportedly has an optical resolution capacity of one meter, provides India with a strategic early warning capability that could help ensure the survivability of its nuclear forces. These satellites could also help improve India's military command, control, communication, and intelligence capacities.

Pakistan, a member of the CWC since 1997, is not believed to possess chemical weapons but, according to a January 2001 U.S. Department of Defense (DOD) has imported a number of dual-use chemicals with commercial applications that could also be used to make chemical weapons. Pakistan, a BWC member since 1974, was assessed by the DOD in 2001 as having the resources and scientific capability to conduct limited biological warfare research and development, but was not believed to possess biological weapons. Information on Pakistan's nuclear weapons arsenal is speculative but some analysts believe that Pakistan possesses between 24 and 48 nuclear weapons configured as both aerial bombs and missile warheads. Despite Pakistani claims of higher yield weapons, seismic measurements from Pakistani nuclear detonations on May 28 and 30, 2002 suggest weaponized yields more along the order of 9-12 KT and 4-6 KT, respectively. It is possible that Pakistan has higher yield weapons that have not been tested.

While Pakistan has obtained a variety of combat aircraft from different nations, many experts believe that the most likely aircraft to be used to deliver nuclear weapons would be the U.S. F-16 fighter. Twenty eight F-16 A (single seat) and 12 F-16 B (two seat) fighters were delivered to Pakistan between 1983 and 1987, and 8 of these original aircraft are believed to be no longer in service. Pakistan's 1988 order of 11 additional F-16 A/Bs and additional orders for F-16s since then have not been fulfilled due to the 1985 congressional enactment of the Pressler Amendment which forbids military aid to suspected nuclear weapons states.

Despite the September 22, 2001 Presidential Determination waiving the Pressler Amendment and other sanctions on India and Pakistan, the Administration's current five- year, $ 3 billion aid package will not include the promised F-16s, despite President Musharraf's request that their sale be approved. Pakistan's current fleet of F-16s is believed to be capable of delivering a 1,000 kg nuclear bomb to a range of 1,600 km. While some analysts believe that Pakistan's Hatf, M-11, and Shaheen short and medium range missiles are nuclear-capable, Pakistan's A.Q. Khan, director of the organization that builds the Ghauri missile, claims that the Ghauri is currently Pakistan's only nuclear-capable missile. In May of 1998, the Pakistani government claimed that it was ready to equip the Ghauri with nuclear weapons.

Stability Factors

A number of factors influences the stability of India's and Pakistan's missile forces. These factors include:

Readiness posture: India's and Pakistan's deployment of missiles and nuclear-capable aircraft as well as nuclear warheads and bombs has been described by some analysts as a "virtual state of de-alert." Regional analysts assert that both India and Pakistan maintain similar readiness postures. Each country claims that its missiles are not truly deployed but, on a day-to-day basis, are maintained in what is described as a state of "induction." Induction is described as the peacetime, nonthreatening activity of acquiring a weapon and testing and training with it.

Deployment is described as a belligerent posture with missiles actually on launchers, deployed to forward locations, and kept in a high state of readiness for use. Both countries have been accused of having deployed their missiles on a number of occasions. During the July 1999 Kargil crisis, U.S. intelligence reportedly detected the Pakistani military deploying nuclear- armed missiles, a fact reportedly unknown to Pakistani Prime Minister Nawaz Sharif who was in Washington D.C. on July 4 conferring with President Clinton in an attempt to de-escalate the Kargil situation. Both countries' nuclear weapons are believed to be stored in facilities separate from airfields and missile units for both security and maintenance purposes. One observer suggested that in order for India and Pakistan to have more credible nuclear postures, both countries should increase the state of alert of their nuclear forces to at least provide a rudimentary capability to launch under attack. He posited that such a posture could be particularly of use to India in terms of China, which is believed to keep a portion of its ballistic missile force on a high state of alert. Many analysts, however, believe that the current state of alert in India and Pakistan is a credible deterrence posture and that any move by either country to increase its posture could have negative consequences.

Command and control: Unlike India, which has declared a "no-first-use policy" for its nuclear weapons, Pakistan has not issued a similar statement. In February

2000, Pakistan announced the creation of a National Command Authority (NCA) comprised of an Employment Control Committee, Development Control Committee, and a Strategic Plans Division. Pakistan's President, General Musharraf, serves as leader of the NCA and likely would exercise ultimate authority over employment of nuclear weapons. Pakistan's NCA membership reportedly includes officials from "foreign affairs, defense and interior ministers, chiefs of all military services and heads of strategic organizations." General Musharraf also reportedly established a Strategic Force Command that is responsible for the deployment of strategic missiles. While some experts consider the establishment of a political-military command and control hierarchy reassuring, others point out that in order for it to be effective there must be clear and undisputed lines of authority and established and practiced procedures.

On January 4, 2003, the Indian government announced the establishment of its Nuclear Command Authority. The Nuclear Command Authority consists of a two-tiered political council headed by the Prime Minister who will be the singular authority for launching a nuclear attack and an executive council chaired by the Prime Minister's national security advisor who will provide input for decision making purposes and execute directives from the political council. As part of the establishment of the Nuclear Command Authority, the Indian government also established a strategic forces command which, according to press reports, would command all strategic assets defined as "aircraft, land-based missiles, and nuclear weapons and bombs."While the Indian government claimed that the establishment of the Nuclear Command Authority and the strategic forces command were logical command and control arrangements, some officials conceded that the creation of these two entities was also a response to international concerns about India's "rudimentary, almost non-existent nuclear command and control structure and also to send a 'firm' message to Pakistan."

Some experts believe that India's motivation for a missile defense capability was a result of Pakistan's acquisition of M-11 short-range ballistic missiles from China in 1992 and its continued development of longer range and more capable missiles. Other analysts note that India's desire for missile defense is also a function of its concern about the Chinese DF-21 medium-range ballistic missiles believed to be deployed in western China. Pakistan's periodic declarations that it would use nuclear weapons against India if it feels threatened likely reinforced New Delhi's desire to obtain a ballistic missile defense capability.

India is reported to be pursuing two approaches to regional missile defense: creating an indigenous system or purchasing a complete system from another country. Since late 1993, India's Defense Research and Development Organization(DRDO) has been involved in efforts to modify the Indian-designed Akash low-to medium altitude surface-to-air missile (SAM) into an interceptor capable of engaging ballistic missiles. While some analysts report that efforts are still underway to develop the Akash into a missile defense system, there have been no open-source reports of the Akash being tested against ballistic missile targets. India also is interested in purchasing the jointly-developed U.S. - Israeli Arrow Missile Defense system from Israel. Because the United States has played a major financial and scientific role in developing the Arrow, any legal export of the system by Israel would likely require prior U.S. approval. Both the Senate and House Armed Services Committees have expressed reservations about a possible sale to India or other countries have the following concerns:

— Although the Arrow is a defensive system, it could possibly be reengineered into and offensive system;

— Its sale could possibly trigger a regional offensive arms race;

— Israel has allegedly transferred or attempted to transfer critical military technologies to countries of concern such as China;

— Such a sale could violate the provisions of the Missile Technology

— Control Regime (MTCR), a missile nonproliferation arrangement to which the United States is a party; and,

— Concern that Israel would profit from the sale of a product largely paid for by the United States and might also constitute competition to Raytheon's U.S. Patriot missile system.

The Arrow 2 missile system is designed to provide terminal phase intercept against short and medium range ballistic missiles and reportedly can detect and track up to 14 in bound missiles at distances as far as 500 km away and then intercept them as close as 16 to 48 kilometers from the missile system. Some experts believe that India would deploy the Arrow system along the line of control separating Kashmir and the India-Pakistan international border to protect population and military centers. India has also reportedly been in negotiations with Russia since 1995 to acquire either the S-300 PMU-1 or S-300V anti-tactical ballistic missile system. In May 2003, an Indian newspaper reported that India had discussed sale of the U.S. Patriot Advanced Capabilities-3 or PAC-3 air and missile defense system with U.S. Deputy Secretary of State Richard Armitage.

According to Indian authorities cited, discussions have been underway with the Bush Administration since May 2002 about such a sale, but the U.S. government has not given Raytheon the go-ahead to provide India with pricing, availability, and other information needed to begin the acquisition process. Observers offer a variety of implications for Indian missile defense. Some feel that India's deployment of a missile defense system could erode Pakistan's confidence that its F-16s and missiles, if vulnerable to intercept, could continue to provide a credible nuclear deterrent against India.

Other analysts believe that an Indian ballistic missile defense capability would break the current state of mutual "non-weaponized deterrence" and lead Pakistan to mount nuclear warheads on deployed missiles which could destabilize the region. Another possibility is that Pakistan may adopt a "use it or lose it" policy whereby Pakistan might employ its nuclear forces early in the conflict to penetrate Indian defenses. Another possibility is that Pakistan could embark on a program to develop a greater number of missiles and nuclear warheads in order to saturate and overwhelm India's ballistic missile defenses. Some analysts reject these possibilities and claim that Indian missile defense would contribute to regional stability but provide little explanation as to how missile defense would actually achieve this.

With the waiver of the Pressler Amendment because of Pakistan's support for the United States in its war on terrorism, the Indian press has reported that Pakistan has initiated negotiations with the United States to purchase a ballistic missile defense system. It claims that Pakistan is attempting to acquire either the Patriot system or the Hawk, or Nike-Hercules system. The Hawk and Nike-Hercules systems are no longer in active service with the U.S. Army and were designed primarily to shoot down Soviet-era long-range bombers. While both systems are in use around the world with a variety of militaries, it is not known how effective they would be against modern aircraft and ballistic missiles.

Some analysts feel that the acquisition of one of these systems could help dissuade Pakistan from further missile development in an attempt to overcome India's ballistic missile defense capabilities. Pakistan reportedly has stated that it would deploy any missile defense systems around nuclear facilities and at sites where missiles are built and stored. Such a deployment might be intended to insure that at least some of Pakistan's nuclear warheads and missiles would survive an Indian strike and be available as a deterrent. If Pakistan did acquire a ballistic missile defense system from the United States, India might react by producing more missiles and nuclear weapons to offset an enhanced capability by Pakistan to intercept Indian aircraft or missiles, particularly if Pakistan acquired the more modern and capable Patriot system. Another concern could be that Patriot technology provided to Pakistan might be transferred by Pakistan to China, North Korea, or Iran and be used in the development of countermeasures to prevent U.S. intercept of their ballistic missiles.

Some experts have expressed concern that India or Pakistan might export their missiles or nuclear technology to other nations, increasing the number of nuclear missile-armed nations thereby increasing the security risk to the United States and other countries. Neither India nor Pakistan (nor China, for that matter) are members of the Missile Technology Control Regime (MTCR), which was established in 1987 to restrict the proliferation of WMD capable ballistic missiles, cruise missiles, and unmanned aerial vehicles (UAVs) and their associated technology. The MTCR is not a legally binding treaty or formal agreement, but MTCR members do voluntarily agree to enforce common export control standards.

Many analysts agree that the MTCR has had a positive impact on slowing missile proliferation. Congress may consider the possibility of renewed U.S. efforts to gain Indian and Pakistani accession to the MTCR. Because of the legally nonbinding aspect of the MTCR and its requirements for effective national export control, MTCR membership might be a first step in helping to promote other bilateral or regional initiatives to address missile proliferation and security concerns. Critics of this approach might cite both countries' long-standing resistance to enter into what Pakistan's Permanent Minister to the U.N. called in 1997 "a cartel formed by some industrialized countries for the purpose of placing controls on the transfer of technology" and "an arrangement for promoting their own security interests only." Technical Assistance.

Various technologies might reduce the risk of an India-Pakistan nuclear exchange. Technical assistance for both countries could take a number of forms. A version of a Nunn-Lugar-type program has been discussed in Congress and some analysts see India and Pakistan as prime candidates for such a program. Other initiatives such as establishing a missile launch notification agreement or hotline might be considered. Military sales designed to help each country safeguard its missiles from accidental launch are also a possible option. Opponents of technical assistance could argue that it would virtually be impossible to extend any form of technical assistance to one nation without arousing suspicion in the other country. What we might consider as safeguarding ballistic missiles from accidental launch could be construed as improving the ability to launch a missile surprise attack by either country. Another consideration is that of equity. Pakistan, with a smaller and less modern military, could argue that it deserves considerably more technical assistance than India- a position that might arouse considerable Indian opposition.

Export controls: Another option that could be explored is a multilateral initiative to assist India and Pakistan in improving their export control systems, particularly as they pertain to missile technology. Such an initiative could be a "stand alone" effort undertaken to improve the overall quality of each country's system, or it could be in anticipation of eventual MTCR membership. In order for a country to become an MTCR member, it must be approved for membership by all current members and meet stringent export control requirements. It is not known how receptive India or Pakistan would be to such an initiative. Export controls are essentially a domestic legal matter and U.S. assistance in this area might not be well received or even appreciated, for that matter. In Pakistan's case, export controls which could limit its missile-related dealings with North Korea and Iran would likely meet considerable resistance from government and military officials.

Confidence-building measures: Confidence-building measures, or CBMs, are described as "measures designed to reduce the risk of deliberate or accidental conflict and build trust by demonstrating the ability of the parties to keep promises." Confidence-building measures are by no means new to India and Pakistan. The 1999 Lahore Declaration entailed a number of CBMs designed to "reduce the risks of a nuclear exchange prompted by an accident or misinterpretation of a nuclear or ballistic missile test." Pakistan's deployment of troops to Kargil and the ensuing fighting in July 1999 effectively derailed the Lahore process and its associated CBMs. Some analysts suggest that the United States could play a role in helping to establish a series of CBMs in the region. Experts point to the previously abandoned hotline, notifications of military exercises, and missile launch notifications

Open skies agreement: If initial joint monitoring flights along the Line of Control proved successful, then deeper, more intrusive flights might be a future option. Other possible measures might involve assisting India and Pakistan in the establishment of a mechanism to settle disputes, perhaps modeled on the U.S. - Russian Nuclear Risk Reduction Centers in Moscow and Washington, or providing technological support in establishing a series of ground- based sensors in critical, disputed areas. Some experts assert that the United States would not necessarily have to be directly involved in all aspects of mediating or monitoring but could provide technological support and advice as needed.

Critics of regional CBMs might emphasize the past failure of CBMs due to the volatile nature of the region. Resurrecting previously-attempted CBMs, only to have them suspended due to a disagreement or incident, could further their argument that the region is not conducive to this particular approach. Perhaps a more practical and cost-effective approach might be to attempt to first settle regional disputes diplomatically and then institute appropriate CBMs on an incremental basis based on equal commitments from both India and Pakistan.

Proliferation security initiative (Counterproliferation): The Proliferation Security Initiative (PSI), announced by President Bush on May 31, 2003, is an international initiative which focuses on the interdiction of WMD and associated delivery systems and technology. Ten nations besides the United States have agreed to take steps to stop the flow of these items including the seizure of shipments as they transit air, land, and sea routes. According to the Administration's Fact Sheet, the PSI principles are "fully consistent with national legal authorities and with relevant international laws and frameworks." The PSI group met in Paris in October 2003 and adopted these principles detailed in the fact sheet. A series of U.S.-sponsored naval interdiction exercises called "Pacific Protector" were conducted in September 2003, involving Australia and Great Britain, as part of the PSI. While the Administration claims that the PSI does not target any particular country, many experts believe that the PSI was developed in response to growing North Korean missile exports and technological assistance to countries of concern. In theory, both India and Pakistan could be subject to seizures of WMD and missile-related items under the PSI.

Congress may further explore the legality of the PSI both in terms of U.S. and international law. Other issues for Congress may include how the PSI complements or detracts from current nonproliferation regimes. Congress might also review the scope of the PSI in terms of India and Pakistan—will proscribed shipments to or from these countries be interdicted or will we choose not to interdict in order to maintain favourable relations with both countries and their continued cooperation in the global war on terror?

The CRS report weapons of mass destruction counterproliferation: Legal Issues for Ships and Aircraft questions the legality of the PSI's intent to interdict sea, air, and land shipments. The report acknowledges that international law recognizes that states have a limited right to interdict vessels and aircraft in specific circumstances, but suggests that the PSI's wide-ranging provisions to interdict and seize WMD and missile-related technologies on the high seas appear "doubtful" under current international law. Suggestions to address this issue range from amending current international laws governing the sea and air to include WMD and missile technologies to amending current nonproliferation treaties. Other Issues Pakistan-North Korea Relations. Of critical concern to both Congress and the Administration is a suspected Pakistan-North Korean proliferation relationship. Both countries stand accused of proliferating missile and nuclear technology, and many analysts believe that rapid advancements in Pakistan's missile and perhaps nuclear program can be directly attributed to North Korean assistance.

Some experts suggest that, as Pakistan's missile programs have matured and advanced, Pakistan may be assisting North Korea in its missile program, primarily by providing North Korea with missile test flight data. Prior to September 22, 2001, when President Bush issued a Presidential Determination waiving a number of sanctions against both India and Pakistan, sanctions were the primary means by which the United States attempted to compel Pakistan to terminate proliferation activities with North Korea. Today, the situation is considerably more complex and may merit congressional attention.

The BrahMos Cruise Missile: Concerns have been raised about current and proposed U.S. missile defense vulnerability to the alleged supersonic, stealthier handed BrahMos cruise missile being developed by Russia and India. Could these missiles in the hands of hostile states and non-state actors, provide them with a dangerous asymmetric military advantage? Another issue is how difficult would it be to develop a nuclear warhead for the BrahMos and what countries presently have the scientific and engineering capability to do so.

Vertical and non-missile proliferation: While U.S. efforts to strengthen the international nonproliferation regime have slowed under the Bush Administration, some observers advocate increasing pressure on India and Pakistan to encourage their accession to such treaties as the NPT and the CTBT. Moreover, the world's nascent nuclear powers watch closely for any new U.S. development and procurement of nuclear weapons, and so U.S. decisions in this realm may have cascading effects on the scope and pace of global proliferation perspectives and behaviours. Thus, while some policy makers believe that new U.S. nuclear weapons would enhance deterrence, others claim that such weapons would undermine U.S. nonproliferation goals.

The ramifications of possibly providing U.S.-developed missile and air defense systems to India and Pakistan are of concern. While some experts contend that providing both countries with these systems would help to de-escalate tensions others argue that it could heighten tensions and possibly invite military "adventurism" by creating a false sense of security. In addition to the impact that missile defense might have on India and Pakistan, its possible effects on Sino-Indian relations could be a serious concern. Were the United States to provide such systems to India and Pakistan, issues related to technology transfer would arise. Policymakers, including many in Congress, would be concerned about the potential for onward transfer of advanced U.S. missile defense technology to countries such as North Korea, Iran, China, and Russia. If these or other countries had access to U.S. missile defense technologies, the potential may exist for them to develop countermeasures and penetration aids that could render U.S. theater missile defenses less effective.

In the new century-and especially after September 2001—South Asia is no longer the "strategic backwater" that it was for many U.S. analysts during the Cold War. The overt nuclear postures of India and Pakistan, and U.S.-led antiterrorism efforts centered on Southwest Asia have made the region's security dynamics a matter of great concern for the United States, where government officials acknowledge that a stable and thriving South Asia would advance U.S. interests. With regard to missile proliferation and South Asian security, many appear sanguine about the future: from the perspective of proliferation optimists, the establishment of nuclear command and control mechanisms and the deployment of reliable ballistic missile capabilities on both sides is seen to contribute to crisis stability through mutual deterrence, and thus to decrease the likelihood of a fourth full-scale India-Pakistan war. However, proliferation pessimism continues among many.

Some years ago, then-Deputy Secretary of State Strobe Talbott warned that, "Unless India and Pakistan exercise genuine restraint and great care, the [nuclear weapons] delivery systems themselves could become a source of tension and could by their nature and disposition increase the incentive to attack first in a crisis." Unlike aircraft, ballistic missiles cannot be recalled after launch and, given the contiguity of the two countries, missiles afford little time for warning and protective measures. So long as terrorism- and Kashmir-related animosity exists between India and Pakistan, making the outbreak of war a substantive risk, the continued proliferation of strategic arsenals in South Asia cannot be viewed with complacence. Among the future developments that could exacerbate regional tensions are the increased influence of Hindu nationalism in New Delhi and/or the increased influence of Islamic fundamentalism in Islamabad. Moreover, many analysts are concerned that continued military rule in Pakistan will hamper efforts at regional entente. In the near term, two issues appear key to South Asian security or its absence:

1) Ongoing violence in the Kashmir region and Pakistani support for or tolerance of Islamic terrorist groups operating from territory under its control; and
2) Afghani instability and ongoing conflict along the Pakistan-Afghanistan border.

Trends in these areas are difficult to determine, but significant violence has continued in both theaters. In the middle and longer term, developments in four areas appear directly relevant:

1) the course of India-China relations and strategic posturing;
2) the extent of positive U.S. engagement with both India and Pakistan;

3) New Delhi's weapons procurement decisions; and

4) the possible deployment of missile defense systems.

Here trends appear to be mixed: New Delhi and Beijing have moved toward more peaceful relations, and the United States is remaining fully engaged with both of South Asia's largest countries. Yet India's energetic acquisition of sophisticated new weapons platforms and pursuit of missile defense systems may bode poorly for regional stability. Moreover, within each of these areas, the progress and scope of regional missile proliferation represents a crucial and interactive facet. The importance of U.S. policies toward South Asia is difficult to deny. Missile proliferation and its implications for South Asian security are worthy of careful monitoring in the future.

New South Asian Policy of US

Given the complex relationship between the United States and India and Pakistan, and the delay in appointing an assistant secretary of state for South Asia, the Bush administration's go-slow policy toward the region is understandable. But critical policy questions must be addressed now. A comprehensive policy review currently underway by the administration will take months, but immediate attention should be given to strengthening and restoring relations with India and Pakistan, respectively. India is emerging as an Asia-Pacific power.

Pakistan remains an important regional power, despite a lack of popular enthusiasm for its military regime and a weak economy. These two countries are also nuclear weapons states, and each interacts, in a different way, with the Chinese nuclear program. The linked conflicts in

Afghanistan and Kashmir threaten to spill over into nearby regions or trigger a new war between New Delhi and Islamabad.

While the last administration's non-proliferation policies angered Indians, and arguably contributed to their decision to test five nuclear devices, President Clinton's highly publicized trip to India in March 2000 did much to restore U.S.-Indian relations. Indians were persuaded that while America and India diverged on some critical issues, there were important common interests, and America did not oppose India's emergence as a major power.

A subsequent visit to the United States by Indian Prime Minister Vajpayee led to a considerable inflation of the rhetoric of rapprochement, as senior American officials echoed Vajpayee's assertion that the United States and India were "natural allies." Yet as Clinton left office, there was no agreement on what constituted a "natural" alliance. There was little progress in resolving the nuclear problem, and Indian officials were urging the United States to take a tougher stance against Pakistan on grounds that it had an undemocratic, military regime and that it was supporting terrorism in India and elsewhere.

The most useful result of these visits was an agreement that the two countries would dramatically expand their high-level political, economic, and strategic dialogue. At the very least, the Bush administration should adhere to the timetable set by Clinton and Vajpayee. This would mean a "summit" meeting this year and perhaps a visit to India by President Bush in 2002. Meanwhile, the dialogue between government experts, military officials, and members of each country's legislative branch should move ahead, especially in such areas as trade liberalization and the nuclear and missile policies of both countries.

While the nuclear weapons issue still carries great symbolic and strategic weight in the U.S.-India relationship, there are other issues that are important, although none as pressing. Washington and New Delhi have divergent-but not necessarily dissimilar-views on questions of global arms control, the development of national and theater missile defenses, humanitarian intervention, and India's quest for a permanent UN Security Council seat. There may also be a dispute over trade policy since New Delhi still has some of Asia's highest tariffs.

These are issues that cannot be resolved easily, but the administration should take advantage of this newly created framework for dialogue with Delhi, and listen carefully to India's positions. American investment in India is increasing, and India has established a foothold in the American high-technology sector. These developments, plus the growth of the Indian-American community, have increased the number of groups and individuals on both sides with a stake in good U.S.-Indian relations. There is every indication that this new relationship will be a departure from the past. India and the United States have moved from a near-alliance in the late 1950s, to apathy in the 1970s, to estrangement by the 1990s. The two countries may not be natural allies, but they are now natural friends.

While America should pursue an "India First" policy in South Asia, this should not become an "India Only" policy, nor should India be given a veto over American relations with Islamabad. Pakistan, once an important American ally, now under three layers of sanctions, remains one of the freest of the Islamic states, and many among its elite are open to relations with the West. Further, Pakistan is now a nuclear weapons state and will, in a few years, be the world's fifth most populous country. It is likely to revert soon to a civilian government, although the military will remain the most powerful political force for the foreseeable future.

The Bush team has a chance to advance important American interests vis-à-vis Islamabad, but must act quickly and creatively. There are several ways the United States can rebuild its relationship with Islamabad regardless of the nuclear question. First, it should renew contacts with those Pakistanis who share Washington's concern over the spread of radical Islam. These include some of the Pakistan army's officer corps, many Pakistani intellectuals and professionals, and most of the business community.

The American military training programs for Pakistanis that were terminated nearly nine years ago should be immediately revived, but for every dollar spent on them, Washington should spend several times that amount to rebuild its contacts with Pakistani civil society. The United States cannot transform Pakistan, but American help for Pakistan's civilian institutions and western-oriented middle class may slow the country's descent into chaos and extremism, and it could be decisive if Pakistanis themselves restart the process of institutional and social reform. Washington should also vote favorably on International Monetary Fund and World Bank loans as Islamabad reforms its economic infrastructure, and the United States should make a long-term commitment that would allow Islamabad to restructure significant parts of the economy without triggering significant political resistance at home.

Finally, both the official and strategic dialogues that were so helpful in addressing U.S.-Pakistan differences in the past should be revived. As the army hands power to a nominally civilian government and reform efforts continue, high-level visits and ties with Pakistan should be resumed.

Indian and Pakistani nuclear policies are driven by calculations of national security and pride, and it will take more than lectures, the blunt application of sanctions, or the example of other states which have chosen not to build nuclear weapons, such as South Africa or Argentina, to significantly influence them.

The Clinton administration developed four benchmarks regarding the Indian and Pakistani programs. These demanded adherence to the Comprehensive Test Ban Treaty (CTBT), movement toward a fissile material production cutoff, a ban on nuclear technology exports to other states, and restrictions on nuclear deployment. A fifth benchmark-that the two states resume talks on Kashmir-was subsequently put in place. The "prize" for adhering to these benchmarks would be the lifting of sanctions, although there would still be limits on the sale or transfer of civilian nuclear technology to both states and, in the case of Pakistan, sanctions on economic and military assistance because of its military coup.

The Clinton administration's approach was too narrowly drawn. The benchmarks should be dismantled and replaced with a cluster of incentives that would give the United States greater leverage in the negotiations that lie ahead. Washington might begin by attempting a fresh start in the area of greatest concern: the spread of nuclear expertise, fissile material, and missile technology from South Asia to other states. In this area, also important to many U.S. allies and friends, Washington should be willing to offer significant inducements if both states are willing to participate in various nuclear and missile control regimes, separate their civilian and military nuclear programs, and allow international inspection of the civilian programs. The most effective inducement would be a reversal of past American policy limiting the transfer of civilian nuclear technology to India and Pakistan. This does not mean condoning these countries' weapons programs, but it does separate military and civilian uses of nuclear energy, thereby strengthening their mechanisms of control.

As India and Pakistan begin the process of separating their programs and allowing full-scale inspections of the civilian side, Washington should start to provide information on nuclear safety and specific assistance concerning the (often unsafe) nuclear reactors operated by both states. Over time, this might even lead to other assistance to the two states' civilian programs or the sale of nuclear power reactors, although the latter would require a change in U.S. law.

The second most critical regional nuclear problem is the lack of reliability and safety of regional nuclear weapons themselves, and the risk of accidental nuclear war or detonation. Here, too, American policy should change. Some have proposed that Washington might provide safety devices for Indian or Pakistani bombs, but this is neither feasible nor necessary, since both countries are able to fabricate these devices. In any case, neither would want a foreign government to have access to its designs, and such assistance could be construed as a violation of the Non-Proliferation Treaty (NPT), which bans the transfer of such technology. However, it is not a violation of the treaty to take steps that would reduce the risk of war triggered by an accidental detonation, a false radar signal, or bad intelligence. To address this problem, the United States should offer to provide hitherto unavailable information to India or Pakistan if they took steps to control or restrain their nuclear deployments, and to make such deployments as non-provocative as possible. The information could relate, for example, to the origin of undeclared missile launches or the origin of a nuclear detonation on their territory.

South Asia is home to three of the world's most intractable ethnic-domestic conflicts:

Afghanistan, Kashmir, and Sri Lanka: Because each is different in both the nature of the conflict and its importance to U.S. interests, each requires a different policy approach. In Sri Lanka, India no longer supports the Tamil Tiger separatists and has allowed the island's capital of Colombo to receive military aid from many countries (including the United States). The war could conceivably end if the grip of the Tigers loosened and if the Sri Lankan government agreed to significant political concessions to the Tamil community. This is not the case with the Afghan and Kashmir conflicts. They threaten to spill into nearby regions and raise deep concern in China, Iran, Russia, and the Central Asian republics.

Kashmir is also a possible trigger point for an India-Pakistan nuclear war. Pakistan is the link between the two disputes. Islamabad supports the Taliban government that controls most of Afghanistan as well as the radical Jehadis in Kashmir, some of whom are veterans of conflicts in Bosnia, Afghanistan, and Chechnya. As long as Pakistan continues this support, the risk of an expanded conflict in both regions remains high. Washington should make a serious attempt to work with Islamabad, reserving the option of developing a more confrontational policy if cooperative efforts fail.

The United States has had no serious peace proposal for Afghanistan in many years but is wrong to dismiss this torn country as irrelevant to American interests. If the Afghan conflict continues, then some of the region's border states (including Iran, India, Russia, the Central Asian republics, and China) might expand their support for the anti-Taliban factions and Pakistan would increase its own commitment to the Taliban. The war in Afghanistan could escalate, turning the country into a battleground and flooding neighbouring countries with radical Islamic movements and terrorism.

Several European states and the European Union have been searching for ways to reduce the level of violence in Afghanistan and undertake its reconstruction. The United States should encourage these states to take the lead in finding a resolution to the Afghan crisis, an effort that might also garner support from China, since it is concerned with the spread of extremist Islam in its western provinces. A collaborative effort that included Pakistan might bring about a ceasefire between contending Afghan groups. Such a policy will need to be reviewed in a year or so, if it does not lead to the prospect of a ceasefire and the moderation of Taliban policy.

Kashmir is South Asia's most critical problem. The conflict has generated considerable terrorist violence, and was the cause of several wars between India and Pakistan-the most recent being the limited war fought in the Kargil region in 1999. Pakistan is too weak to seize Kashmir, but is able to stoke violence in the Valley. India is strong enough to retain Kashmir, but has not been able to govern it properly.

The traditional culture of the Kashmiri people cannot survive the present large-scale violence. The Kashmiri leadership is weak and confused, and neither the United States nor the UN can impose a solution. However, the United States can take a number of steps. It could:

— Urge India to start a meaningful dialogue with Kashmiri leaders of all political persuasions.

— Offer assistance to New Delhi to increase counterterrorism.

— Make the case to Islamabad that continued support for non-Kashmiri and terrorist groups will qualify it for inclusion on the list of states that support terrorism.

America should work with allies and friends to prepare for a time when the parties involved in the Kashmir conflict are amenable to outside help. At that point, and with Indian and Pakistani concurrence, discussions over an agreement that could include monitoring and verifications mechanisms could commence, with the goal that all parties would adhere to the final agreement. In the meantime, the United States should actively encourage discussion of alternative solutions to the Kashmir problem, but remain impartial. In recent years, there has been resistance in Washington to increasing American involvement in either the Afghanistan or Kashmir conflicts. This view is shortsighted. Neither dispute is ready for resolution or for a major American role as mediator or peacemaker. But if the current situation continues, it is likely that other countries will be drawn into the Afghanistan problem, and that the Kashmir dispute eventually will lead to another India-Pakistan war. Besides the obvious consequences for the Afghan and Kashmiri peoples, these disputes affect the interests of a number of important states, and in Kashmir, the conflict carries the danger of a nuclear confrontation.

American policy should be carefully crafted to permit somewhat greater engagement, with the United States turning first to its allies and friendly powers for partners in an ameliorative diplomacy approach. However, the United States must also be prepared to intervene more weightily in Kashmir if India and Pakistan appear headed for war.

The Department of Defense, the Department of State, and the National Security Council each handle India and Pakistan differently. The Defense Department, which would like to resume military exercises with India and restore its long-standing and useful relationship with the Pakistan Army, divides them between two regional commands. The State Department unites them in the South Asia Bureau-the smallest bureau at State and one that was pushed aside during the Clinton administration by other bureaus with greater political clout.

The National Security Council has separated South Asia from the office of Middle East affairs, placing it under the jurisdiction of the Special Assistant for Asia. The CIA and Congress also have different ways of allocating responsibility for the two countries. It is probably impossible to streamline all of the various South Asia policy arms in the executive and legislative branches, but the process can be tightened up in three ways.

— regional economic, arms control, and military issues have been poorly served within the State Department's South Asia Bureau, while the other offices that deal with these issues have in the past regarded the Bureau as guilty of "clientitis," or pursuing regional interests ahead of U.S. interests. If the regional bureaus are going to carry more weight in the policy process-as seems to be Secretary of State

Colin Powell's goal-then the functional capabilities of the South Asia bureau in particular need to be enhanced.

— The South Asia Bureau at the State Department needs to be larger to attract and maintain a core of regional experts. At a minimum, the Central Asian republics should be included in the bureau. It would still be the smallest of the regional bureaus, even though its jurisdiction includes over a quarter of the world's population.

— Better interagency coordination is essential. At the policy level, interagency meetings should take into account India's rising economic and strategic influence in the Middle East and Southeast Asia, and Pakistan's critical importance in Central and Southwest Asia. Similarly, South Asian experts must be consulted in arms control and strategic policy decisions that affect China.

While it may not be possible to streamline all of these offices and programs, better interagency coordination would go a long way towards enhancing the effectiveness of American policy in South Asia.

3

Corruption in South Asia

Corruption afflicts South Asia at all levels of state and society. Scarce government resources that ought to be financing basic health, nutrition and education programmes are often allocated to huge arms deals and infrastructure projects that offer officials and politicians prospects of lucrative kickbacks. At the individual level, high levels of corruption impose disproportionate costs on the majority of South Asians, as they are forced to pay bribes in order to gain access to basic social services. Democratic and authoritarian governments alike wax lyrical about the need to combat corruption, but the region's political, bureaucratic and military elites are rarely held accountable.

The largest country, India, has the strongest democratic institutions in the region, but it is as plagued as Bangladesh, Nepal and Pakistan by systemic public and private sector corruption. Sri Lanka, which has the highest Human Development Index ranking, also suffers from this menace. Foreign donors have played a significant role in influencing the region's development as a whole over the past decades, pushing in recent years for good governance. But their role in the fight against corruption generates much controversy. Some argue that the direction of foreign aid in the region is still dictated by political and strategic considerations, rather than the economic needs and policy performance of recipients. There is no evidence that less corrupt governments receive more aid. Recent opinion polls indicated mounting public awareness that corruption has increased in politics, administration and the judiciary.

Growing democratisation, coupled with the liberalisation of media ownership, has stimulated the emergence of a vocal civil society. People understand that corruption cripples their institutions, undermines the rule of law, hurts the environment and distorts social and economic development. For government officials, corruption has emerged as a key issue around which political battles are fought. Increasingly, South Asian governments stake their own legitimacy on the lack of accountability of political opponents, as events during 2000-01 clearly showed.

The state's standard response to the demand for corruption control is to implement new strategies, laws, regulations and institutional mechanisms. These provide governments with a measure of legitimacy and serve to deflect public pressure, but it is questionable whether fundamental change is thereby achieved. In India, convictions of high-level politicians in the year 2000 restored a small measure of hope in the rule of law. In October 2000, P.V. Narsimha Rao became the first Indian prime minister to be convicted on charges of corruption. Along with a former home minister, he was sentenced under the Prevention of Corruption Act of 1988 to three years' imprisonment for bribing four minority MPs to alter their vote. In the same month, the leader of the All India Anna Dravida Munnetra Kazhagam (AIADMK) party, Jayaram Jayalalitha, was sentenced to five years' imprisonment in two cases relating to the purchase of state-owned land at undervalued prices while she was chief minister of Tamil Nadu. Despite electoral disqualification, Jayalalitha was again sworn in as chief minister when her party swept the state elections the following May.

At an All India Conference of State Vigilance Commissioners in January 2001, Prime Minister Atal Behari Vajpayee vowed to 'provide a clean, efficient and transparent administration' and to 'adopt a policy of zero tolerance while dealing with corruption'. His words boomeranged as an arms bribery scandal exposed by the news website Tehelka.com rocked the ruling coalition government of the National Democratic Alliance (NDA). A video-taped sting operation conducted by two journalists posing as arms dealers appeared to show politicians, senior military personnel and Defence Ministry bureaucrats receiving bribes. Minister for Defence George Fernandes subsequently resigned, although he had not been filmed. Bangaru Laxman, President of the Bharatiya Janata Party (BJP), and Jaya Jaitley, President of the Samata Party and close aide of Fernandes, also stepped down. The Central Bureau of Investigation (CBI) - the primary law enforcement agency entrusted with investigating corruption - arrested the chief of India's Central Board of Customs and Excise in April 2001 for possessing assets disproportionate to his known sources of income. The CBI later raided other senior officials for alleged involvement in a smuggling racket. Earlier, in October 2000, the CBI charged the three Hinduja brothers for their role in the Bofors scandal that had led to Rajiv Gandhi's defeat in the 1989 elections. Allegedly Bofors paid them millions of dollars in illegal commissions.

The Hindujas admitted receiving the payments from the Swedish firm, but denied they were linked to a controversial howitzer deal. In January 2001, the Hindujas appeared in a CBI court charged with 'conspiracy to bribe and cheat'. In December 2000, the Board of Control for Cricket in India imposed a life ban on former captain Mohammad Azharuddin and test-player Ajay Sharma, and suspended two other team members for five years, for fixing matches in exchange for bribes. The decision came in the wake of a CBI report on match fixing which blew the whistle on a global cricket-betting racket.

In Pakistan, the military regime of General Pervez Musharraf that ousted a democratically elected government in 1999 pursued a vigorous 'accountability' campaign, ostensibly aimed at recovering defaulted loans worth Rs 211 billion (US $4 billion) from the country's politicians and industrialists. The military's anti-corruption arm, the National Accountability Bureau (NAB), secured its first major conviction in July 2000 when a court sentenced ousted prime minister Nawaz Sharif to 14 years' imprisonment. Though several other corruption charges were pending against Sharif and his close family members, he was pardoned and exiled to Saudi Arabia in December 2000.

In June 2001, General Musharraf consolidated his authority further when he declared himself President. In August 2000, allegations of kickbacks in arms deals, which implicated two army chiefs, one naval chief and two air force chiefs, hit the Pakistani headlines. The arms deals reportedly amounted to US $2.7 billion worth of submarines, jets and tanks from French and Ukrainian companies. In April 2001, at the request of the Pakistani government, the US authorities arrested former naval chief Admiral Mansur ul-Haq, who opted for voluntary extradition.

A corruption charge against him is pending before a Pakistani accountability court. In 2000, the Auditor General of Pakistan reported misappropriation of Rs 12 billion (US $240 million) in the World Bank Social Action Programme, prompting the Bank to dispatch a team to investigate the embezzlement. In March 2001, the Supreme Court set aside the conviction of former prime minister Benazir Bhutto and her husband on corruption charges and ordered a retrial in the wake of an exposé of intelligence tapes revealing the manipulation of her trial by the Sharif government. Meanwhile, the Court also instructed the government to amend the NAB ordinance and reduce the remand period of suspects in corruption cases from 90 days to 15 days, and the disqualification period for public office from 21 years to 10 years.

The Court ruled that from 2002, accountability courts should be under the discipline of high courts, and not the government. In Sri Lanka, allegations of major irregularities in defence deals surfaced in June 2000 as bidding procedures were reportedly set aside to put the government's US $800 million arms procurement drive on a fast track. In March 2001, the chief of the navy cancelled a US $20 million gunboat deal with a state-owned Chinese firm amid allegations of kickbacks pocketed by defence officials and middlemen. Allegations of corruption led to resignations of the President of the Ceylon Electricity Board and the Chairman of the Board of Investment in 2001. Meanwhile, a multi-billion rupee expressway project was in disarray as President Chandrika Kumaratunga, in her capacity as Finance Minister, sought cabinet approval to award the tender to a South Korean joint venture, Daewoo-Keangnam, despite its disqualification in the initial bidding process. Mass rigging, electoral malpractice and violence in many districts that, according to the Centre for Monitoring Election Violence, had a major distorting impact on the outcome of the polls, marred parliamentary elections held in Sri Lanka in October 2000. Mylvaganam Nimalrajan, a Jaffna-based journalist investigating the electoral malpractice, was shot dead at his residence by unidentified attackers during a curfew.

The Swiss newspaper Le Courrier made startling disclosures of the heroin smuggling, money laundering, extortion and human trafficking networks that greased the war machine of the Liberation Tigers of the Tamil Ealam (LTTE), who are fighting the Sri Lankan government in the north of the country. The Central Bureau of Investigation report on match fixing also accused two star Sri Lankan cricketers, Arjuna Ranatunga and Aravinda De Silva. In November 2000, the Board of Cricket Control in Sri Lanka (BCCSL) appointed an inquiry committee to look into the allegations.

A few months later, the BCCSL was itself dissolved amidst allegations of financial irregularities. In Nepal, the government of Prime Minister Girija Prasad Koirala, which came to power on an anti-corruption platform in 1999, announced plans to combat corruption through three proposed anti-corruption measures: a Prevention of Corruption Bill, an amendment to the Commission for Investigation of Abuse of Authority (CIAA) Act, and provisions for a special Anti-Corruption Court. Ironically, parliament remained deadlocked in early 2001, with opposition parties calling for Koirala's resignation for his alleged involvement in a controversial Boeing lease fraud.

After months of investigation, the CIAA filed corruption charges against officials accused in the case, including the civil aviation minister at the time. Stopping short of prosecuting the Prime Minister, the CIAA strongly rebuked him for his role in approving foreign exchange for the deal.

In March 2001, the CIAA sought the Prime Minister's permission to proceed against Govindaraj Joshi, the Minister for Local Development, for his allegedly dubious intentions in amending selection guidelines for teachers when he was education minister in 1997. Joshi filed a petition in the Supreme Court challenging the CIAA's action. The CIAA is also fighting another battle in the Supreme Court against the Attorney General, who filed a writ petition challenging the CIAA's authority to question his decision to drop proceedings in a currency smuggling case. In Bangladesh, official anti-corruption efforts continued to target political opponents of the ruling Awami League government.

In August 2000, Hussein Mohammed Ershad, head of his own faction of the opposition Jatiya Party, was sentenced to five years' imprisonment, banned from contesting elections for five years and fined Tk50 million (US $1 million) for misuse of office and corruption during his presidency. A month later, Khalida Zia, a former prime minister and now leader of the main opposition Bangladesh National Party, along with two former ministers and seven officials, was charged with receiving kickbacks of Tk1.7 billion (US $32 million), allegedly paid during the purchase of two French airbus passenger jets for state-run Biman Airlines during the party's 1991-95 rule. Ershad was released on bail in April 2001.

The year 2000-01 was one of the worst for freedom of the press in Bangladesh as several journalists were killed, harassed, assaulted or received death threats for reporting on corruption and other criminal activities.

Anti-corruption Drives

The thin line between accountability for corruption and political victimisation often appears blurred in South Asia. In India, the decline of the opposition Congress Party and the rise of new regional and sectarian parties has intensified political competition. Indian politicians now find it expedient to use anti-corruption accusations as a strategy against political opponents. Similarly, increased political instability and electoral competition in Pakistan and Bangladesh have spurred insecure governments to settle political scores using official anti-corruption drives. 'For maximum political mileage,' argued Pakistani political analyst Mohammad Waseem, 'special emphasis is placed on high-profile convictions of opposition leaders.'

In India, the government in power often uses the Central Bureau of Investigation (CBI) to promote its partisan objectives. The filing of the charge sheet in the Bofors arms case in October 2000 was seen in political and media circles as an attempt to malign Sonia Gandhi, President of the Congress Party. This was also the case with the disproportionate assets case filed against her personal secretary. The misfortune of the former Tamil Nadu chief minister Jayalalitha after falling out with the BJP was captured by The Hindu newspaper: 'As long as the AIADMK leader Ms Jayalalitha was part of the Vajpayee political entourage, questions about her corruption were conveniently put on the back burner. The moment she parted company with the BJP, she was again discovered to be corrupt.' When it was the government's turn to clean up its act in the wake of the Tehelka allegations, the focus of its inquiry was superficial to the point of cynicism: corruption was not the issue, but rather the fact that allegations of corruption had been made and published at all.

In Pakistan, five successive elected governments have been dismissed on charges of corruption and mismanagement since 1988. Most recently, the Sharif government's alleged manipulation of the trial judge in the Bhutto case, and Sharif's exile to Saudi Arabia in the 'national interest', left little doubt as to the political motives of official anti-corruption drives.

Political observers and human rights activists in Pakistan questioned the legality of the National Accountability Bureau (NAB) ordinance that until recently allowed detention of suspects for 90 days without a trial, but which explicitly excluded from its purview serving military personnel and judges. While politicians useful to the military's political machinations were also excluded from investigation, those belonging to Sharif's faction of the Pakistan Muslim League (PML) were prime targets as the regime tried to use the stick of accountability to effect defections to the pro-military faction of the PML.

'The cases brought by the NAB look politically motivated, and none has seriously touched the army, source of much of the graft,' said The Economist. The only high-level case, brought against former navy chief Admiral Mansur ul-Haq, also seemed to be driven by political motives. In Bangladesh, the anti-corruption drive of the Awami League (AL) government fares no better. In 1999, as many as 70 cases were pending against opposition MPs and activists, ranging from corruption to murder. Political observers claim that the Bureau of Anti-Corruption (BAC), which investigates cases after approval from the Prime Minister's office, is engaged in political witch-hunts. This behaviour is not limited to the current government. The opposition Bangladesh National Party (BNP) also used the Bureau to settle its political scores when it was in power.

The case against former president Ershad is an example of these pendulum politics. Jailed for corruption in 1990 by the BNP, Ershad was released on bail in 1997 after he decided to support the AL's 'government by consensus'. Soon after he parted ways with the AL and joined the opposition BNP in August 2000, Ershad was again convicted of corruption. After he was released on bail in April 2001, Ershad bade farewell to the four-party opposition alliance, lending credence to allegations that he had struck a deal with the AL government.

The Daily Star said in an editorial: 'Such alternating political expediency on the part of major political parties in the country, centring around a single person with a reputation for changing loyalties, hurts people's political sensibilities and diminishes their faith in democracy.' However, the independent Commission for Investigation of Abuse of Authority (CIAA) in Nepal may be making more progress. The anti-corruption agency filed corruption cases against high-profile officials and an ex-minister and rebuked the Prime Minister for approving the Lauda Air deal. It is too early to assess the long-term impact of these developments on official corruption levels, and they clearly represent only a beginning. Nevertheless, in 2000-01, CIAA initiatives demonstrated to South Asia that autonomous public anti-corruption agencies backed by constitutional provisions can make a difference, and avoid falling under the sway of partisan objectives. Even so, the prevailing climate of political competition mobilised around corruption issues remains a threat to the fight against corruption, in Nepal as elsewhere. A further problem is the absence in the region of functioning judicial systems. While all South Asian countries have rigorous anti-corruption laws, conviction rates are low and sentences rarely carried out. The judicial process is open to manipulation and cases drag on for years.

The intensification of the India-Pakistan conflict in the aftermath of the May 1998 nuclear tests, the Kargil conflict in 1999, and the raging civil war in Sri Lanka, continue to fuel strategic priorities and the demand for military hardware in the region. The heavy secrecy that shrouds arms deals in South Asia makes it difficult to corroborate the allegations of widespread corruption relating to them. Many defence analysts and former officials agree that defence purchases offer the widest scope for corruption as governments invoke national security considerations to avoid scrutiny. 'If corruption is pervasive in civilian procurement despite extensive checks and balances,' argued a defence analyst, 'one can imagine the extent of corruption in secret arms deals involving billions of dollars.' Military spending in South Asia is higher than in any region other than the Middle East. In 1999 alone, the region spent a whopping US $20 billion on military expenditures, with Pakistan, India and Sri Lanka allocating 5.7 per cent, 3.4 per cent and 5.1 per cent of their respective GDPs to defence. This contrasts sharply with the GDP allocated for health, which hovers around 1 per cent across the region.

In India, the evidence of high-level arms bribery revealed by the Tehelka tapes was a crude reminder of the rot that plagues defence procurement. The editor-in-chief of Tehelka.com wrote that: 'Of course all Delhi knows that an entire subculture of staggering influence ... survives on defence kickbacks.' While an interim report by the Central Vigilance Commissioner (CVC) on irregularities in defence deals gathers dust in the Defence Ministry, the Tehelka tapes provided stunning disclosures of the nexus of middlemen, politicians, military officers and their civilian counterparts 'who make hundreds of crores cranking the machinery of Indian defence'.

In Pakistan too, defence procurement deals are notoriously corrupt. 'The military in Pakistan, which takes away most of the budget, is accountable to no one,' according to a Pakistani defence analyst. 'There is no procurement system, little accountability and the interaction of buyers and sellers is dangerously close,' argued another. The former chief of the defunct Accountability Bureau claimed in an interview in September 2000 that US $1 billion was paid to senior military officers in kickbacks in eight defence deals. The amount, he alleged, was more than the combined misappropriations in all the civilian projects his team had investigated.

In Sri Lanka, arms deals 'spawn billionaires' overnight. According to independent observers, politicians and officials don't want the civil war to end, since defence deals promise the most lucrative payoffs. 'There is no transparency or oversight,' according to defence journalist Iqbal Athas. 'Deals are shrouded in secrecy and bidding procedures are usually set aside for crisis purchases.' Basic consumer items are subject to a 6.5 per cent defence tax and prices are frequently increased to raise extra money for arms procurement. 'Sri Lankans are compelled to pay for the sins of those who make millions and get away with it,' Athas pointed out. In Bangladesh too, corruption in arms deals is endemic. Opposition leader Khaleda Zia claimed in April 2000 that the Awami League government had misappropriated Tk4 billion (US $75 million) during the purchase of MIG 29 fighter jets from Russia.

The Parliamentary Standing Committee on Defence is investigating allegations of kickbacks in another deal involving the purchase of frigates worth Tk5 billion (US $90 million) from South Korea. No discussion of corrupt arms deals in South Asia would be complete without mentioning the ubiquitous role of the foreign arms manufacturers, who factor in commissions to deals. Journalists and officials often accuse armament firms of handing out millions to win contracts. In the late 1980s, the Swedish firm Bofors paid vast kickbacks to President Rajiv Gandhi and middlemen in what became the worst corruption scandal in Indian history. The government of Pakistan collected evidence against three French firms who allegedly paid US $8.3 million in kickbacks to former navy chief Admiral Mansur ul-Haq, in connection with the purchase of submarines and related equipment.

Role Media and Civil Society

Defence and political observers in the region welcome the OECD Anti-Bribery Convention, but say that it remains to be seen whether OECD governments will enforce its standards, at the risk of alienating a powerful industry that provides extensive revenue and employment to their domestic economies. Investigative capacities are low, employment conditions poor and ownership-related political influence and other forms of censorship constrain reporting. However, with the onset of democratisation and overall liberalisation of information media, a vibrant press, with a healthy tradition of exposing corruption in high places, is emerging. Corruption exposés are turning the heat on governments and providing an impetus for reform.

The Tehelka revelations, which spurred the Indian government to speed up defence procurement reforms, are a spectacular instance of this dynamic. In the aftermath of the devastating Gujarat earthquake, media exposure of collusion between cabinet ministers, senior officials and construction firms to allow lax building codes provided urther evidence of the investigative tradition in the Indian media coming into its own. In a region where the lectronic media is still largely state-controlled, satellite news channels are now breaking news 'as it happens', making it doubly difficult for governments to hide their misdeeds. In Pakistan, the media has clawed back some f the ground lost during decades of authoritarian ensorship. The power of the press was evident in the way he Sharif administration was pressured to abandon its ntimidation campaign against the Jang Group, the country's largest newspaper company.

The regular exposure of corruption reinforces a strong ublic appetite for 'frying the big fish' - and for pushing overnments to institutionalise accountability. Exposure of orruption in the military has tainted the army's 'sacred ow' status in popular perceptions, spurring a lively debate the media on the need to regulate arms procurement particular, and military budgets in general. In Nepal, ne media adopted corruption as its main theme in 2000-1. 'Brazen corruption prevalent five years ago,' said the litor of Himal magazine, 'is impossible now as the media ill take anyone to town.' While news programmes on the radio can only be broadcast on government stations, private FM stations sidestep regulations by hosting lively discussions with intellectuals and officials on corruption and other issues of popular concern. In Sri Lanka, the tradition of investigative journalism is kept alive by the private media which regularly exposes official corruption despite draconian censorship regulations. The press is lobbying parliament for comprehensive media reform, including the enactment of a freedom of information act and an independent press complaints commission.

Democratisation, though incomplete and reversible in some cases, has created an opportunity in South Asia for public debate on corruption, including the hitherto taboo subject of corrupt practice in defence procurement. In the last five years, the perception that corruption hurts the economy, undermines institutions and impedes human development has led to vigorous debate among the informed public on the need for reform. It is clear that without adequate public pressure, governments are unlikely to enforce probity in public office.

But groups such as the Centre for Media Studies in India, Transparency International in Bangladesh, and Media Services International in Nepal are articulating public perceptions through opinion surveys, making it harder for governments simply to dismiss corruption allegations out of hand. The Public Interest Litigation Centre, Common Cause in India and other NGOs and individuals are effectively employing public interest litigation to redress public grievances. At the local level grassroots movements have demonstrated the crucial role collective citizen action has to play. The Mazdoor Kisan Shakti Sangathan (MKSS), or Association for the Empowerment of Farmers and Workers, in Rajasthan

India, is campaigning for the right of ordinary citizens to access official information and organising public hearings where government records are cross-checked against the evidence provided by service users. While authorities are reluctant to supply information and few officials have been punished for corruption, the movement has been instrumental in 'mobilising rural people to prioritise the seemingly abstract right to information as a key element in their struggle to achieve accountability from local authorities and enhance their livelihood prospects'.

The Nepalese government introduced its key anti-corruption measures under sustained pressure from the media, the public and NGOs. In Sri Lanka, the government moved to institute a parliamentary select committee to investigate allegations of corruption in arms deals amid demands for accountability from the opposition and media. Freedom of information bills, the distinguishing mark of democracy around the world, are on the legislative table in India, Nepal and Pakistan. The region's judiciaries, parliamentary committees, auditor generals and independent election commissions are also turning the screw on corruption. Growing anti-corruption sentiment is reflected in the aggressive postures of influential public figures.

The Central Vigilance Commission in India posted lists of corrupt officials on its website. Sri Lankan Justice Minister Batty Weerakoon openly attacked politicians and bureaucrats for their collusion with arms dealers and plans to bring amendments to the Bribery Act, including provision for forfeiture of assets acquired through illegal means. In Nepal, the Speaker of the House of Representatives Tara Nath Ranbhat castigated the Prime Minister and the cabinet for corruption; and the Public

Accounts Committee chairman earned the public's respect for his committee's active role in probing corruption in ministries. Official accountability drives in South Asia have capitalised on the need to weaken and undermine political opposition as insecure leaders seek to legitimise their hold on power.

Governments claim the moral high ground by pursuing one-sided accountability investigations in the belief that, as long as the public's attention is focused on the corrupt deeds of previous regimes, their own will be overlooked. The seesaw politics of official anti-corruption drives has served to politicise administrations and the judiciary, increasingly calling on them to take sides in political battles. Grand corruption in arms deals imposes huge economic costs on one of the world's poorest regions, as its resources are diverted from social development priority areas. Corrupt arms deals also undermine genuine national security needs, as procedure is bypassed in favour of pay-offs.

The need for greater transparency in military expenditures and arms deals calls for urgent attention. Regulating the role of middlemen, reducing discretion and secrecy, ensuring the participation of all civilian and military actors in the decision-making process, and parliamentary oversight are some options for making arms deals more transparent. There is a belief in the region that the OECD Anti-Bribery Convention fails to make parent companies act with sufficient responsibility for the corruption of their subsidiaries or local agents. Defence analysts recommend that firms involved in bribery in South Asia should be blacklisted.

Analysts also draw attention to the menacing role of the global arms trade in fuelling a nuclear arms race in the region that has grave consequences for international security. While the anti-corruption movement still has a long way to go, the proactive stance of the news media, civil society groups and key public figures pushed corruption to the top of the public policy reform agenda in 2000-01. Growing public anger against petty and grand corruption is due in no small measure to the media, which routinely points out corruption at the highest levels of state.

The deterrent effects of the threat of public exposure remain a potent check on malfeasance in public office. However there is a danger that frequent allegations of corruption may create widespread public disillusionment with leaderships of all persuasions. Ironically, the electoral fortunes of politicians so far remain largely unaffected by corruption investigations, as shown by the continued popularity of many leaders accused of corruption. As South Asian countries grapple with critical social, political and economic transformation, corruption is unlikely to decrease in the short run.

Political instability, underpaid civil servants and unresponsive state institutions are compounded by rising poverty and unemployment. Political violence, increasing military expenditures spawned by intra-state and inter-state conflict, and massive debt burdens are also major problems. All these factors limit the capacity of states to institute the meaningful institutional reforms necessary for economic development and reducing corruption. Media and public pressure, collective citizen action and the consolidation of democratic institutions could, however, turn the tide in the medium term.

Public expenditure on basic and critical services like drinking water, education, health and security represents a significant allocation of the scarce resources in all of the South Asian countries. The outcome and effectiveness of this spending, however, is not easy to observe and measure. Governments typically monitor the amount of expenditure on each and every service and scheme, and measure achievement in terms of the physical assets and benefits created as recorded by the officials involved. But whether these assets and services are actually delivered efficiently and meet the real needs of the people cannot be determined by expenditure monitoring or head counts alone. Services may be delivered, but they may be of low quality or entail unwarranted delays or other costs for the users. Assets may be acquired, but yield low benefits because of the neglect of maintenance or lack of responsiveness on the part of public officials.

Policy statements may declare certain services as free-of-charge, yet in reality hidden costs such as bribes and delays may negate these benefits. The productivity and effectiveness of public expenditure can be greatly reduced by these shortcomings. Yet the latter are seldom monitored, let alone analysed and remedied. The observation that corruption is endemic and rampant in South Asian countries is by now a well documented and loudly articulated concern. The never-ending saga of high-profile exposés and racy media coverage of graft in recent years offer a disquieting reel of vignettes on the magnitude of corruption in all spheres of life. The level of corruption has been exposed by the annual Corruption Perceptions Index (CPI).

Table 1. Corruption in South Asia

Country	*Transparency International Corruption Perceptions Index scores (1995-1998)*							
	1995	*1996*	*1997*	*1998*	*1999*	*2000*	*2001*	*2002*
Bangladesh	N/A	2.29	N/A	N/A	N/A	N/A	0.4	1.2
India	2.78	2.63	2.75	2.9	2.9	2.8	2.7	2.7
Pakistan	2.25	1.00	2.53	2.7	2.2	N/A	2.3	2.6
Sri Lanka	N/A	N/A	N/A	N/A	N/A	N/A	N/A	3.7

Taking into account the fact that Nepal does not figure in the table above, it is quite clear that other countries in the region have scored very poorly in terms of integrity. This poor performance, however, assumes a critical dimension when one contrasts it with development indices. The picture is troubling. South Asia accounts for 30 to 40% of the world's poor and 45% of the region's 1.4 billion population live in poverty. The following table depicts the strong undercurrents linking corruption to development indices.

The link between corruption and development has been explored quite deeply by researchers and analysts. Interestingly, one of the earliest contributions argued that corruption was likely to have beneficial effects in developing countries suffering from restrictive private monopolies and government practices. However, since then various studies have clearly shown how corruption undermines development in the long run. To quote some studies on the South Asian experience: If India were to reduce corruption to the level that exists in the Scandinavian countries, investment could be increased by 12 percent and the GDP growth rate by 1.5 percent per annum.

Similarly, Bangladesh could increase its GDP growth rate by half a percent if profiteering practices were reduced to the level found in Uruguay. And, if Pakistan were to reduce its level of corruption to be on a par with Singapore, GDP growth rates could increase by two percentage points. Given these well documented facts, the growing debate on good governance, and the various reform agendas jointly explored by international donors and national governments, why have the systems in South Asia failed to break out of the poor governance cycle? A major reason seems to be the weak demand for mobilisation around critical governance themes.

Most governance initiatives appear to be externally driven or top-down, with little or no ownership inside the country, specifically among the critical stakeholders—the citizens. This explains to a large extent why there are very few civil society initiatives that link up to the ongoing macro reforms. It may also be the reason why countries from the region score poorly on governance indicators, as depicted below:

Table 3. Key Governance Indicators in South Asia

Country	*Selected Governance Indicators*					
	Polity Score	*Press Freedom*	*Voice & Accountability*	*Law & Order*	*Government Effectiveness*	*Graft Corruption*
Bangladesh	6	60	-0.20	2.0	-0.54	-0.64
India	9	42	0.66	4.0	-0.17	-0.39
Nepal	6	57	-0.06	N/A	-1.04	-0.31
Pakistan	-6	57	-1.43	3.0	-0.48	-0.79
Sri Lanka	5	74	-0-23	3.0	-0.44	0.00

Regional Survey on Corruption

It is in this context that the role of Transparency International (TI) - a global coalition against corruption - assumes critical significance. The TI movement by design has demonstrated the potency of linking up grassroots initiatives to policy issues. By addressing corruption at various levels - international conventions, private sector, multilateral and bilateral donors, national governments and civil society organisations - TI has been able to address the growing menace of corruption in an informed manner. A major tool developed by TI to widen its anti-corruption framework is the Corruption Perceptions Index (CPI). The CPI quantifies a hitherto abstract phenomenon and provides a basis (a country's ranking) for comparison and reform. The CPI is one of a series of new initiatives that have tapped in to the potency of indicators and databases as tools for awareness raising, diagnosis and reform.

A major fault-line in governance where corruption appears to be rampant and impinges directly on the everyday life of citizens in South Asia is the domain of public services. The state in all of the countries in the region is all-pervasive and in most cases, has a monopoly on providing critical public services such as drinking water and power.

For the vast majority of the poor, the state is the only accessible source for health and education. Given the overarching nature of the state in the overall governance framework, it is not surprising to see that for large numbers of the population there is no real 'exit' option to move from a corrupt and inefficient public service provider to another source. Given this highly disabling environment, the only option for change comes from 'voice' mechanisms. Experiences from various countries increasingly point to the growing potency of citizen feedback surveys as highly effective 'voice' mechanisms. Surveys highlight an interesting array of useful information that enables service providers to carry out meaningful diagnostic exercises and at the same time empowers other stakeholders to demand more accountability from the state.

Underlying the survey is the belief that feedback from the people who are at the receiving end of public services can effectively fill the gaps in assessing public expenditure. Citizens who interact with service providers are not experts in the technology and delivery systems of the services they receive. Nor can they produce overall assessments of the performance of the public agencies involved. These are some of the reasons why such feedback is neglected in conventional evaluation and monitoring exercises. Nevertheless, experience based user feedback can shed light on the efficiency and effectiveness of those who plan and deliver these services.

From a civil society perspective, credible information gained through user feedback surveys is a powerful tool to generate public awareness of the key problems. Dialogue and campaigns will be more purposive and meaningful when people are armed with information that is well focused and pertinent to a given situation. Civil society institutions can potentially play an active role in assembling and using such information to incite public agencies to improve their services.

Transparency International has a strong presence in South Asia and TI national chapters are now active in most countries of the region. The TI chapters realised early on, in working with various stakeholders in designing anti-corruption programmes, that objective databases such as citizen feedback surveys are highly effective voice mechanisms. When the citizens' voice consists of objective assessments of both the qualitative and quantitative aspects of different public services that are based on first-hand interaction with the agencies providing these services, it is possible to rank the agencies according to their level of performance.

This 'score card' can be used to stimulate collective action by citizens, and provide leaders with a basis to design reforms. This collective interest led to the design of a pioneering project in South Asia to make an objective assessment of the levels and forms of corruption in the five major countries of the region. What makes this initiative unique is that a common survey instrument was used to capture perceptions and experiences, thereby rendering it possible to study emergent trends in the region. The range of public services in South Asia is wide. It would be difficult to include all of them in a single survey. Not only would it unduly add to the cost of the survey, but it would also strain the attention span of respondents. For the purposes of this survey, a decision was made to focus on a set of services that are essential for the majority of the population, especially the poor and disadvantaged sections of society. The selected services which were examined through the common questionnaire in all countries are: healthcare, education, power, land administration, taxation, police and the judiciary.

The regional survey will be carried out on a sample size of 3,000 households evenly distributed in rural and urban areas and administrative areas in each of the selected countries.

Methodology

The appearance of an increasing number of user surveys reflects a growing awareness of the potency of empirical approaches to provide a trigger to effectively mobilise stakeholders around a common demand. Empirical approaches have helped to quantify and give shape to many themes, including corruption, that hitherto existed in the realm of the abstract. The methodology adopted for this survey attempted to capture credible and representative data from users of different public services.

Sample size for selected countries was originally envisaged to be 3000; it was proposed, however, that India should have a larger sample size. To facilitate a common reference point for determining the sampling framework, a template was drawn up. Each country was then given the choice to follow this template or any other format subject to the condition that it is scientific and does not affect the analysis of the regional survey findings.

Sample Profiles

Country	*Total Sample Size*	*Rural Sample Size*	*Urban Sample Size*
Bangladesh	3030	2305	725
India	5157	2289	2868
Nepal	3060	2610	450
Pakistan	3000	800 (semi-urban)	2200
Sri Lanka	2278	1953	325

The following issues were covered in the questionnaire:

i) Interaction and process of interaction of the sectors;

ii) Types of corruption;

iii) Actors who may or may not have participated in corrupt practices;

iv) Irregular costs due to corruption;

v) Nature of interaction;

vi) Causal factors leading to corruption in service delivery.

Semi-urban refers to a geographical enclave between a town and a rural village. From past experience with similar household surveys in rural areas, it was felt that collecting sufficient response from rural areas would be difficult. The literacy rate and remoteness of villages in Pakistan are further constraints. For these reasons, we substituted semi-urban locations for rural samples.

Demographic Profiles

	Bangladesh	*India*	*Nepal*	*Pakistan*	*Sri Lanka*
			Gender		
Male	73	74	71	97	75
Female	27	26	29	03	25
Educational status					
Illiterate	32	15	19	06	03
Non formal	-	02	16	02	04
Primary Education	37	07	19	08	34
Secondary/ Equivalent	20	29	26	18	46
Higher Secondary/ Equivalent	06	29	14	20	10

Bachelor Degree/ Equivalent	04	16	05	29	02
Post graduate /Equivalent	01	02	01	17	01
No response	-	-	-	-	-
Occupational Status					
Service (Govt. & Private)	10		12	41	15
Business	13		19	28	11
Lawyer				02	-
Farmer	34		41	02	
Fisherman				02	21
Labourer	07		05	04	4
Student	04		07	05	-
Housework	24		10	01	08
Retired	02		02	06	09
Self-employed	03		01	04	05
Unemployed	01		02	02	16
Other02		01	03	11	

Country Profiles

Countries	*Three sectors perceived as most corrupt*		
Bangladesh	Police (39%)	Health (25%)	Land Administration (18%)
India	Police	Health	Power
Nepal	Land (50%) Administration	Customs (41%)	Police (24%)
Pakistan	Police (28%)	Power (15%)	Taxation (13%)
Sri Lanka	Police (39%)	Health (5%)	Education (4%)

Prior to being asked about their actual interactions with the sectors, respondents were questioned on which of the seven sectors they perceived to be most corrupt. Very clearly, the police comes out as the sector perceived to be extremely corrupt in all five countries, except Nepal. This finding points to the need for law enforcement reform - a concern repeatedly expressed by various civil society organisations. Equally worrying is the finding that health figures prominently in the list of most corrupt sectors in three out of the five countries.

Bangladesh

— The police is perceived to be the most corrupt public agency, followed by health and land administration.

— While 13% of respondents reported irregular admission processes, a far larger percentage (38%) indicated that corruption is pervasive in the regular functioning of government institutions. More than 87% of the victims of corruption identify teachers as the major facilitators. Direct extortion of bribes was reported by 87%. One in two respondents identified weak accountability as a major factor facilitating corruption in the education sector.

— More than half of the users of government hospitals report that they accessed the service through irregular processes. Payment of money was widely reported to be the most common form. 80% of inpatients and 45% of outpatients report they were victims of corruption. 56% of the victims identify the doctor as the major facilitator of corruption and more than 60% said that bribes were demanded directly by the major facilitator. Weak accountability (67%) and poor transparency (45%) are quoted as the major causes of corruption in the health sector.

— More than one-third of the total users of the public power utility report irregularities in accessing the services; the percentage was significantly higher in rural areas (45%) than in urban areas (23%). Of those respondents reporting irregularities in getting energy connections, almost all of them report that they paid bribes. A third of regular users report of some corruption in their dealings with the department. Meter 13 readers (26%) and department officers are identified as the major facilitators of corruption. Almost 80% of the victims of corruption cite extortion as the main form of graft. Lack of accountability (57%) and a monopoly power (47%) are identified as the key factors contributing to corruption in the power sector.

— An overwhelming 73% of users interacting with the land administration report corruption. Surveyors (43%) and Tehsildars (27%) are quoted as the major facilitators of corruption, and extortion of bribes was reported by more than 80% of the victims. Lack of accountability (64%) and discretionary power (55%) are identified as the key facilitating factors.

— Very few respondents reported interactions with the tax department; one in five users reported corruption. Surprisingly, a good majority of the victims (67%) was unable to identify the key facilitator. More than half (56%) of the victims reported that bribes were directly demanded. Lack of accountability (40%) and discretionary power (27%) were identified as the key facilitating factors.

— 84% of respondents who interacted with the police department reported corruption. In 96% of the cases, bribes were paid for a release after arrest under a false pretext. While a third of the victims could not identify the facilitator, 24% identified duty officers and 19%, investigating officers. Direct extortion of bribes was reported by 84% of the victims. Lack of accountability (76%) and discretionary power (73%) were identified as the key facilitating factors.

— About 75% of users of the court system (lower judiciary) reported incidences of corruption. Interestingly, one in two users report being the accused. Court officials were identified as the major facilitator of corruption by 66% of the victims of corruption and bribes were demanded directly in 73% of cases. Lack of accountability (68%) and discretionary power (61%) were identified as the key facilitating factors.

India

— The Police Sector is perceived to be by far the most corrupt sector in the country, followed by health and power.

— The survey found that 18% of those using the education sector got admission through an irregular process. The two main forms of corruption in the admissions process are donations (57%) and use of an influential relative (19%).

— Payment of money through staff was the most common irregular process encountered for admission to hospitals, followed by direct payments to physicians. The dominant form of corruption after getting admission was improper care including medicine, food, and treatment from doctors and nurses. 25% of those who interacted with the healtl sector said that money was demanded. The key actors facilitating corruption in this sector were identified across the region as physicians (77% followed closely followed by hospital staff (67%).

— 'Improper supply of electricity' and 'payment o excessive bill' were the key forms of corruption facec by users of the power sector. About 50% respondents who had interacted with the power sector in the pas year 14 had to pay bribes to office staff. Of these money was directly demanded in 67 percent of cases The key facilitators in corruption in this sector were linesmen (37%) and officers (24%).

— On average, 36% of those who interacted with the land administration department said that bribes hac been demanded; and of these cases direct extortior was reported in 60% of the cases. The key beneficiaries of corruption named in this sector were surveyors (45%) and revenue officers (30%).

— The tax department surprisingly earned a lowe 'corruption score' in comparison with other sectors The key corruption faced was cited as 'paying fo getting a reduced or correct assessment'. However only about 11% reported paying bribes. The ta officer (44%) and tax department clerk (35%) were cited as the key facilitators of corruption in this sector.

— 53% of respondents reported that politica intervention was the main form of corruption they faced in their interactions with the police department 14% said that money was demanded for making ar First Information Report (FRI). 50% of all those whc interacted with the police admitted paying bribes. The police officer on duty (54%) was seen as the chief beneficiary.

— The major form of corruption prevalent in the judiciary was found to be bribing court officials. To add to the justice seeker's misery, money sometimes needed to be paid to the public prosecutor and even the opponent lawyer.

Nepal

— The public service frequented most was education, followed by health, power and land administration. The departments of taxation, police and judiciary had the fewest users, with judiciary being the least used.

— Land administration is perceived to be the most corrupt sector followed by the customs department. Police and judiciary were ranked as third and fourth most corrupt sectors respectively. However, the actual usage profiles, seen from respondents answers about their own experiences, indicated that the police (42%) and judiciary (48%) are the most corrupt sectors.

— While 7% of the respondents questioned on the education sector complained of irregular admission processes, one in four regular users reported corruption in the day-to-day functioning of educational institutions. The key facilitators of corruption cited in this sector were teachers followed by members of the management committee.

— Government hospitals were found to be the main institution used for health care in the country. While

8% of those who frequented public hospitals reported irregular methods of access, about 18% of users reported corruption during regular visits. Paying extra for prescribed medicines and being forced to buy medicines from specific pharmacies were cited as the main forms of corruption. Doctors and hospital staff 15 were named as the major facilitators of corruption in the public health service.

— About a quarter of respondents with access to electricity reported getting connections through irregular means. Interestingly, the percentage reporting corruption in their regular interaction with the power service was quite low at 12%. Paying extra for an uninterrupted supply of electricity and bribes to correct over-billing were the most commonly named forms of corruption. Linesmen were cited most often as the main facilitators of corruption, followed by meter readers.

— About 17% of those who used the services of the department of land administration during the past year said that they had encountered corruption. The Tehsilder was reported as the main instigator of corruption in this sector, followed by surveyors.

— Fourteen percent of respondents said they interacted with officials from the tax department during the past year. Service users were concentrated in urban areas and the most common form of service was the payment by users of income tax. A quarter of service users said that they had encountered corruption in this sector. Employees of the department were found to be the main facilitators of corruption.

— Only seven percent of respondents reported interaction with the police sector during the past year. Almost half of those reporting interaction (48%) said that they had encountered corruption in this sector. The police officer was found to be the main instigator of corruption, followed by the department clerk.

— The service used the least was the judiciary, with only 5% of respondents reporting that they/their family members had needed the service during the past year. Nearly 42% of service users reported encountering corruption in this sector. Court employees and public prosecutors were cited as the main facilitators of corruption.

— Across all sectors, extortion was quite common and a lack of accountability was identified as the major reason for corruption.

Pakistan

— Of the 3000 respondents surveyed, 1,724 (57%) recalled using the services of one or more than one of the seven government departments during the past year. The department perceived to be the most corrupt was the police, followed by power and taxation.

— About 70% of respondents who interacted with educational institutions cited the existence of irregular methods of gaining admission. Teachers and members of the management committee were cited as the most involved. The main causes of corruption identified were a lack of accountability and low salaries.

— Sixty five percent of all patients visiting a hospital reported irregular admissions and 96% of those who were admitted said they were 16 victims of corruption. Hospital staff were identified as the key facilitators of corruption by 65% of the users and direct extortion was reported in 60% of the total cases of corruption. Lack of accountability and monopoly power were quoted as key contributing factors.

— A very high percentage (65%) of users with access to electricity reported irregular processes in acquiring it; a much higher percentage reported of corruption in regular interaction with the department. (96%). Meter readers and billing employees were identified as the key facilitators; extortion was reported by 72% of the victims. A lack of accountability and low salaries of employees were identified as major contributory factors.

— Only eight percent of respondents reported interactions with the land administration department. All of those who used the services of the department, however, reported incidences of corruption. Surveyors and revenue officers were identified as the major facilitators. Bribes were directly demanded in 64% of cases and a lack of accountability, discretionary powers and low salaries were cited as the key causes of corruption.

— Eight percent of respondents interacted with the tax department during the past year. Corruption was perceived to be rampant, with 99% of users reporting corruption. A third of all incidences of bribes were paid to reduce a customer's assessed tax. Tax officers and employees of the department were identified as the major facilitators and in most cases (61%) bribes were extorted. A lack of accountability was identified as the major reason for the prevalence of corruption in the tax department.

— Nearly a third (32%) of all respondents reported using the services of the police during the past year. All of those who interacted with the police reported encountering corruption; one in two victims identified the police officer as the key perpetrator. Extortion was reported by 74% of the respondents. A lack of accountability and low salaries were quoted as the major contributory factors.

— Only six percent of respondents reported using the services of the judiciary during the past year; almost half of the users interacted in their capacity as a complainant. 96% of users reported encountering corruption; 44% of cases involved bribing court officials. Court officials (41%) and judges (24%) were identified as key facilitators; in most cases (61%), bribes were demanded directly. One third of the respondents said that a lack of accountability was the main factor contributing to corruption in the judiciary.

Sri Lanka

— The police was perceived to be the most corrupt sector in the country, followed by health and education.

— Government institutions dominate the education sector. Almost 55% of users reported that they had accessed the institutions through irregular means. An alarming 61% of those who interact regularly with the institutions report encountering corruption;

irregular fees of various 17 kinds constituted the most common form of corruption cited. Sixty-two percent of the victims of corruption reported that money was directly demanded. Teachers and the members of the management committee were identified as the major facilitators in this sector. Excessive bureaucracy and discretionary powers were identified as the main reasons for corruption in the education sector.

— Most of the users (97%) of health services visit public hospitals; 18% of them reported using irregular processes to access the services. More worryingly, 92% of users report of corruption after admission, with the highest number of cases reported for getting prescribed medicines and also for receiving proper treatment. Hospital staff were identified as the major instigator of corruption in the sector. While 30% report of extortion in the corrupt exchanges, 19% said they paid bribes voluntarily to ensure proper services. Monopoly and discretionary powers were cited as the primary reasons for the prevalence of corruption; interestingly, 23% identified a shortage of resources as a major cause.

— Securing an electricity connection through irregular channels was found to be very common (63%); most of these connections were made by paying bribes to the office staff. A similarly high number of respondents (63%) reported encountering corruption in regular interaction with the power department, with 42% of the victims paying bribes to ensure proper power supply. Repairmen and department officials were identified as the key facilitators of corruption in the power sector. An equal number (33%) of cases of extortion and voluntary bribery was reported. Monopoly power and low salaries were cited as the major factors contributing to corruption in the power sector.

— Only 9% of respondents reported interactions with the land administration department. An overwhelming 98% reported encountering corruption; interestingly, more than half of the victims of corruption (54%) were unable to identify the perpetrators. Monopoly power and a lack of transparency were quoted as the key facilitating factors for corruption in Land Administration.

— All respondents who interacted with the police department during the past year reported encountering corruption. Police officers and investigating officers were identified as the key perpetrators of corruption; one-third of the respondents reporting of corruption paid bribes voluntarily. Discretionary powers and influence of powerful interest groups were cited as the major factors contributing to corruption in the police department.

— Very few respondents (6%) reported interacting with the judiciary during the past year; 44% of them interacted in the capacity of an accused. Corruption in the judiciary was reported by all users; interestingly, most victims could not identify the key perpetrator. Monopoly power and excessive bureaucracy were cited as the key contributory factors.

4

Recent Developments in South East Asia

The spread of information technology (IT) in a society has the potential to alter power relationships between citizens and their state. Politics and governance rely on the communication of messages and ideas, and technology can bolster political power by influencing the speed, destination, and anonymity of those communications. IT is never the sole motivator for political flux, but a medium by which it occurs. Harnessing IT may alter the momentum in a political contest, and a shift in momentum can become a shift in political reality. IT can affect the internal politics of a state in several ways. For example, IT can make it easier for fringe political parties, NGOs, or dissenters, whether formally organized or not, to challenge a ruling party or a given policy by distributing messages broadly and by allowing supporters to organize easily.

When information flows more freely, citizens can more easily gather facts with which to hold leaders accountable, particularly when the traditional media will not challenge the government. When opposition groups harness its transgressive power, IT can actually assist in regime change by facilitating the distribution of criticisms and protest venues.

Influence of IT Revolution on Politics

Politics in different Asia-Pacific countries have felt the IT revolution in a variety of ways. In some Asian countries, IT has already clearly influenced political events. In others, IT has not affected politics noticeably at all. In yet others, a future influence is highly likely.

The internal politics of some current and former Asia-Pacific one party dominant states, such as Indonesia, China, and Malaysia, have clearly been influenced by IT. Other such regimes, such as North Korea, Myanmar, and Singapore, have not been the locus of notable political activity enhanced by information and communications technology (ICT). For one-party dominant states, the Internet and IT pose a paradox they must resolve-they offer enticing commercial advantages yet can empower dissent and threaten regimes by giving citizens access to new information and a platform for discussion. Controls that limit the Internet's political potential also reduce its commercial value.

The most dramatic example of information technology's political effect on an Asia-Pacific dictatorship is Indonesia, where IT contributed to the downfall of President Suharto. In the last years of his 30-year reign, "the Internet was used extensively by the urban middle-class opposition to get around the regime's censorship of broadcast media. Within hours of its posting, hundreds of pages of faxes poured in from around the world to the Office of the President, the Department of Defense, and the Department of Foreign Affairs. The village girl from East Java became a workers' heroine. A few years later, when political momentum for Suharto's ouster had reached a critical point, students used the Internet to "plan their moves" in the massive nationwide demonstrations that lead to the regime's collapse in 1998. Students occupying the parliament building used laptops to send messages to the outside world. Sen and Hill postulate that it was not just the utility of the Internet as a political platform that made it a popular tool of opposition groups, but that "the very freedom of the Internet became a constant reminder of the absence of openness and freedom in other media." Although Internet penetration was then and is still now relatively low in Indonesia, several factors allowed the net to empower those in opposition to Suharto.

— Many Indonesians share passwords and accounts, thus reducing costs to get online.

— Internet cafes, or "warnet," were starting to become popular and brought affordable access. There are now some 2,000 such cafes in Indonesia. Some proprietors helped their clientele locate the opposition sites. Government-sponsored public Internet kiosks also multiplied.

— The traditional media covered much of the online political discussions, thus both advertising the existence of the forums and carrying their message.

— The Indonesian government was not willing or able to censor the online political activity.

It wanted, as many other Asian countries, to encourage the information economy and did not have the technical or legal structures in place to block sites or monitor e-mail traffic.

IT has also influenced politics in China, albeit in a more nuanced way. China is unique in the Asia-Pacific region-no other government is attempting to both encourage and control IT as completely. Because the Chinese Communist Party (CCP) realizes that it must sustain economic growth to keep its hold on power, the government is promoting information technology growth of every variety, investing billions in infrastructure, and encouraging competition in the telecommunications industry. The Tenth Five Year Plan for the economy issued in 2001 even mentions the importance of "popularizing" information technology. At the same time, the government blocks Internet users from accessing certain political websites based overseas and encourages a high degree of self-censorship among domestic commercial websites through a plethora of strict regulations. A number of activists, academics as well as ordinary citizens, have been arrested for voicing anti-party ideas on the Internet. Moreover, any formal, organized challenge to the political authority of the CCP, online or off, is forbidden. Thus, unlike in 1990s Indonesia, technology is not used widely for antiregime political organizing in China because there is little such activity.

Despite these measures, the Internet in China is a much more free and pluralistic medium than traditional newspapers, magazines, and TV. Ideological challenges to government policies abound on the Internet, although most users are not seeking subversive political information. And to the extent that there have been, in the recent past, attempts to organize political parties, as in the case of the nowoutlawed China Democracy Party, the Internet did play a critical role.

Although dissidents are not gaining much traction, Chinese political dynamics, at the central and local levels, are nonetheless being altered by IT. The potentially most powerful political effect of increased technology access in China comes not from ideological challenges, but from ordinary citizens with an increased ability to hold their government accountable. Information about what their governments do (and do not do) is more freely available online, and Internet forums offer a place in which to discuss such information safely. Websites and bulletin boards that encourage discussions of political topics such as corruption, pollution, women's rights, and HIV have created a new public sphere for political discussion. The Chinese Academy of Social Sciences has found that users in China do view the Internet as a forum to express their political opinions and as a source for political information.

Regime criticism is also directed at the central government. The Hainan Island spy plane incident in 2001, in which a Chinese pilot died and an American flight crew was held by China for 12 days, prompted strong anti-American but also anti-Beijing sentiment. Until censored, chat-room visitors chided their leaders for being "soft" and too old. These sorts of incidents are rare so far, but they illustrate the power of information technology to spread quickly politically sensitive information that can be used against governments. They show how Internet is "crystallizing public dissatisfaction with government." In the long run, at times of crisis, this dynamic could facilitate political change. If China's strong economy falters badly, or some other incident triggers a major political disruption, IT would make the story almost impossible to contain. Citizens could learn what foreign media were reporting about the incident and could talk to each other online in a way that would have been impossible earlier. If momentum for protests built up, e-mail would make them easy to organize. And unlike at Tiananmen Square in 1989, the country would learn how authorities handled the protesters.

Malaysian citizens are also looking to the web for accurate information on political events. The Barisan Nasional Party has ruled since 1969, and because the regime controls the traditional media very tightly, citizens search the Internet for information. Unlike in China, though, the Malaysian government has decided not to censor the Internet for the most part. The government has pinned its hopes for the growth of its mostly market-driven economy on information technology and the Internet. Prime Minister Mahathir bin Mohamad has promoted the "knowledge economy" as a centerpiece of his regime and has invested millions in the "Multimedia Super Corridor" (MSC), Malaysia's answer to Silicon Valley. It promotes and enables Internet access, even for the poor, and places few or no restrictions on online political content. To ensure that no policy would hinder IT growth, the Malaysian government made a clear, public decision, codified in the MSC "Bill of Guarantee," not to censor the Internet, including foreign websites.

Dissident groups and NGOs also use the web in Malaysia. When Prime Minister Mahathir fired his reform-minded deputy, Anwar Ibrahim, in 1999 and imprisoned him on dubious charges, dozens of pro-Anwar sites sprung up, many hosted in the United Kingdom and the United States, to organize international condemnation. NGOs in Malaysia have used international listservs to organize campaigns to pressure the government on human rights issues, including the struggle of the indigenous peoples in Sarawak. Although IT has not been responsible for a dramatic political shift in Malaysia, the media and others' use of the Internet has certainly changed the tenor of political dynamics and has created a channel and audience for any future political movement. IT does not necessarily alter politics in closed regimes. There are a number of one-party dominant states in the Asia-Pacific region where IT has had no major effect.

Myanmar and North Korea have been successful in controlling the Internet, as they do all other media, very strictly. They do so in large part by restricting access to IT. In North Korea, Internet access is illegal. No Internet service providers and no North Korean servers allow citizens to access the Internet. (North Korea, however, does vigorously promote computer literacy and has opened one Internet cafe for foreigners.) The current regime in Myanmar, the State Peace and Development Council (SPDC), has made unauthorized use of a computer or modem punishable by 7-15 years in jail. Recently, one government-controlled Internet cafe opened in Yangon, but exorbitant membership charges prevent all but about 600 citizens from having e-mail accounts. Few people in either country have mobile phones. There are also complete restrictions on political organizing of any kind. Thus, civil society and political parties, to the little extent they may exist inside North Korea and Myanmar, are not using technology for political change. This situation could change if either country were to open up their economies in an effort to promote growth. Now that countries must compete for highly valuable but mobile and often fickle foreign capital, countries without IT infrastructure and Internet access will have great difficulty winning over investors.

Despite the controls within Myanmar, opposition groups based outside the country, many in Thailand, have been increasingly active. These groups, supplied with laptops and Internet connections by international democracy-promotion organizations, have linked with other campaigners around the world "to form a transnational movement that has pressured the SPDC to an extent many assert would have been impossible without Internet use." An umbrella organization, the Free Burma Coalition, has used grassroots online organizing to pressure the U.S. government to impose sanctions and convince large corporations to withdraw from Burma. It is unclear whether these efforts have had a notable political effect within Myanmar, but they have certainly affected the international debate.

Vietnam is pursuing a strategy similar to that of China- allowing IT but attempting to control its influence. Internet cafes have been blossoming by the thousands in urban Vietnam, and "doing the chat" is popular among teenagers. Yet, the government built a firewall beginning in 1998 that reportedly blocks well over 3,000 political and pornographic sites. Authorities shut down offending websites and have arrested individuals for posting articles about democracy. The government is now considering penalties for cafe owners who allow customers to visit antigovernment or pornographic websites. Although antiregime discussions among Vietnamese and the diaspora are commonplace, it is unclear what the political import of those discussions will be.

IT has not had an effect on politics in the illiberal democracy of Singapore either. Singapore, ruled by the People's Action Party since 1959, is not restricting IT in the least. In fact, the government is encouraging, even forcing, its population to adopt information technologies. Per-capita use of the Internet in Singapore is very high. But government controls and political apathy have teamed to make Singapore cyberspace fairly apolitical. Just as the government closely controls all traditional media, it also keeps careful watch on any online political activity. In 1996, the Singapore Broadcast Authority (SBA) issued the Internet Code of Practice, which prohibits all material on the Internet that might threaten the "public interest, public morality, public order, public security, [and] national harmony" or that "offends against good taste and decency." Regulations make website hosts legally responsible for any content that appears on their sites. ISPs must register with SBA but "are not required to monitor the Internet or its users." These regulations encourage self-censorship, but the SBA claims that it "has not taken action against anyone for objectionable content on the Internet."

A few widely publicized incidents in the 1990s revealed, however, that the government had been monitoring individual web browsing. Current policy states, "SBA does not regulate personal communications, such as Internet Relay Chat (IRC) and e-mail. It does not monitor individual access to Web pages." Recently, with the presence of opposition parties growing on the Internet, and the then-approaching November 2001 elections, the government drafted new rules to allow closer monitoring of political websites. Nevertheless, opposition party websites do exist and do carry criticisms of the ruling party. A few NGOs also host independent political websites that likewise post critiques of government policies. But "these sites have a long way to go before they may be in a position to make some significant impact on the political scene. As one journal commented, "Singapore is a safe, modern, high-rent enclave in an increasingly dodgy neighborhood. Why fool around with opposition politics?" Liberal Democracies IT has played a role in the politics of liberal democracies as well as in the one-party dominant states of the Asia-Pacific region.

The most profound example of IT's role in an Asian democracy comes from the Philippines where, as in Indonesia, IT has been credited with a role in actual regime change. Even before the corruption accusations against then-President Estrada began to surface in 2000, text messaging and the Internet had become channels for political debate and organization among citizens. Websites that criticized and poked fun at his regime-some 200 by one estimate-proliferated soon after Estrada took power.

Most important to the actual organization of protests were mobile phones. Mobile phone penetration is high in the Philippines and text messaging is a wildly popular application, with many millions of messages sent each day. Filipinos were swapping thousands of jokes and slogans about President Estrada through their handsets well before the Senate impeachment trial got under way in early 2001. Some of the websites that hosted anti-Estrada discussions added text messaging to their distribution channels. Then, in January 2001, when a committee of senators voted to keep sealed financial evidence widely believed to be incriminating of Estrada, the public began to gather at a historic shrine less than an hour later. Anti-Estrada forces relied on text messaging to organize these efforts -sending out details of planned gatherings-meeting times, locations, and proper attire. Eventually, as many as a million citizens joined the protests, and Estrada stepped down less than a week later. One mobile phone company found its daily average jump by nearly 60 percent to 70 million a day during the week of protests, and other estimates put the total over the four-day period at 160 million per day. Some companies had to supplement their equipment with mobile cell sites to continue providing reliable service.

In the case of the Philippines, the various technologies reinforced one another-websites and listservs built a community, text messaging and e-mail organized the community, and TV images motivated the community. IT certainly changed how events transpired, although it likely did not change the ultimate outcome. Now "cyberactivism," as one Filipino commentator dubbed it, continues in the Philippines. Even local candidates develop websites and many send out campaign text messages, although the number they can send is limited by election laws. A number of independent election sites host discussions of candidates and issues, and sites such as PCIJ's continue to investigate and publicize possible government corruption.

In Indonesia, with the transition to a democratic system now complete, political parties still use the Internet. But because of the media freedom that has come with democracy, and the still low percentage of users, it is not as critical a technology to internal politics as it was in the transition period when Suharto was ousted. Activists, students, and NGOs, however, have continued to use the Internet to rally the international community, as Burmese activists have. A leader of a separatist group in Aceh recently argued that the Internet is the only way his independence movement can communicate with international powers, a critical factor for success.

In South Korea, a democracy with now expansive media freedom and very high Internet penetration, the 2002 Presidential election became a textbook example of the power of IT. Analysts argue that the success of Roh Moo-hyun was "largely due" to his Internet-based supporters' organization, called "Nosamo." With 80,000 members, the group was able to raise more than $7 million over the Internet and bring thousands to campaign rallies with text messaging, without the typical payments for lunch or bus fare. Half a million visitors logged onto Roh's site every day. The April 2000 national parliamentary elections were an earlier example of IT's political influence. Six hundred small civic groups banded together to press the National Elections Commission (NEC) to release criminal records of all the candidates. When the NEC did so, on its official website, the umbrella group used the information to create a "blacklist" of 86 candidates, many of whom were revealed to have serious criminal records. The NEC site registered 1.1 million visitors on election day, according to the supervising official who called the response "explosive" and "beyond imagination." Importantly, although the mainstream papers did not report the damaging information at first, once the information was widely available on the Internet, they did. In the end, 58 of the 86 blacklisted candidates, including some with well-established careers, lost their contests. The coalition organizers concluded that the collaboration of groups was possible only through "meetings" on the Internet, and one analyst who followed the race closely stated that without the Internet, the coalition's effect would have been "very much limited." Finally, South Korean NGOs, thousands of them, lobby the government for various policies, often using the Internet as a base and connecting with NGOs abroad.

As in the case of closed regimes, there are a number of democracies in Asia where IT has not had a discernible effect on politics. In Japan, despite its leadership in technology production, the Internet and other new technologies have not yet been greatly influential in politics. This reflects a general lack of dynamism in Japanese politics as the ruling Liberal Democratic Party (LDP) has a firm grip on power. One impediment has been the 1950 law that governs elections, which has been interpreted to prohibit online campaigning. A government task force is evaluating that policy and will likely recommend changes.

To comply with regulations, they do not update the sites during election season. Another factor that contributes to the lack of IT influence in Japanese politics is the disproportionate influence of rural voters who have less Internet access. An incipient exception to the otherwise sleepy state of IT influence on politics might be the activism of NGOs in Japan. In one case, Japanese consumer groups opposed to genetically modified foods have established websites to promote their view and have used the Internet, in part, to organize coordinated rallies across Japan.

In India, local governments have made impressive strides in using technology, especially for a relatively poor country. However, at this stage, technology has not played an influential role in India's politics. Many of the large political parties do have websites, and some of them are updated frequently. But parties are not using the Internet or other advanced technology to mobilize citizens or to gather input from them in part because IT penetration is quite low among the general population. NGOs appear to be using the web, as in other Asian countries, to network with international counterparts and to raise awareness of certain policy issues. For example, according to one account, in 2001, an Internet-based campaign by India's grassroots organizers and a network of environmental activists in Maine managed to redirect 20 tons of mercury headed for India back to the United States. Australia. Australia's political parties are using the Internet, but the effects of this trend are not yet significant. Although many parties have robust informational sites, there is little evidence to indicate that the parties are using IT to interact with potential supporters or in other innovative ways.

Future Trends

Technology does not discriminate by regime type in its influence. Technology has contributed to regime change in Indonesia and the Philippines, helps Chinese citizens hold their government more accountable, affects the international debate on Myanmar, empowered the East Timorese independence movement, and is changing elections in South Korea. IT has had a strong effect in select authoritarian and democratic regimes and no effect in others. More research is needed to draw definitive correlations, but some preliminary observations are possible. First, and obviously, some degree of flux in the underlying politics of a state must be present before IT can have an effect on changing politics. In a country with staid politics, for whatever reason, be it a democracy such as Japan, where bureaucracy is so thick that it resists any change, or a dictatorship such as North Korea, where the regime allows no political challenges, or an illiberal democracy such as Singapore, where neither the regime nor the populace seems to crave change, IT will have little political effect because there is no underlying political movement.

A second condition that must be met for IT to have an effect on politics is some degree of technology penetration, at least among the middle class. In every Asian country, some more than others, the "digital divide" is large. But when the middle class has access, citizens can use those channels for political change, as they did in Indonesia and the Philippines. Last, government controls of the media have a bearing on the political effect of IT. In such countries as Myanmar, where not only is access limited but those few with access to the Internet can surf only a list of preapproved sites, there is little room for political activity. Although it restricts online content somewhat, China nevertheless permits citizens to engage in political activity on the web if they stop short of calling for an end to the regime. We also observe that a frequent presumption about one-party dominant states-that all are trying to control the Internet as much as possible for fear of its political effect-is not truc. One-party dominant states are responding to IT in a wide variety of ways.

At one extreme, North Korea and Myanmar are attempting to exclude the Internet. On the other end of the spectrum is Malaysia, which is encouraging its spread and not censoring its use. China and Singapore are adopting compromise approaches. It is not clear that one-party regimes that welcome IT are more likely in the long run to be undermined than those regimes that exclude it. The economic growth that IT can generate may benefit a sitting regime more than the increased political opportunities of its citizens will hurt it. That is certainly true for Singapore. Malaysia and China are also taking this bet, hoping that liberalizing cyberspace will lead them to a future like Singapore, not Suharto's Indonesia.

In Asian countries with sizable IT penetration, at least among the middle class, IT will no doubt play a role in future moments of political crisis or disjuncture. This is especially true in countries where the likelihood both of significant political disruptions and of technology penetration is high, such as in China and Malaysia. Also, if closed regimes that have excluded IT, such as Myanmar and North Korea, attempt to open their economies to stimulate growth, they will have to permit IT, and then they may experience disruptions as their disenchanted populations find national and international online communities. In addition, IT will be used increasingly by

NGOs to bring domestic and international pressure to bear for certain policy changes. As in every other region of the world, the international community will have an increasing influence in internal Asian politics, as the examples of Myanmar and East Timor reflect. Finally, political parties in the liberal democracies will likely increase their use of IT, but this effect will be sporadic and will depend upon the rise of political challengers that eschew traditional channels.

In addition to the sometimes profound changes IT has enabled in bottom-up politics, IT is also reshaping the way Asia-Pacific governments conduct the business of government. Trends in e-government are what this section will examine.

Since the mid-1990s, countries from every corner of the earth have embraced IT. Technology was often portrayed as a miracle cure for all the many ills of government. IT, it was argued, would single-handedly save money, bring government closer to more people, increase transparency, and reduce corruption. ."E-government initiatives can have three primary benefits-increased access to information about government programs and policies, better service delivery to citizens and businesses, and greater citizen involvement in government decisionmaking. In some countries, simply the increased transparency associated with readily available, but static, information about the identities of responsible government officials, about how to contact them, or about the proper procedures for a given service, is a potentially large change.

For many governments, the holy grail of e-government is Internet-based transactions that save money and allow citizens and businesses easy, anytime, anywhere service. To achieve this sort of "one-stop shop," historically "stove-pipe" government agencies must coordinate their activities because "transformation comes not from moving services online, but from redesigning the organization and processes to put the citizen at the center, integrating across agencies to simplify interaction, reduce cost and improve service." Last, IT has the potential to enhance democracy by allowing citizens to participate in debates as they happen, overcoming boundaries of geography and giving many people and organizations access to information once restricted to the powerful few.

As with the effect of IT on politics in Asian countries, the picture when looking at top-down e-government is quite varied in Asia. Some countries are e-government leaders where others have but simple websites. Overall, IT's "wonderful potential has been hardly used in most Asia-Pacific countries" for e-government. Unlike with the case of internal politics, IT has not lead to dramatic changes in the substance of government in any country. In some countries, however, changes in the form of government have been so substantial that they are approaching changes in substance. In others, such as China, e-government could lead to actual changes in governance in the future by disguising government reform under the cover of hardware and software. The Asian governments that routinely place within the top ten in the world for e-government according to various survey groups include Australia, Singapore, Hong Kong, New Zealand, and Taiwan.

Others are devoting significant amounts of time and resources to e-government but have not reached a level of global sophistication; those include Thailand, the Philippines, and Malaysia. Countries such as India and

China have remarkable pockets of innovation in local polities but are in the early stages overall. North Korea, Myanmar, Vietnam, and Indonesia have not developed robust e-government programs.

Singapore finds itself in a neighbourhood still largely recovering from economic and political crises. There are mixed signs of recovery in parts of Southeast Asia, but Indonesia's "multidimensional crisis" has the widest regional implications of all. Malaysia, Singapore's other near neighbour, is, by comparison, far more politically and economically stable, but not without its political vicissitudes.

The accession of Megawati Sukarnoputri to the presidency of the Republic of Indonesia on 23 July 2001 cleared the political impasse that had virtually paralysed the executive, under Abdurrahman Wahid (or Gus Dur), since the beginning of 2001. Megawati came to power with low expectations on what she could achieve. Her initial cabinet was stronger than most had anticipated—greeted with a strong market rally—but with the passage of time the low expectations have returned as the government has failed to confront the major challenges facing Indonesia in a meaningful way. On the positive side of the ledger, Megawati's presidency brings far more political stability to Indonesia, in no small measure due to her being far less vulnerable to the political process that removed Wahid. At the very least, talks with the International Monetary Fund (IMF) have resumed after a worrying hiatus under the Wahid administration. However, this political capital has so far not been used to create a political momentum that will tackle the economic, political, and regional problems that beset Indonesia. When Megawati came to the Indonesian presidency many feared that Indonesia may have landed itself a super-nationalist leader, instinctively in favour of centrism, inclined to use a heavy hand in Aceh and Irian Jaya, close to the military, and possibly an economic nationalist. Much of the speculation was extrapolated from Megawati's nationalist rhetoric, and a heavy conflation by many with her father's policies. It is also clear that Megawati considers the presidency as a birthright, being the daughter of Indonesia's founding father, rather than based on a coherent policy programme that she can offer the Indonesian people. Notable for her silence on issues while she was a party leader, this seems to have carried over into the Presidency.

In August 2001, some two weeks after her selection by the Indonesian Upper House, Megawati unveiled the 32 member "Gotong Royong" Cabinet. With a few exceptions, the new cabinet was widely hailed as a very strong line-up. It was a mixture of technocrats and political appointees from a number of parties. Wahid's gravest error was to increasingly sideline important political blocs in favour of his own appointees to the executive. With around 10% of the vote in parliament, this placed him in a vulnerable position. Megawati has so far avoided this mistake. The cabinet includes appointees from the three leading blocs in the Indonesian legislature: Megawati's own party, Indonesian Democracy Party-Struggle (PDI-P), Golkar, and Poros Tengah (Central Axis. An olive branch was extended to Wahid's National Awakening Party (PKB) with one important cabinet post.

The military retain four positions, although a civilian heads the defence ministry. Indonesia's creaking and groaning political system is badly in need of an overhaul. The zeitgeist of Reformasi, which swept the country in

1998, ushered in an era of democratization—which is to say that Indonesia became relatively more democratic than it had been under Soeharto's authoritarian rule. Although the era was marked by genuine checks and balances, free elections, and freedoms in media and public comment, critics have pointed out that democratization has brought with it chaos and the inability to muster the strength and resources needed for strong and effective governance. However, the ineffective governance of Indonesia has more to do with the failure to implement strong political institutions within a democratic framework, than a failure of democracy per se.

Indonesia's 1945 Constitution, still used to this day, is a very basic document designed to serve Sukarno's revolutionary presidential-style government (while in opposition to the Dutch), and has altered only marginally since. While the 1945 Constitution was a vague document to begin with, subsequent MPR sessions have made amendments but failed to coherently build a coherent governing structure. This is largely because constitutional amendments and supplementary laws are usually the result of compromises within Indonesia's multi-party environment—which has resulted in a system that may fall between two rocks. Indonesia's government has uniquely combined these systems and is governed by elements of both. In 2001 it was decided that Indonesia would move to a direct election for president by 2004, but compromises amongst the various factions may mean that unless a single candidate gains more than 50% in the vote (which is very unlikely), the president will be chosen by the Upper House—thus reverting back to the status quo.

The electoral rules are another case in point. Although largely a proportional system, it contains elements of the district system. But, unusually for a proportional system, it contains no effective threshold. This means that there is little incentive for parties to cohere—in fact all of the major parties are in serious danger of splintering. Megawati presides over Indonesia's largest party, PDI-P, which gained 30% of the parliamentary seats in the last election. This puts Megawati is the (relatively) strongest political position. PDI-P is a marriage of urban liberals, nationalists, and a large number of "common people" (*massa*) who have fond memories of Sukarno and/or respect for Megawati as an opponent of Soeharto. However, there are serious divisions opening within the party, and some officials have been very unhappy with the perceived dominance of Megawati's husband—Taufik Kiemas. The next largest party, Golkar (24% of seats), faces a two-fold problem.

— Some of its leaders are under suspicion of corruption, including party leader, Akbar Tanjung, who is accused of diverting US$4 million from Bulog into the coffers of his party.

— Golkar in the post-Soeharto era has become dominated by representatives from eastern Indonesia (especially Sulawesi) and they may seek to challenge the party's Java based leadership at some point.

All of the main parties that espouse some form of Islamic identity, either merely as a political constituency or as a political agenda, face the prospect of a split. Wahid's PKB is experiencing a very open feud between two factions. Amien Rais' PAN and Vice President Hamzah Haz's PPP are also split. Ever since the Vice President and his lieutenants began to push for an explicit mention of Islam in the Constitution, a section of the party, called PPP Reformasi, has threatened to split. Even the tiny, yet radical, PBB, is in open conflict. With few incentives for parties to remain together, the possibilities for splinter factions grow. In the run up to the 2004 elections we should expect to see some splintering, reordering, and perhaps even reconstitution of the political parties, especially the "Islamic" parties. The terrorist attacks in the United States have forced Megawati to walk a tightrope. Megawati's scheduled visit to the US was not postponed in the wake of the attacks as many had thought, but given some prominence. While Indonesia's political elite, from most parties, have condemned the terrorist attacks, supporting the US response has run up against domestic opinion.

Demonstrations, opinion polls, and newspaper commentary in Indonesia's main dailies indicate that a significant portion of the Muslim population is deeply concerned about a US counterattack against other Muslim countries and are demanding that greater evidence be produced against Al-Qaeda. Aside from displays of co-religionist tendencies on behalf of the moderate (and largely pro-democratic) mainstream, there are a number of small, but increasingly radicalized, Islamic groups who continue to be a cause for concern. The most well known group is Laskar Jihad, which has waded into the Maluku conflict through the contribution of armed militia. Other groups have engaged in "sweep" operations looking for American citizens, or made threats to the US Embassy and its personnel—although none of this has amounted to anything. Greater pressure will come on the Indonesian government to control or shut down these groups, some of whom are believed to be linked to terrorist networks outside the country and are deeply antagonistic to the west and global capitalism, and continue to cause havoc in their own country.

Despite the serious independence challenges in Aceh and Irian Jaya, and the communal violence in Maluku, Kalimantan and central Sulawesi, Indonesia is in no immediate danger of breaking up. The handling of regional issues, and centrifugal forces in the periphery, will determine the question of Indonesia's long term future as a state. However, Indonesian nationalism remains, on the whole, quite strong. Aceh has quickly become Indonesia's most serious regional problem, with 2001 being the worst year on record for conflict deaths, due to the effective break down of peace talks and the full scale resumption of the police-led security campaign. In both Aceh and Irian Jaya, the military and the police have demonstrated a propensity to deal violently with "treasonous" elements, often involving the targeting of unarmed government critics, and the human rights abuses of the past have not ended.

The security forces have operated without effective civilian control, but there are signs that key members of the Megawati government are pushing strongly for an end to the military "solution", while stressing negotiations, greater autonomy, devolution of resources, and the reestablishment of law and order. While special autonomy deals are being prepared for Aceh and Irian Jaya, the other regions are subject to the standard regional autonomy deal. This means devolution to the district level of all government functions except defence, foreign affairs, justice, overall monetary and fiscal policy, religious affairs, and the development of strategic and natural resources. The regional autonomy package is confusing and flawed, but a major step forward from the previous centralization. Many districts in resource rich areas are already doing far better in terms of social development, while a dark cloud hangs over the resource poor provinces with a shrinking centralized public purse. Investment and concession rules are still in need of clarification. President Megawati Sukarnoputri has now inherited a position that requires her to govern one of the world's most complex nation states, compounded by the multidimensional crisis that now afflicts it.

There are signs of improvement, with a stronger economy being the most obvious means to potentially diffuse unmet expectations and improve social conditions. The flaws within regional autonomy have not been addressed so far, however the devolution of resources is a step in the right direction, as the total centralization of capital and power of Indonesia's recent past now seems largely unacceptable in the provinces. Nonetheless, rumours persist that the Megawati administration will seek to re-centralize some aspects of power. Indonesia's foreign policy is largely continuous with Soeharto's time, and normalised relations continue within ASEAN. However, since the fall of Soeharto, bilateral flare-ups have occurred, with a number of these involving Singapore. Habibie and his supporters expressed their anger with Singapore, which seemed to stem from a perceived slight by Singapore's Senior Minister, Lee Kuan Yew, and the expectation that Singapore should have provided capital assistance to Indonesia in its time of need. In late 2000, Abdurrahman Wahid made several barbed comments about Singapore, including the suggestion that the Singapore government looks down upon Malay peoples. These bilateral spats should be put in context, as there is a largely positive diplomatic and commercial relationship between Singapore and Indonesia. However there has been frustration expressed on both sides over the Jemaah Islamiyah (JI) movement. JI operatives have been arrested in Singapore and Malaysia, but cohorts of the group in Indonesia have not yet been arrested. Indonesia has not only failed to act in this case, but openly questioned whether the evidence would be enough to convict.

There are a number of factors to this issue. Both Singapore and Malaysia have made use of the Internal Security Act (ISA), while during Indonesia's reformasi process there has been a repeal of similar provisions, including the Anti-Subversion Law. There has also been a general run-down of state capacity in terms of enforcing and investigating law and order. Furthermore, the Megawati administration has been determined not to alienate key Muslim groups, and is sensitive to their demands. This is not to say that these groups are extremists or sympathetic to Al-Qaeda, but that some may see the general response to the events of September 11 to be directed unfairly at Islam and Islamic groups. Recent remarks by Singapore's Senior Minister provoked a nationalist reaction in Indonesia, causing key members of the Indonesian government to label this as interference in Indonesia's domestic affairs.

Members of the Islamic Defenders Front protested at the Singaporean Embassy, although these demonstrations were small. With each bilateral spat, often at the leadership level, lower level bureaucrats have worked to downplay differences between the two states and smooth over ruffled feathers.

Malaysia's leader, Dr Mahathir Mohamad, has now served for more than two decades as Prime Minister, and is thus the country's longest serving head of government. Throughout his 20-year rule he has proved his capacity for being politically tenacious in pursuing his agenda, and very firm in dealing with his political opponents. The jailing of Anwar Ibrahim sparked a serious political crisis in Malaysia, given his appeal within some sections of Malaysia and the perception of injustice in this case. Although the government's popularity has been greatly tested, as evidenced by the losses in the last general election, and in various by-elections, there are signs that BN's fortunes have revived in recent times. Political damage to the BN was evident in the last general election returns. The twin issues of Anwar and the growing concern over KKN (corruption, collusion, and nepotism) saw UMNO have its worse returns since 1969, being reduced to just 72 seats (from 94) in the 193-seat parliament. Nonetheless, UMNO and its coalition partners in the ruling Barisan Nasional (BN) were able to gain a total of 148 seats.

The government's fortunes were boosted by UMNO's coalition partners, as a large number of Chinese and Indian votes were captured, as well as continued dominance in Sarawak and Sabah. The 27 September 2001 state polls in Sarawak saw the BN win 60 out of 62 state assembly seats, providing a psychological boost to the ruling coalition in Malaysia. In the Malay community, the traditional bedrock of BN political power, however, UMNO may have captured less than 50% of the vote. The two opposition Malay-based parties, keADILan (National Justice Party) and PAS (Pan-Malaysian Islamic Party), gained 5 and 27 seats respectively. Despite growing public discontent with the Mahathir-led government, various factors have strengthened his hand.

— A rally in economic indicators has boosted some confidence in the administration.

— The opposition Barisan Alternatif (BA) has fallen apart and,

— The events surrounding the September 11 have allowed Mahathir to discredit the Islamicist opposition.

— Recent corporate restructuring, since the resignation of Daim as the Finance Minister, has given the impression that the government is serious about correcting the KKN problem.

The BA, which included keADILan, PAS, Parti Rakyat Malaysia (PRM) and the Chinese dominated Democratic Action Party (DAP), has now fallen into disarray. The anticipated divorce occurred on 22 September 2001, when DAP withdrew. These parties do not represent natural alliance partners—large numbers of non-Malays continued to give their support to the BN and in the 1999 election in part out of fear of the PAS vision for an Islamic state. The issue of Malay Dominance in government and society has also driven a wedge between DAP and the Malay dominated keADILan and PAS. The split within BA clearly strengthens Mahathir's political fortunes. The terrorist attacks of 11 September 2001 have had some domestic impact on Malaysia. Aside from a general economic slowdown (linked to global trends), the issue has sparked a further round of debates about the role of Islam in society. Mahathir very publicly condemned the September 11 attacks, but expressed strong reservations about the counterattack against Afghanistan.

The response of PAS demonstrated a far more hardline streak. Not only did PAS supporters demonstrate outside the US Embassy, but the party declared a Jihad against the US and urged its followers to consider going to Afghanistan. Such a radical response has played into Mahathir's hands. He has been able to demonstrate himself to be a more moderate Muslim leader, and arrests of alleged terrorists with Al-Qaeda links who have been imprisoned under the ISA. Before the terrorist attacks the government arrested eleven suspects, allegedly belonging to the Kumpulan Mujaheedin Malaysia (KMM), including Nik Adli, the son of Kelantan Chief Minister (and PAS leader) Nik Aziz. Also, Nik Adli, a former religious teacher, and eight other Muslim militants, were ordered to serve a 2-year detention under the ISA for, according to Malaysian police, plotting to overthrow the Mahathir government, planning assassinations, and sending fighters to take part in religious clashes in Indonesia's troubled Maluku province. After the September 11 terrorist attacks there was a second round of KMM arrests as well as the incarceration of suspected members of the group.

The Malaysian government has found it easier, for various reasons, to imprison those it deems to be a threat to society, than Indonesia—not least of all because it strengthens Mahathir's position. Malaysia has also committed itself to cooperation (diplomatic consultations, intelligence sharing) in trying to undermine the perceived global threat from terrorism. In all of this are UNMO attempts to win back Malay support. September 11 portrayed UMNO as a moderate party vis-à-vis PAS, which may have convinced a more moderate middle ground to come back to the UMNO fold. The government has also made attempts to deal with KKN through the removal of some corporate leaders. UNMO itself has also mounted a grass-roots campaign at local levels to recruit and to explain BN policies to the Malay public. So far the main indication of how successful this is comes from the outstanding success in a recent Perlis by-election, where UMNO dramatically increased its majority.

It is passé to suggest that ethnic politics remain the sine qua non of the Malaysian polity. As such, relations between the three core groups—Malays, Chinese, and Indians— are of considerable import in Peninsula Malaysia. On the whole these groups have learned to coexist to the extent that there is no suggestion of the return of race riots. However, ethnicity, a division reinforced by government classification and distinction in policy making, continues to need attention and management. UNMO's BN partners have openly challenged the aspects of Ketuanan Melayu, and Mahathir himself has said (or warned) that this system may one day come to an end.

The Malaysian Indian Congress (MIC) president Samy Vellu, a partner in the ruling BN, now advocates the implementation of a quota system for Indians in the public service to stem the tide of marginalization in the Indian community. This idea, and proposals put forward by the Malaysian Chinese Organizations Election Appeals Committee (Suqiu) for removing discrimination against non-Malays, were met with strong rebuke by Mahathir and UMNO stalwarts who conveniently interpreted Suqiu's 17-point proposal as a demand to abolish constitutionally-enshrined Malay rights and privileges. However, Mahathir has 10 always been cognizant of the fact that non-Malay support played a crucial role in the UMNO-led BN coalition victory in the 1999 elections—and hence the need to placate the non-Malays, especially the Chinese, by conceding to the establishment of an MCA-run tertiary institution (Universiti Tunku Abdul Rahman, so named for Malaysia's founding prime minister). Knowing the sensitivities of Chinese and Indian Malaysians regarding their right to vernacular education, Mahathir assured both communities that the presence of many Chinese and Tamil schools in the country was "solid proof of the government's commitment to protect the interests of all races especially in educational development". Mahathir, while generally committed to Ketuanan Melayu, has appeared to speak against the issue on occasion. He has openly cautioned against the blind continuation of such Malay privileges as it made them complacent and uncompetitive vis-à-vis the non-Malays. This may reflect Mahathir's view that the intended recipients of the New Economic Policy have been ungrateful.

In terms of relations with Singapore, like the relationship with Indonesia, the Malaysian relationship is a substantial one. Intimate diplomatic and commercial ties exist between the two near-neighbours—as well as strong links of kith and kin. Formal defence ties exist between Malaysia and Singapore as members of the Five Power Defence Arrangements (FPDA). A high profile visit by Singapore's Senior Minister in 2001 has done much to demonstrate the positive aspects of the relationship. Nonetheless, there are bilateral issues and arguments that need negotiation from time to time. Many of these issues are well known: arrangements over the use of Malaysian airspace, the Tanjong Pagar Malayan Railway station and customs checkpoint, land reclamation to the north of Singapore, CPF money belonging to Malaysians, and negotiations over the water supply for Singapore. Currently, discussions over water centre around the price per 1000 gallons. Commentary in Malaysia about the "tudung issue" in Singapore's primary schools was perceived as interference in Singapore's internal affairs.

Interdependent neighbours will inevitably have bilateral difficulties that will need management and negotiation—and this is the experience of states the world over. The Malaysia-Singapore partnership should be seen in this context. It is largely an intimate relationship, but is at times beset with difficulties and misunderstandings. Mahathir has tightened his grip on the reins of power in Malaysia. This is not to say that the public discontent over the Anwar arrest has been totally assuaged, but several factors have played into the BN's hands. Under Malaysia's Westminsterstyle, first-past-the-post electoral system, the inability of the opposition to unite under a single electoral pact spells doom for their chances of gaining power. Serious differences have been evident within BA for some time over the issues of Malay dominance and PAS' notion of an Islamic state. While the BN Malay-vote has dramatically fallen away, votes from non-Malays have come to Mahathir's rescue. September 11 further strengthened Mahathir, as the main opposition party, PAS, severely discredited itself by declaring Jihad against the United States. The question of leadership succession remains an open one. Mahathir has hinted on a handful of occasions that he may step down, but in more recent times he has indicated that he is still needed in order to maintain secure political leadership. It seems unlikely that Mahathir will step down in the short term—indeed many commentators believe he will remain in office as long as humanly possible.

The President, Gloria Macapagal-Arroyo, is now firmly entrenched as the chief executive after some extraordinary events saw the removal of her predecessor, Joseph Estrada, in January 2001, and subsequently resulted in competing claims to the presidency. By May 2001, Estrada's supporters had failed in their bid to restore him, and Macapagal-Arroyo was reinforced by a narrow victory in senatorial elections that month—although in the Philippines faction-ridden parties, her grip on the Senate is tenuous at best. Economically, the Philippines is showing positive signs of modest growth for the first time since the lethargy of the Estrada years—with 3.3% for 2001. But daunting problems remain, including a projected population growth of over 3% per annum. September 11 has, for the Bush administration, brought the Philippines into sharp focus—or at least a certain region of it. The Muslim south, Mindanao, has been a restive region for more than two decades. A peace deal with the Moro National Liberation Front (MNLF), saw leader Nur Misuari become head of the Mindanao autonomous region. Fighting continued against the splinter group, Moro Islamic Liberation Front (MILF). Nur Misuari's removal as provincial chief in 2001 saw him return to fugitive status, as he has been linked to insurgent activity.

In the aftermath of the September 11 attacks, the United States has inserted several hundred Special Forces advisers to assist in targeting another splinter faction—Abu Sayyaf. Abu Sayyaf have gained notoriety in recent times through a series of high profile kidnappings, which have generated millions of dollars for the rebel group. Founded by veterans of the Soviet War in Afghanistan, Abu Sayyaf stands accused of fostering links with Osama bin Laden and Al-Qaeda.

In January 2001, the Thai electorate delivered a serious blow to the then ruling Democrat Party, and handed power to the Thai Rak Thai (Thais Love Thais - TRT). Created by business magnate, Thaksin, TRT was able to secure 248 seats in the 500 member House of Representatives through a combination factors, including: dissatisfaction with the Democrat-led government's handling of economic and political issues, a clever marketing campaign, and Thaksin's promises on a range of issues from farm subsidies to health care to economic nationalism. TRT's popularity, which dovetails with new constitutional election arrangements, have created a polity less reliant on multi-party coalitions. The new rules offer a mixture of district and proportional seats, which favour larger parties and have seen smaller parties fold.

The 2001 election was the first time that a single party had come close to achieving a majority and was the greatest electoral win in Thai history. Now that TRT has swallowed smaller parties, Seritham and the New Aspiration Party (NAP), and made secure coalitional arrangements with Chat Thai and Chat Phatthana, it has secured a solid majority in the house. Serious doubts have emerged about the Thaksin administration's ability to deliver on its myriad of promises to the electorate. Even the King of Thailand is on record as expressing his concern over this. Nonetheless, Thaksin, who survived a legal challenge to his rule in 2001, appears to be firmly entrenched in power for the moment—although influential sections of the middle class and the intelligentsia are turning against the Prime Minister. Controversy has recently been stirred over the expulsion of Far Eastern Economic Review journalists and reports of other types of media interference.

More than eleven years after the May 1990 elections, in which the National League for Democracy (NLD) won convincingly, the ruling military junta, now known as the State Peace and Development Council (SPDC), has yet to announce the time table for a return to civilian rule, and thus remains largely an international pariah. The Malaysian diplomat Razali Ismail, as the United Nations (UN) Secretary General's special envoy, appeared to have brokered a breakthrough in the decade-long impasse in Myanmar politics by facilitating "landmark talks" between the junta representatives and NLD leader Daw Aung San Suu Kyi. More than 200 NLD members have been released from detention with the onset of these talks. However, the oscillation of the military on this issue in recent years has given some cause for pessimism about whether the negotiations will amount to anything substantial. Tangible progress is needed soon for the level of engagement to be enhanced so that Myanmar can reap substantive benefits that would increase its capacity to tackle the complex problems of economic and political transition, with the attendant humanitarian issues relating to health, education and social welfare.

Meanwhile, the recent revelation by the ruling junta of a coup plot, apparently hatched by former leader Ne Win's immediate family, and the subsequent shake up of the military hierarchy, have complicated the political situation and have led to concerns over national security and regime stability. It remains to be seen whether these events will seriously affect the ongoing political reconciliation process between the junta and the opposition.

Prime Minister Hun Sen and the ruling Cambodia People's Party (CPP) have gained a stranglehold on government, and consolidated this position after the 1998 national elections. The commune elections (local body) reconfirmed this status with final results. CPP garnered 67 % of total commune positions, from 61 per cent of valid votes, and a whopping 98% of commune leader positions. The only remaining opposition figure of any note remains Sam Rainsy and the small, yet vocal, Sam Rainsy Party. The trauma of the past continues to loom large in political calculations—both domestic and foreign. There has been considerable international pressure for war crimes trials of senior Khmer Rouge figures, which Hun Sen has wavered on—but it is pretty clear that without international pressure the government would not have pursued this agenda. However, the UN has now withdrawn from the process, and Hun Sen has decided to press ahead with trials. There is concern that these trials will not be impartial and free of political considerations.

Military demobilization is still incomplete despite the end of the civil war some years ago, and this remains a sore point in foreign relations with the west. Border issues remain with both Thailand and Vietnam, although relations are constrained by considerations of cordial ties within an ASEAN context. Despite starting from a very low basis, the Cambodian economy is expected to grow at between 5-6% over the next few years. Although under an increasingly authoritarian regime, the absence of serious political instability and civil war for the first time since the 1970s bodes well for a period of economic stability. Nonetheless, Cambodia is highly dependent on foreign aid. Social problems remain enormous for Cambodia, with AIDS reaching epidemic proportions, and widespread drugs use.

During the year 2001, the principal political event in Vietnam was the 9th Party Congress, which, in the absence of contestable elections, stands as the major event of the body politic. A new party chief, Nong Duc Manh, was named in 2001, but this seems to be part of a pattern of high turnover for the top position since 1991. Reforms in Vietnam have been in the economic, rather than political, realm. Lessons from the decline in foreign investment and a sluggish economy have made an impact on Vietnam's leadership, and have sparked interest in reforms that include removal of a lot of bureaucratic red tape for foreign and domestic investors. Vietnam continues to pursue a mixed economy, but strong emphasis is being given to the free market. The depressed mood of the business sector from 1997 to 1999 is being replaced by a buoyant outlook, and Vietnam's economy is arguably one of the bright spots in the region. In time, political reforms will need to keep pace with economic changes, such as a clear division of power between different institutions, and between central and regional governments, and also the even application of the rule of law. This type of governance will be needed to run a modern market economy and keep it on track. Domestically there are growing signs of unrest with ethnic minorities in the Central Highlands—although this now seems to have been brought under control.

Southeast Asia, on the whole, is more stable than it was several years ago. However, in a region as diverse as Southeast Asia, it is difficult to draw generalizations, without taking note of greater complexities and exceptions. The region is still recovering from economic crisis, and political change. Countries that continue to show signs of difficult times ahead are Myanmar, with its unyielding junta, and Indonesia, which is still struggling with democratization. However, in Indonesia's case, despite the continuing difficulties over stability, there is now far less talk about the disintegration of the Republic —and regional autonomy may have played a leading role in this.

5

SAARC and Nuclear Confrontation

The idea of regional cooperation in South Asia was first raised in November 1980. After consultations, the Foreign Secretaries of the seven countries met for the first time in Colombo in April 1981. This was followed a few months later by a meeting of the Committee of the Whole, which identified five broad areas for regional cooperation. The Foreign Ministers, at their first meeting in New Delhi in August 1983, adopted the Declaration on South Asian Association for Regional Cooperation (SAARC) and formally launched the Integrated Program of Action (IPA) in the five agreed areas of cooperation: agriculture; rural development; telecommunications; meteorology, and health and population activities. Later, transport; postal services; scientific and technological cooperation; sports, arts, and culture were added to the IPA.

The SAARC seeks to promote the welfare of the peoples of South Asia, strengthen collective self-reliance, promote active collaboration and mutual assistance in various fields, and cooperate with international and regional organizations.

Meetings of Heads of State or Government: Meetings are held once a year. To date, 10 meetings of the Heads of State or Government have been held: Dhaka (1985), Bangalore (1986), Kathmandu (1987), Islamabad (1988), Malé (1990), Colombo (1991), Dhaka (1993), New Delhi (1995), Malé (1997), Colombo (1998), Kathmandu (1999), and Pakistan (2000). The Heads of State or Government during the Ninth SAARC Summit agreed that a process of informal political consultations would prove useful in promoting peace, stability, amity, and accelerated socio-economic cooperation in the region.

Council of Ministers: The Council, comprising the Foreign Ministers of Member States, meets twice a year. The Council may also meet in extraordinary circumstances by agreement of Member States.

Standing Committee of Foreign Secretaries: The Committee provides overall monitoring and coordination, determines priorities, mobilizes resources, and approves projects and financing. It may meet as often as deemed necessary but in practice normally meets twice a year and submits its reports to the Council of Ministers. The Standing Committee may also set up Action Committees comprising Member States concerned with implementation of projects per Article VII of the Charter. The Standing Committee is assisted by a Programming Committee, an ad hoc body, comprising senior officials, to scrutinize the Secretariat Budget, finalize the Calendar of Activities, and take up any other matter assigned to it by the Standing Committee. The Programming Committee also has been entrusted to consider the reports of the Technical Committees and the SAARC Regional Centers and submit its comments to the Standing Committee.

The position is held by the Secretary-General, who is appointed by the Council of Ministers for a two-year term and is rotated among Member States, six Directors, and a General Services Staff.

Development of SAARC

1985: The Heads of State or Government at their First SAARC Summit held in Dhaka on 7-8 December adopted the Charter formally establishing the South Asian Association for Regional Cooperation (SAARC).

In the declaration of the First SAARC Summit the Member States expressed concern at the deteriorating international political situation and the unprecedented escalation of the arms race, particularly in its nuclear aspect. They recognized that mankind was confronted with the threat of self-extinction arising from a massive accumulation of the most destructive weapons ever produced and that the arms race intensified international tension and violated the principles of the UN Charter. The Member States called upon the NWS to undertake negotiations on a CTBT leading to the complete cessation of testing, production, and deployment of nuclear weapons. In this connection, they welcomed the recent meeting between President Reagan and General Secretary Gorbachev in Geneva and expressed the hope that the meeting would have a positive effect on international peace and security.

1986: In the declaration of the Second SAARC Summit in November, in Bangalore, India, the Member States noted with deep disappointment that the promise held out by the US-Soviet Summit in Reykjavik could not be realized. They, however, noted with satisfaction that the proposals made at the Summit were still on the table and expressed the earnest hope that the negotiations would be resumed without delay so that a decisive step could be taken towards realizing the ultimate goal of eliminating nuclear weapons altogether. The Member States called for the early conclusion of a CTBT.

1987: At the Third SAARC's Summit in Katmandu, Nepal, there was disagreement over a proposal by Pakistan for a South Asian treaty banning nuclear weapons; the final declaration simply noted SAARC's resolve to "contribute" to nuclear disarmament. The States also called for the early conclusion in the Geneva CD of a CTBT and a Convention to Ban Chemical Weapons, declared their intention to continue their efforts to contribute to the implementation of the objective of halting the nuclear arms race and eliminating nuclear weapons, and declared their resolve to support every effort to conclude a treaty prohibiting vertical and horizontal proliferation of nuclear weapons.

1988: In the declaration of the Fourth SAARC Summit in December, in Islamabad, Pakistan, the Member States called for the early conclusion by the CD of a CTBT and a Convention to Ban Chemical Weapons. They declared their intention to continue their efforts to contribute to the realization of the objective of halting the nuclear arms race and eliminating nuclear weapons, as well as declared their resolve to support every effort to conclude a treaty prohibiting vertical and horizontal proliferation of nuclear weapons.

1990: In the declaration of the Fifth SAARC Summit in November, in Malé, Maldives, the Member States expressed the hope that the talks between the United States and USSR on arms control would culminate in the conclusion of an agreement for substantial reduction in their nuclear arsenals leading to the total elimination of nuclear weapons. While welcoming the measures being considered for arms reduction at the global level, they were convinced that the objective could be best achieved through the promotion of mutual trust and confidence among the Member States. They underlined the inherent relationship between disarmament and development and called upon all countries, especially those possessing the largest nuclear and conventional arsenals, to re-channel additional financial resources, human energy, and creativity into development.

Member States expressed their support for the banning of chemical weapons and early conclusion of a CTBT. In this context, they welcomed the convening of the UN Conference in January 1991 to consider amendments to the Partial Test Ban Treaty to convert it into a CTBT.

1991: In the declaration of the Sixth SAARC Summit in December, in Colombo, Sri Lanka, the Member States assessed current international developments in the political sphere particularly those that affected the lives of the people of South Asia. They noted the changing power structures in international relations and the reduction of confrontations and tensions, particularly among the United States and USSR. These have contributed to the receding of the threat of nuclear confrontation and to agreements on disarmament measures. The Member States hoped that these developments would restrain the pursuit of military power in all areas of the world and expressed hope that the peace dividend would be used for promoting the further development of developing countries. They welcomed the trend towards popularly based democratic governments in different parts of the world, including in South Asia.

1993: In the declaration of the Seventh SAARC Summit in April, in Dhaka, Bangladesh, the Member States noted a number of recent positive developments in the area of nuclear, chemical, and conventional disarmament, including the agreements on bilateral arms reductions between the United States and Russia. They expressed their hope that the implementation of the far-reaching arms reduction agreed to in the Washington Agreement of June 1992 and START II signed in Moscow in January 1993 would be successfully carried out. The Member States urged all NWS to collectively endeavour to attain the ultimate goal of complete elimination of nuclear arsenals in the shortest possible time.

1995: In the declaration of the Eighth SAARC Summit in May 1995, in New Delhi, India, the Member States noted that while the international community had successfully created a norm against chemical and biological weapons, it had, unfortunately, been unable to do the same with regard to nuclear weapons. They expressed the conviction that more needed to be done and at a far greater pace. They reiterated that the utmost priority was to be given to nuclear disarmament, given the danger posed by nuclear weapons. The Member States urged the CD to negotiate an international convention prohibiting the use or threat of use of nuclear weapons under any circumstances and to undertake negotiations for the complete elimination of all nuclear weapons within a specified period of time.

1997: In the declaration of the Ninth SAARC Summit in May, in Malé, Maldives, the Member States recognized the need for the international community to pursue nuclear disarmament as a matter of highest priority. In this regard, they recognized the need to start negotiations through the CD and to establish a phased program for the complete elimination of nuclear weapons within a specified framework of time, including a Nuclear Weapons Convention.

1998: In the declaration of the 10th SAARC Summit in July, in Colombo, Sri Lanka, the Member States were of the view that stability, peace, and security in South Asia could not be considered in isolation from global security environment. They noted that the great power rivalry, which the Non-Aligned Movement (NAM) had consistently opposed, no longer posed a serious threat and the danger of a global nuclear conflagration had abated. However, some States still sought to maintain huge arsenals of nuclear weapons and the NPT and the Comprehensive Nuclear Test Ban Treaty (CTBT), to which some SAARC Members were signatories, had not led to any progress towards nuclear disarmament nor prevented proliferation.

The Member States underscored their commitment to the complete elimination of nuclear weapons and the need for promoting nuclear disarmament on a universal basis, under effective international control. They recognized that global nonproliferation goals could not be achieved in the absence of progress towards nuclear disarmament and in this context called upon all NWS, whether party or nonparty to the NPT, to engage constructively through a transparent and credible process of negotiations at the CD. The Member States urged the CD to commence negotiations on a comprehensive, universal, and nondiscriminatory international instrument prohibiting the use or the threat of nuclear weapons as well as eliminating such weapons in existing arsenals.

2002: On 21-22 August, the session of the SAARC Council of Ministers was held in Kathmandu, Nepal. In recognition of the need to update the SAARC Convention on Suppression of Terrorism on account of the obligations devolving on Member States under UNSC Resolution 1373 and the International Convention for the Suppression of Financing of Terrorism, the Council decided to hold a meeting of senior officials assisted by legal experts. The meeting of the senior officials, which is to be held in Sri Lanka, will also prepare the ground for a Ministerial-level meeting. The 11th SAARC Summit was convened in Kathmandu on 4-6 January. In the Summit declaration, the Heads of State or Government were of the view that stability, peace, and security in South Asia should be promoted together with efforts to improve the global security environment. They underscored their commitment to general and complete disarmament including nuclear disarmament on a universal basis, under effective international control.

They agreed that global nonproliferation goals could not be achieved in the absence of progress towards nuclear disarmament and in this context called upon all nuclear weapon States (NWS), whether party or nonparty to the Non-Proliferation Treaty (NPT), to engage constructively through a transparent and credible process of negotiations at the Conference on Disarmament (CD). The leaders also recognized the linkage between disarmament and development. The Heads of State or Government recognized that due to their particular vulnerability, small States require special measures for support from the international community for the safeguarding of their sovereign independence and territorial integrity. They reiterated that the real protection of small States should be firmly rooted in the scrupulous adherence to the UN

Charter, and the rule of law and the strict adherence to universally accepted principles and norms related to sovereign rights and territorial integrity of all States, irrespective of size.

The Heads of State or Government were convinced that terrorism, in all its forms and manifestations, is a challenge to all States and to all of humanity, and cannot be justified on ideological, political, religious, or on any other ground. The leaders agreed that terrorism violates the fundamental values of the United Nations and the SAARC Charter and constitutes one of the most serious threats to international peace and security in the 21st century. In this regard, they emphasized the need for the urgent conclusion of a Comprehensive Convention on Combating International Terrorism. They also emphasized that international cooperation to combat terrorism should be conducted in conformity with the UN Charter, international law, and relevant international conventions.

They also reiterated their support of UNSC Resolution 1373 of 28 September 2001 and affirmed their determination to redouble efforts, collectively as well as individually, to prevent and suppress terrorism in all its forms and manifestations Such efforts would include increased cooperation and full implementation of the relevant international conventions relating to terrorism to which they are parties. In this context, they called on all States to prevent and suppress the financing of terrorist acts by criminalizing the collection of funds for such acts and refraining from organizing, instigating, assisting, or participating in terrorist acts in States or acquiescing in organized activities within its territory directed towards the commission of such acts.

The leaders reaffirmed that the fight against terrorism in all its forms and manifestations had to be comprehensive and sustained. The Heads of State or Government were unanimous in recognizing the distinct ominous link between terrorism, drug-trafficking, money laundering, and other transnational crimes and emphasized the need to coordinate efforts at the national and regional levels to strengthen the global response to this serious challenge and threat to international security. They called upon the international community to assist Member States of SAARC to deal effectively with the adverse economic effects of terrorism in general and to meet the rising insurance and security-related costs in particular.

The Heads of State or Government reaffirmed their commitment to the SAARC Regional Convention on Suppression of Terrorism, which, among other things, recognizes the seriousness of the problem of terrorism as it affects the security, stability, and development of the region. They also reiterated their firm resolve to accelerate the enactment of enabling legislation within a definite time-frame for the full implementation of the Convention, together with strengthening the SAARC Terrorist Offences Monitoring Desk and the SAARC Drug Offences Monitoring Desk.

Nuclear Confrontations in South Asia

The 1998 nuclear tests by India and Pakistan dramatically worsened the security situation for over a billion people in the subcontinent. Since then the two countries have continued to engage in a slow but steady arms race involving qualitative and quantitative developments and a gradual consolidation of nuclear weapon infrastructure. Nuclear use doctrines are taking shape. There have also been two major military crises, both prominently featuring nuclear threats.

Once the incendiary rhetoric characterizing the immediate aftermath of the nuclear tests had subsided, India and Pakistan appeared to take their first steps towards arms control and détente, partly in order to assuage domestic and international fears. As with the superpowers during the cold war, India and Pakistan sought to move the terms of the nuclear debate away from disarmament and towards managing the nuclear threat. The culmination of this process was the Lahore summit meeting in February 1999 between Indian Prime Minister A. B. Vajpayee and Pakistani Prime Minister Nawaz Sharif. The Lahore Declaration committed both countries to 'take immediate steps for reducing the risk of accidental or unauthorized use of nuclear weapons and discuss concepts and doctrines with a view to elaborating measures for confidence building in the nuclear and conventional fields, aimed at prevention of conflict'.

The accompanying Memorandum of Understanding signed by the foreign secretaries of the two countries called for limited transparency measures. Unfortunately, even these steps were not implemented. Nevertheless, the Lahore Declaration offers a possible basis for limiting the threat of nuclear weapons in the region and initiating nuclear disarmament, should the two countries reach a period of better diplomatic relations. The Kargil War The slight hopes that the Lahore meeting offered for restraint in South Asia were dashed within a few months. In May 1999, just one year after the nuclear tests, two months of bitter fighting broke out when Pakistani soldiers and

Islamic militants crossed the Line of Control (LOC) dividing Pakistani Kashmir from Indian Kashmir and occupied a mountain ledge near the town of Kargil. To dislodge them, the Indian Army both literally and figuratively had to fight an uphill battle, taking heavy casualties in the process. Estimates of the total number of casualties sustained by both sides vary from 1200 to 2000.

For the first time since the 1971 war that led to the independence of East Pakistan and the creation of Bangladesh, India used its air force to launch attacks. In response Pakistan put its air force on 'red alert', scrambled its own fighters and tested air raid sirens in its capital city, Islamabad. Both countries conducted army exercises at various points along the borders and both navies were put on alert. Political leaders, strategic analysts and sections of the media in both countries called for a more aggressive war and the opening of new fronts. There were calls in India for the bombardment of Pakistani supply routes to Kargil. Some went even further. Kushabhau Thakre, then national president of the ruling Bharatiya Janata Party (BJP), suggested that the ultimate aim, after evicting infiltrators from the Kargil region, should be to take back the part of Kashmir held by Pakistan.

Pakistan denied that its armed forces were involved and claimed that the fighters were Kashmiris fighting for independence, but the international community was not convinced and demanded that Pakistan order the fighters to withdraw. As Indian troops gained ground and Pakistan stood isolated diplomatically, Nawaz Sharif flew to Washington, where President Bill Clinton bluntly told him he should withdraw Pakistani forces or be prepared for fullscale war with India. Based on information from intelligence sources, Clinton informed Nawaz Sharif that the Pakistani Army had mobilized its nucleartipped missiles. Unnerved by this disclosure and the resulting potential for disaster, Nawaz Sharif agreed to immediate withdrawal, shedding all earlier pretensions that Pakistan had no control over the attacks. There are also reports suggesting that nuclear weapons were kept ready on the Indian side.

The most credible of these reports claimed that India 'activated all its three types of nuclear delivery vehicles and kept them at what is known as "Readiness State 3"- meaning that some nuclear bombs would be ready to be mated with their delivery vehicles at short notice'. These temporary deployments may well become regular practice, driven by the belief attributed to Indian policy makers that 'Pakistan's willingness to exploit its nuclear weaponry for even the most mundane ends might require India to consider developing at least a small set of rapid-response capabilities'. While some have tried to underplay the seriousness of the Kargil War-to the extent of not even classifyng it as a war-it was the first large-scale military engagement between two states with nuclear weapons.

Kargil therefore represents a failure of deterrence, at least as defined by nuclear advocates in South Asia who promoted nuclear weapons in the two countries with the promise of lasting peace. Pakistan's nuclear tests may even have provoked this war. Benazir Bhutto, a former Prime Minister of Pakistan, has stated that in 1996 Pakistani military officers had presented her with plans for a Kargil-style operation, which she vetoed. It would therefore seem that the nuclear weapon tests convinced Pakistan's political and military leaders that the operation might be feasible with a nuclear shield to restrict any possible Indian response. As a consequence, the lessons taken from the war by leaders in the two countries have been very different.

For Pakistan, Kargil represented proof that its nuclear weapons would prevent India from launching a massive military attack. For India, Kargil meant that India would have to find ways of waging limited war that would not lead to the eventual use of nuclear weapons.

The 1999 Military Coup

The coup in Pakistan in October 1999 led by General Pervez Musharraf was a key development. Musharraf was seen in India as the architect of the Kargil War and relations between the two countries deteriorated sharply. The only major meeting between the leaders of the two countries' governments, the Agra Summit of 14-16 July 2001, produced no agreement. The coup has also allowed India to portray differences between itself and Pakistan as a conflict between a democratic nation and a dictatorship-with mixed success. This is encapsulated in the argument, put forward by some Indian leaders, that India and the United States have a special relationship as 'the largest democracy and the oldest democracy'-an argument that has, at best, received a lukewarm reception in the USA.

On 13 December 2001, Islamic militants attacked the Indian Parliament in Delhi. Fourteen people were killed, including five of the assailants. Claiming that the Islamic militant group Lashkar-e-Taiba was responsible for the attack, Indian leaders issued an ultimatum warning of dire consequences if Pakistan failed to close down the offices of the Lashkar-e-Taiba and those of another militant group, the Jaish-e-Mohammed. Although Musharraf probably did not order or authorize the attack, India cut off communications with Pakistan. The Indian ambassador in Islamabad was recalled to Delhi, road and rail links were closed, and Pakistani airlines were banned from using Indian airspace. At the height of the ensuing crisis, over half a million troops, about two-thirds of them Indian, were moved to the border.

According to Indian Defence Minister George Fernandes, the Indian military was 'raring to go'. He also warned Pakistan not to consider using nuclear weapons, saying: 'We could take a strike, survive, and then hit back . . . Pakistan would be finished'. Pakistan Foreign Minister Abdul Sattar was quoted as saying that his anxieties were 'mounting not only by the day but by the hour'. Perhaps because of concerns about the possibility of an Indian strike on Pakistani airbases, the Pakistani Air Force practiced landing and taking off from the Islamabad-Lahore highway. Fortunately, the Indian Government did not launch an attack, in part because of General Musharraf's statement on 12 January 2002 that he was banning the Lashkar-e-Taiba and the Jaish-e-Mohammed, and the situation settled down somewhat. In May 2002 two attacks were carried out in Kashmir within two weeks, the first of which was on the wives and children of Indian soldiers posted in the region.

Once again India claimed that the attacks were perpetrated by gunmen who had crossed from Pakistan 'three or four days' before. As proof, it claimed that a chocolate bar made in Pakistan was found in a pocket of one of the attackers. India moved five warships from its east coast to the Arabian Sea. On 22 May, Prime Minister Vajpayee told front-line troops in Kashmir that the time had come for a 'decisive fight', adding 'we will win again'.

Soon after, an Indian Army officer briefed a senior journalist about plans for a quick attack that would set back 'Pakistan's military capability by at least 30 years, pushing it into the military "dark ages"', adding that 'casualties in men and machines in such an operation will be high and the military has firmly told the politicians to prepare the nation for losses and delayed results, as fighting will be fierce'.

Details of the plans for attack, with a 'D-day' of 15 June 2002, have since been confirmed by the current Indian Army chief. Leaders on both sides made a number of nuclear threats. Fortunately, the situation cooled down within weeks. In a parallel with the 1962 Cuban missile crisis, there were also incidents that could have accidentally led to war. In March 2002, a senior Indian Air Force officer flew a transport plane across the LOC and spent 11 minutes in Pakistan's airspace, during which time a surface-to-air missile was fired by Pakistan, damaging his aircraft. The Indian officer then tried to hide his mistake by reporting to the chief of the air force that the incident was minor and had created no problems. It was only when the Indian Army forward posts filed their reports, which were eventually passed on by the chief of the army to the air force, that the magnitude of the incident became clear.

Although it did not develop into war, there are a number of factors that make the 2002 crisis more dangerous than the Kargil War-especially in its implications for India-Pakistan relations in the future. Unlike Kargil, where Pakistan is clearly seen to have lost-especially politically-the 2002 crisis is claimed as a victory by both sides. On the Indian side, General Musharraf's January 2002 promise that he would rein in Pakistan-based militant organizations is seen as proof that India's 'coercive diplomacy' worked. Indian leaders also emphasize that the military crisis forced the international community to recognize Pakistan's support for terrorism. Pakistan claims the opposite. Despite the huge build-up of forces by the Indian side, and much talk of attacking so-called terrorist camps within Pakistan, India did not actually conduct any military attacks. That a massive military confrontation with strong nuclear overtones is seen as a victory for one side is dangerous enough, but both sides viewing it the same way increases the likelihood that similar incidents will occur in the near future.

There are also those in India who see General Musharraf's concessions as not being particularly effective in controlling the militancy in Kashmir. However, the conclusion drawn from this is not to seek a different political strategy but instead to call for a more aggressive military response, including strikes into Pakistan. This again makes the situation very unstable.

The international context for the South Asian military confrontation in 2002 was set by the terrorist attacks on the USA of 11 September 2001. Indian leaders used the opportunity to portray the Kashmir issue as primarily one of terrorism and India as its victim. It was quick to offer airbases and other logistical support to the US military with the aim of isolating Pakistan. The USA, on the other hand, wanted to exploit Pakistan's geographical advantage and its close ties to the Taliban. Realizing the dangers of civil instability that could arise from allying with the USA, Pakistani leaders hesitated but, in the end, agreed to provide support for the USA's military campaign in Afghanistan.

The key impact on the 2002 crisis came from the decision by the USA to unilaterally bomb Afghanistan without a UN Security Council resolution. Immediately, several Indian politicians, media commentators and military personnel called publicly for India to follow the USA's lead and attack facilities in the part of Kashmir held by Pakistan. In November 2001, for example, even before the attack on the Indian Parliament, a meeting of high-level Indian army officers recommended '"hot pursuit" of terrorists in Pakistan-occupied Kashmir and destroy[ing] their training camps'. These sentiments may have been accentuated by the response of US leaders to the 13 December attack. Both President George W. Bush and Secretary of State Colin Powell were reported to have said that India had the right to self-defence. Many media commentators interpreted this to mean that the USA wanted India to destroy purported terrorist camps in Pakistan, as was done in Afghanistan. The trend has continued. Soon after the crisis subsided, Indian Foreign Minister Jaswant Singh claimed that every nation had the right of pre-emption, adding, 'It is not the prerogative of any one country'. While India has not so far attacked across the border, this opinion is now an accepted part of the political and strategic discourse within India.

Role of the International Community

India and Pakistan have been among the largest importers of conventional arms for many years. After 11 September, traditional suppliers continued to sell weapons, in some cases to both countries. However the USA, which had previously followed a highly restrictive approach regarding arms exports and military assistance to India and Pakistan, became more active in selling weapons and offering military assistance to India and Pakistan as part of its efforts to influence policy in the region. The arms race is unequal. Pakistan has a smaller economy and lower rate of economic growth. Seeking to persuade the USA to increase military aid to Pakistan, Pakistani leaders have argued that peace in the region can be neither guaranteed nor durable because of the growing disparity in conventional weaponry. It is ironic that the same argument was used to advocate nuclear weapons prior to the 1998 tests. General Musharraf has claimed that Pakistan's conventional deterrence prevented the war.

With India and Pakistan vying for US support, it is not surprising that US diplomacy was able to play a role in the de-escalation of tensions. Anxious not to have India and Pakistan get in the way of the prosecution of its war in Afghanistan, US leaders made a number of promises to both sides. In particular, sanctions imposed after the nuclear tests of 1998 were lifted and Indo-US military ties increased to a level described as 'unprecedented' by General Richard B. Myers, Chairman of the US Joint Chiefs of Staff. Several highlevel officials made visits to the region and the crisis received the personal attention of President Bush and others. This balancing act paid off. However, in the event of other militant attacks, or similar triggers, in the future it is not certain that the situation could be resolved in a similar way.

Indian Doctrines

In August 1999, shortly after the Kargil War, the Indian National Security Advisory Board released its draft report on Indian nuclear doctrine. Although the board's recommendations have not been accorded the status of official policy, the DND remains the most comprehensive view of India's emerging nuclear posture. Largely modelled on the doctrines and deployment postures of the nuclear weapon states, the DND states that 'India shall pursue a doctrine of credible minimum nuclear deterrence'. According to the DND, this requires:

a) sufficient, survivable and operationally prepared nuclear forces;

b) a robust command and control system;

c) effective intelligence and early-warning capabilities;

d) planning and training for nuclear operations; and

e) the will to employ nuclear weapons.

The requirement for India to have 'operationally prepared' nuclear forces is usually interpreted to mean deployment of nuclear weapons on delivery vehicles. Deployment of India's nuclear weapons would, according to the DND, involve a 'triad of aircraft, mobile land-based missiles and sea-based assets' structured for 'punitive retaliation' so as to 'inflict damage unacceptable to the aggressor'. The DND envisaged an 'assured capability to shift from peacetime deployment to fully employable forces in the shortest possible time'. In January 2003, the Indian Government published a brief official nuclear doctrine. This reiterated some of the elements of the DND, including the plan to build and maintain a 'credible minimum deterrent' and the statement that 'nuclear retaliation to a first strike will be massive and designed to inflict unacceptable damage'. In common with the DND, the official statement does not define 'minimum', leaving open the possibility of a constantly expanding arsenal. Although it claimed to have a posture of no-first-use, wherein 'nuclear weapons will only be used in retaliation against a nuclear attack on

Indian territory or on Indian forces anywhere', it went on to significantly weaken the policy by claiming the right to nuclear retaliation if India was attacked using chemical and biological weapons (CBW). In this it appears to be following the lead of the USA, which had also announced that it would consider responding to a CBW attack with nuclear weapons.

The policy may also reflect the advice of the National Security Board, which had recently argued that India should drop the no-first-use policy. The caveat about CBW attacks may well be the first step in completely repudiating the no-first-use policy. Parts of the military and the more hawkish sections of the strategic community are the main players pushing for the development of a larger and more usable nuclear force. The triad structure recommended by the DND is an example of their influence. The armed services support this structure because each service would like to have nuclear weapons of its own. They have also been involved in a struggle over who would control the nuclear arsenal. The growing role of the military is also likely to generate pressures for a launchon-warning posture for the nuclear arsenal that brings with it a grave risk of accidental nuclear war.

Pakistani Doctrines

In Pakistan, the overwhelming dominance of the army has left no scope for other political and bureaucratic players and institutions. There has been no official pronouncement on nuclear weapons use or deployment doctrines in Pakistan. A newspaper article by Agha Shahi, Zulfiqar Ali Khan and Abdul Sattar, former Foreign Secretary, Air Marshall and Foreign Minister, respectively, may illuminate the typical thinking of Pakistani policy makers. With regard to the use of weapons, the article argued in favour of following NATO's flexible response strategy of using nuclear weapons even in response to a conventional attack. 'The assumption [is] that if the enemy launches a general war and undertakes a piercing attack threatening to occupy large territory or communication junctions, the "weapon of last resort" would have to be invoked.'

Another account, based on comments by General Khalid Kidwai, Director of the Pakistani Army Strategic Plan Division, states that nuclear weapons will be used only 'if the very existence of Pakistan as a state is at stake'. This would include situations where:

a) India attacks Pakistan and takes a large part of its territory;

b) India destroys a large part of Pakistan's armed forces;

c) India imposes an economic blockade on Pakistan; or

d) India creates political destabilization or large scale internal subversion in Pakistan.

Finally, it has also been suggested that, if India were to penetrate to a line joining Gujranwala, Multan, Sukkur and Hyderabad, then 'it is likely Pakistan would have to accept defeat or employ nuclear weapons'. It seems fairly clear that Pakistan's policy makers envisage the use of nuclear weapons in a variety of contingencies, although these contingencies are perhaps delineated in the hope that they may never come to pass. India, reflecting its conventional military superiority over Pakistan, has claimed that it has a no-first-use policy, although, as noted above, this policy has been weakened somewhat in the recent nuclear doctrine. In response, Pakistan has asked India to sign a no-war pact. Since India has refused to sign such a pact, there has been an impasse.

Nuclear Force Developments

India and Pakistan continue to produce fissile materials and develop missiles. There have been no official statements regarding plans for the eventual size of nuclear arsenals from either side. While it is possible to find semiofficial arguments for arsenals involving anywhere from 100 to over 400 nuclear weapons, the size of the nuclear forces are currently, and will remain, limited by the constraints of their fissile material and missile inventories. Pakistan's nuclear arsenal is smaller and will almost certainly remain so. Currently, neither country is believed to keep its nuclear weapons mounted on missiles and ready for launch. However, they would be able to prepare their nuclear weapons for launch within a fairly short period of time-possibly within a few hours. This time period could be significantly shorter if the weapons were fully integrated into the armed forces.

India has been gradually moving towards this position. Should India continue along this path, Pakistan is certain to follow. In the midst of the 2002 crisis, both India and Pakistan tested new nuclear capable missiles. India began in January 2002 with a test of a 700-km version of the Agni-clearly specific to Pakistan since it is not capable of reaching any significant targets in China. Pakistan responded by testing three missiles later in the year. In December 2001, India moved the short-range nuclear-capable Prithvi missile to locations close to the border, bringing major Pakistani cities such as Islamabad, Rawalpindi, Lahore and Faisalabad within striking range

The following month, it was reported that Prime Minister Vajpayee had granted authorization for the armed forces to use the missile at their discretion.

In March 2002 the Indian Government announced its decision to induct the 2000-km range Agni-II missile, capable of delivering a nuclear warhead, into the military. Unlike the prototypes developed in the 1980s, the newer versions of the Agni missile are solid-fuelled, enabling them to be fired rapidly. A special missile regiment has been formed to operate the missile. There have been other, less publicized, signs of the imminent military deployment of nuclear weapons. Military officers have reportedly been undergoing training in the handling of nuclear devices at the Bhabha Atomic Research Centre. India conducted large-scale military exercises in May 2001, during which Indian President Abdul Kalam-the 'father' of the Indian missile programme-revealed that the armed forces were training to use nuclear weapons. It is known that the Indian armed forces have been making detailed plans for operations involving nuclear weapons.

Following the publication of the DND in 1999, the three armed service headquarters were reportedly involved in drawing up detailed schemes for inducting a variety of nuclear armaments and ancillary and support equipment in their orders-of-battle . . . [and] appropriate command and control frameworks'. Subsequently, the air force publicly announced that it had decided on its operational plans. There may, of course, be other more secret preparations. In January 2003, the Indian Government announced that it had set up a two layered structure called the Nuclear Command Authority (NCA) to manage its nuclear and missile arsenals. The NCA is comprised of the Political Council, chaired by the prime minister, and the Executive Council, chaired by the national security adviser to the prime minister. According to the announcement, the Political Council is the sole body able to authorize the use of nuclear weapons. However, 'arrangements for alternate chains of command for retaliatory nuclear strikes in all eventualities' are also mentioned, that is, it anticipates contingencies in which someone other than the prime minister may have to, and will be able to, order the use of nuclear weapons.

On 9 January 2003, the Ghauri missile was inducted into the army. Receiving it, President Musharraf, who is also the army chief-of-staff, stated that it was 'a proud day' for him 'to accept the Ghauri on behalf of the army's Strategic Forces Command' and expressed the hope that the induction would 'radiate the necessary effects of deterrence'. The 750 km-range Shaheen-I was handed over to the military in March. These ceremonies were largely formalities-in reality the Pakistani Army has always controlled the nuclear and missile programmes. The domination by the armed forces is also reflected in the organization responsible for formulating policy and exercising control over the development and employment of Pakistan's strategic nuclear forces-the National Command Authority, created in February 2000.56 Pakistan's National Command Authority has three components: the Employment Control Committee, the Development Control Committee and the Strategic Plans Division.

The military's representatives are in a majority in all of them. The Employment Control Committee is chaired by the head of the government and includes the cabinet ministers of foreign affairs, defence and the interior; the chairman of the Joint Chiefs of Staff Committee (CJCSC) the military service chiefs; the director-general of the Strategic Plans Division (a senior army officer), who acts as secretary; and technical advisers. This committee is thought to have been charged with making nuclear weapon policy, including the formulation of policy on the decision to use nuclear weapons. The Development Control Committee manages the nuclear weapon complex and the development of nuclear weapon systems. It has the same military and technical members as the Employment Control Committee but lacks the cabinet ministers that represent the other parts of government. The Development Control Committee is chaired by the head of the government and includes the CJCSC (as its deputy chairman), the military service chiefs, the director-general of the Strategic Plans Division and representatives of the weapon research, development and production organizations. These organizations include the A.Q. Khan Research Laboratory in Kahuta; the national development complex; and the Pakistan Atomic Energy Commission.

The committee also includes the newly created National Engineering and Scientific Commission, headed by Samar Mubarikmand, who was formerly the head of technical development at the Pakistan Atomic Energy Commission and led the team that conducted the nuclear weapon tests. The Strategic Plans Division is located in the Joint Services Headquarters under the CJCSC and is led by a senior army officer. This division acts as the secretariat for the NCA and has responsibility for planning and coordination and, in particular, for establishing the lower tiers of the command-and-control system and its physical infrastructure.

One of the recurring themes in recent South Asian military crises has been the threatened use of nuclear weapons by leaders in India and Pakistan, following the practices of Soviet and US leaders during the cold war. These tactics predate the 1998 nuclear tests. While formally denying that they possessed nuclear weapons, Pakistan's leaders at times played on the widely held belief in the international community that Pakistan did have a nuclear weapon capability. Although the facts remain controversial, it is widely believed, especially in Pakistan, that Pakistani leaders resorted to nuclear threats during the military crises in 1987 and 1990 as a way of signalling their determination to forestall potential Indian attacks or invasions. During the Kargil War, Indian and Pakistani officials and ministers delivered indirect and direct nuclear threats no fewer than 13 times.

The 2002 crisis was no exception to this pattern. Jana Krishnamoorthy, president of the ruling BJP, set the tone when he warned in December 2001 that, if a nuclear weapon is used by Pakistan, 'its existence itself would be wiped out of the world map'. For his part, Prime Minister Vajpayee warned that 'no weapon would be spared in self-defence. Whatever weapon was available, it would be used no matter how it wounded the enemy'. Indian Army Chief General Sundararajan Padmanabhan claimed that if Islamabad dared use its nuclear weapons: 'The perpetrator of that particular outrage shall be punished, shall be punished so severely that the continuation of any form of fray will be doubtful', and expressed his readiness 'for a second strike' since he felt that India had 'enough' nuclear arms.

Leaders in both India and Pakistan see the 2002 crisis as having been resolved in their favour-at least partially. Since India had a greater military presence on the border and was threatening to attack, albeit in a limited fashion, it should not be surprising that Pakistani leaders have credited their nuclear weapons with having deterred India. Indian leaders have also asserted the efficacy of nuclear deterrence and the power of their nuclear weapons. However, 'they cannot agree on what this power is or does, and even contradict each other on its role and function'. First, Prime Minister Vajpayee claimed that the recent crisis showed that India had, in effect, successfully called Pakistan's nuclear bluff. Next, President Abdul Kalam claimed that nuclear weapons had averted any kind of war. Finally, General V. P. Malik, former Chief of Army Staff, stated that nuclear weapons were largely irrelevant for conventional warfare and played no deterrent role during the Kargil War or in the 2002 crisis.

Indian views on the role of Pakistani nuclear weapons are even more puzzling. A section of the Indian nuclear policy-making community has had a tendency to belittle Pakistan's nuclear capability. In the past, leading scientists have declared that Pakistan could not have enriched uranium to the levels required to make a bomb. The nuclear tests by Pakistan ended such speculation. However, the idea reappeared in a different guise during the 2002 crisis. K. Subrahmanyam, an influential Indian strategist, suggested that, in the aftermath of 11 September, and with the increased US presence in Pakistan, if Pakistan were to deploy any nuclear missiles the USA would destroy them. Pakistan would not therefore be able to use its nuclear weapons—a comforting, if fallacious, idea.

The most important lesson of the Kargil War for Indian leaders was that India would have to find ways of waging limited war without provoking Pakistan to cross the nuclear threshold. In other words, India has embarked upon a search for strategic space in which to act. In

January 2000 Defence Minister George Fernandes, once a trade union leader and one of the few prominent political leaders to oppose the 1974 nuclear test, declared that the Kargil War had shown that the nuclearization of India and Pakistan had not made conventional wars obsolete. Instead, it 'simply imposed another dimension on the way warfare could be conducted'. More recently, Fernandes warned that if Pakistan launched a nuclear attack, it would be 'wiped out'. This should be seen in conjunction with his stated desire to find the strategic space in which a limited war could be waged. By promising massive retaliation, rather than flexible response, there is an expectation that limited war will stay at the conventional level.

6

South Asia: Role of India and the World

South Asia has continental dimensions and is home to nearly 1.4 billion of the world's six billion or so inhabitants. This alone tells us that the big global issues cannot be settled without the involvement of this region, and especially India. However, the natural features, the internal and external situation of individual South Asian countries, their economies and cultures, are so unalike that in defining and pursuing interests in the region we have to differentiate accordingly.

The nations of the Indian subcontinent have a multilateral institution with scope for development in the form of South Asian Association for Regional Cooperation (SAARC), but the prospect of forging a common political will is still very remote. It is nevertheless apparent that they are interwoven to such an extent, not only geographically and historically but also in terms of contemporary tensions and interactions, that we have to develop relations with them within the framework of the overall situation.

India, with a population of about one billion, is the second largest country on earth and the largest democracy. It has a secular structure and while most of the population are Hindu it has the second largest Muslim community in the world (150 million). It is the country with the greatest ethnic, linguistic and religious diversity, and extreme social disparities. In the North West (Kashmir) and the North East (especially Assam), the country is having to quell armed secessionist groups. After decades of modest development India now appears to be developing into another Asian superpower, not on account of its nuclear weapons or the size of its population but because of the gradually visible results of economic reforms and an outward-looking policy initiated many years ago. It is a secularized Muslim state but Islamization has been increasing since the mid-eighties. The aim of a deeply rooted established democracy has not yet been achieved, partly on account of mismanagement, partly due to the erosion of administrative structures. Many times, most recently in 1999, elected governments have been ousted by military regimes. In 2001 President Musharraf presented a "Roadmap for Democracy".

Despite the many common historical, cultural and linguistic roots with India, Pakistan's relations with its larger neighbour have been marred by a bitter rivalry ever since the country's foundation. Hostilities have repeatedly broken out over Kashmir. Pakistan, too, has declared itself a nuclear power. With a population of 128 million, Bangladesh is the country with the greatest population density and at the same time one of the poorest countries in the world. Democracy is not yet firmly rooted.

Since the Soviet invasion of 1979 and the subsequent civil war, the institutions of government had gradually disintegrated. Until the Anti-Terror Alliance began its operations in October 2001, the Taliban, a fanatic religious group, had kept up to 95% of the country under strict military control. The rest of northern Afghanistan was in the hands of the Northern Alliance of mostly Tajik tribes. The Taliban would not allow the people to exercise even the most fundamental human rights and they offered refuge and training to Islamic terrorists. Following the country's liberation from the Taliban by the international alliance seeking to destroy the Al-Quaida network, Afghanistan was given an opportunity for political, economic and social reconstruction.

The Afghan Interim Government is striving to restore the institutions of state authority in a country torn by civil war and inter-ethnic conflict. Sri Lanka (population approximately 18.6 million), seen in terms of per-capita GNP ($820), is, relatively speaking, the wealthiest country on the subcontinent.

The Himalayan kingdom of Nepal has some 24 million inhabitants and is one of the poorest countries in the world. Occupying a sensitive geographical position between India and China, it maintains an impartial course. The threat to domestic peace is increasing again as a result of violent clashes with "Maoist" rebels. The second Himalayan kingdom, Bhutan, has a population of about 640,000. This country, and the island state Maldives (approximately 245,000 inhabitants), are among the tiniest countries in the world. In the year 2000 we established for the first time consular relations with Bhutan.The main objective against this background is to use the tremendous opportunities for this region's cooperative development and global integration, notwithstanding the strife, conflict and underdevelopment in many areas. We must act accordingly: through dialogue and partnership, we must encourage the nations on the subcontinent to develop systems to settle their disputes peacefully and to appreciate the value of cooperative security structures.

The propensity to settle conflicts by force is currently a dominant factor on the subcontinent. We must clearly understand, however, that the ongoing conflicts can only be terminated by those concerned, without intervention from the outside. But where we can lend support, whether in fostering political dialogue between India and Pakistan, participating in Afghanistan's recovery, or helping overcome the consequences of warfare in North-Eastern Sri Lanka, we will continue to do so. Particularly in multi-ethnic and multi-religious South Asia, aim must be to encourage and mobilize democratic thinking based on secular tolerance serving to bolster stability. This is also the key to the permanent establishment and protection of human rights in the region.

South Asia will be drawn into a maelstrom of impoverishment if it cannot adopt speedy and resolute measures to reduce population growth and modernize national economies through a consistent policy of privatization and decentralization. India leads the way in activating the region's globalization potential: the success of its software industry shows how new, mutually profitable partnerships can emerge at the global level. A more outward-looking approach would create fresh development opportunities for South Asia also. The policy in this region must also take account of the new situation in Central Asia (Kazakhstan, Kyrgyzstan, Tajikistan, Turkmenistan, Uzbekistan). Since the disintegration of the Soviet Union this region has clearly been developing closer relations with Asian neighbours in the south. The gradual improvement in relations between South and Central Asia after 1991 would have been very welcome if the main focus had been on trade, freedom of movement, cooperative exploitation of national resources, and cultural exchange. In fact, once Central Asia's borders to the south had opened the region became the target for militant Islamism originating mainly in Afghanistan (and Pakistan) and succumbed to international terrorism as well as trafficking in weapons and drugs.

India's Relations with Neighbours

Relations with Afghanistan

India closely monitored the continuing fratricidal conflict in Afghanistan, a country with which it has historical ties of friendship and cooperation. India maintained close contacts with various parties and groups within Afghanistan. India believes that there can be no military solution to the internecine war which is being fuelled by foreign involvement, principally from across Afghanistan's southern borders. India continued to send humanitarian assistance to Afghanistan both bilaterally and through the UN. Based on cultural and civilisational affinities and historical interactions, India's ties with Iran continued to grow. As a part of the process of highlevel exchange of visits which have contributed to building mutual trust and confidence, Dr Seyed Kamal Kharrazi, Foreign Minister of Iran, accompanied by a high-level delegation, visited Delhi on 2-3 June 1998. Economic and commercial interaction between India and Iran continued satisfactorily. The first meeting of the Indo-Iran Joint Business Council was held in Tehran in May 1998 and the second meeting at New Delhi on 24 February 1999.

Relations with Pakistan

India continued its efforts to build a relationship of trust and confidence with Pakistan, to put in place a stable structure of cooperation, and address out standing issues through peaceful bilateral negotiations. India emphasised the value of reactivating a sustained and comprehensive dialogue, which would not be issue-fixated, but which would enable the relationship to move forward in a broad-based manner.

India's concerns regarding Pakistan's continued, and active involvement in instigating and sponsoring terrorism in J&K and other parts of India, were made clear to them on several occasions during the year and reiterated during the composite dialogue, and conclusive evidence to this effect was also presented. It was emphasised that India's resolve to defeat cross-border terrorism and to safeguard its security interests was total. India has advised them that abandonment of this activity, and full respect for their commitments under the Simla Agreement, including avoidance of provocative acts across the LOC and hostile propaganda, were essential steps. In keeping with India's overall policy, the Prime Minister took the historic initiative of travelling to Lahore, on the inaugural run of the Delhi - Lahore-Delhi Bus Service on 20-21 February 1999.

The Lahore Declaration, the MOU on CBMs and the joint statement issued during the PM's visit, represent in their totality, a vision for the development of the relationship. They spell out concrete steps to be taken by the two countries in translating this vision into reality, including, in particular, a joint commitment to work through a bilateral process in the framework of the Simla Agreement—for establishing a durable structure of cooperation, of building confidence and of resolving outstanding issues through peaceful, bilateral negotiations. There was mutual keenness on the part of both India and Bangladesh to promote understanding and to strengthen bilateral relations during the year. Several high level visits contributed to this process.

Relations with Bangladesh

The Foreign Minister of Bangladesh, Mr Abdus Samad Azad, visited India in April 1998. The Bangladesh Prime Minister, Mrs Sheikh Hasina visited India on 16 June 1998 and on 27-28 January 1999 to inaugurate the 24th Calcutta Book Fair. The system of institutional dialogue to discuss matters relating to security and border management continued during the year.

Relations with Sri Lanka

India's relations with Sri Lanka continued to be marked by warmth and cordiality. The visits of the Sri Lankan Foreign Minister, Mr Lakshman Kadirgamar to India in March and June 1998, as a Special Envoy of the Sri Lankan President provided opportunities for useful, high level exchanges between the two Governments. The Prime Minister's visit to Colombo from 28-31 July 1998 to attend the Tenth SAARC Summit helped to further cement the multifaceted ties between the two countries. The President of Sri Lanka, Mrs Chandrika Bandaranaike Kumaratunga, paid a state visit to India from 27-30 December 1998. During the visit, the two sides signed an agreement to establish a Free Trade Area between India and Sri Lanka which is expected to lead to a steady growth of trade and investment through graduated reduction of tariffs. The two countries also signed an MOU to set up the

India-Sri Lanka Foundation which would promote bilateral exchanges in various spheres and be governed by an independent board. India continued to provide trade concessions to Sri Lanka within the SAPTA framework with a view to improving market access for Sri Lankan products in India. India-Maldives relations continued to remain close and friendly. India kept up assistance to the Maldives in its developmental efforts including in the area of Human Resource Development. There was regular interaction through the exchange of high level visits. President Maumoon Abdul Gayoom visited India in his capacity as Chairman of SAARC from 30 June to 1 July 1998. The Vice President visited the Maldives from 10-13 November 1998.

Relations with Myanmar

India has a stable and cooperative relationship with Myanmar. Focused efforts were made to diversify and broadbase areas of contact and cooperation. The Commerce Secretary led an Inter-Ministerial delegation in October 1998 to explore means of expanding trade and economic linkages including cross border projects in areas such as power, mining, and oil and gas. The Myanmar Deputy Minister for Industry, visited India in November to identify sectors for collaboration. Possibilities of cooperation in the fields of science and technology, herbal medicines, satellite telecommunication, etc., are being explored. In areas of vital interest such as border management and drug-trafficking, regular interaction was maintained through bilateral institutional mechanisms.

Relations with Nepal

The President of India made a State Visit to Nepal from 28-30 May 1998. Their Majesties King Birendra Bir Bikram Shah Dev and Queen Aishwarya Rajya Laxmi Devi Shah of Nepal paid a State Visit to India from 24-29 January 1999. The King was the Chief Guest at the Republic Day celebrations on 26 January 1999. Among the other high level bilateral contacts, notable are Prime Minister Shri A.B. Vajpayee's meetings with his Nepalese counterpart Mr G.P. Koirala on the fringes of the NAM Summit in Durban and the SAARC Summit in Colombo.

The second meeting of the Joint Working Group (JWG) on Border Management was held in Delhi on 16 and 17 June 1998. A number of decisions with the objective of preventing misuse of the open border between India and Nepal by undesirable elements were taken by the two sides. A Nepalese delegation headed by Director General, Taxation attended the second meeting of the India-Nepal Joint Commission set up under the Double Taxation Avoidance Agreement (DTAA) held in New Delhi from 28-30 July 1998. A renewed Transit Treaty between India and Nepal was signed on 5 January 1999.

India's contribution to Nepal's economic development in diverse areas has increased over the years. Major projects funded by the Government of India currently under implementation include the construction of 22 bridges on the Kohalpur-Mahakali sector of the East-West Highway, establishment of the B.P. Koirala Institute of Health Sciences at Dharan, construction of an Emergency and Trauma Centre at Bir Hospital in Kathmandu, broad-gauging of Raxaul-Sirsiya Rail Link and several other projects that form part of India's commitment under the Mahakali Treaty.

Relations with Bhutan

His Majesty the King of Bhutan visited India from 5-8 October 1998. The Minister of Power led a high-level delegation to Bhutan from 26-29 October 1998 to discuss issues relating to development of hydel power in Bhutan. The fifth Joint Technical Level Meeting on the Bilateral Survey Collaboration Project was held in Thimphu from 6-9 August 1998. This project aims at developing indigenous capacity in Bhutan for survey and mapping, and includes supply of equipment and technology transfer in this field. Indian assistance to Bhutan's eighth Five Year Plan (1997-2002), has focused on areas of infrastructure such as the construction of roads, bridges and hydro-power capacity. Special emphasis has also been placed on the implementation of projects in social sectors such as education and health. Larger projects that are being jointly developed with the Royal Government of Bhutan include the Tala Hydroelectric Project, Kurichu Hydroelectric Project and the Dungsum Cement Project.

India continued its active participation in the ongoing SAARC process for regional cooperation in South Asia. These efforts gained further momentum during the year, especially through the consolidation of cooperation in the core economic area, with the conclusion of the third round of the negotiations for setting up a South Asian Preferential Trading Arrangement (SAPTA) in November 1998 and the agreement among the leaders of SAARC countries, on establishing a South Asian Free Trade Area (SAFTA), and to commence negotiations for this purpose in early 1999

India also contributed substantially to the exercise conducted by the Group of the Eminent Persons, a non-official body, constituted by the SAARC leaders in 1997, for working out a perspective plan for further development of SAARC. The report presented at the Tenth Summit in Colombo in July 1998, sets out a broad agenda for economic integration in three phases, and for cooperation in the social sectors up to the year 2020.

India strongly support the consensus reached by the SAARC leadership at the Tenth Summit, reaffirming the desire to further strengthen regional cooperation, particularly in the economic sphere. India took further constructive initiatives to help trade liberalisation and stimulate investment within the region—i.e., the decision to lift quantitative restrictions on imports from SAARC countries into India, with effect from 1 August 1998; the further raising of the ceiling for Indian investment in SAARC countries; proposals for enhanced exchanges in Science and Technology, and for a regional energy grid; and suggestions for strengthening cooperation in the social sectors, as also in working out common positions on key international economic issues.

Relations with South East Asia and the Pacific

India's relations with the countries in the South East Asian region have expanded and diversified and more so since the conscious adoption of 'Look East' policy which sought to strengthen existing linkages and forging new ones with the ASEAN countries. India's ties with ASEAN have been developing satisfactorily since India became a Full Dialogue Partner of the ASEAN in 1996. Shri Jaswant Singh,

Deputy Chairman, Planning Commission and a special envoy of PM led the Indian delegation to the 31st ASEAN Post Ministerial Conference (PMC) and the 5th ASEAN Regional Forum (ARF) meetings held in Manila in July 1998. The ARF Meeting was significant for India as it was the first time after nuclear tests that all nuclear weapons States were interacting in a security related forum. The meetings provided opportunities for important bilateral interactions with ASEAN and ARF members. India maintained friendly and close relations with Cambodia. On Cambodian Government's request, a team of five officials led by Deputy Election Commissioner was deputed to Cambodia from 19-29 July as election observers. India donated medicines worth Rs. five lakh to the internally displaced persons in Cambodia.

General Ke Kim Yan, Chief of General Staff, Ministry of Defence of Cambodia led a 3-member delegation for participation in the Aero India 1998 at Bangalore from 6-14 December 1998. India's relations with Laos People's Democratic Republic continued to be close and cordial. Dr Souli Nanthavong, Vice-Minister of Science, Technology and Environment and Vice-Minister of Commerce, Mr Siaosavath Savengsuksa visited India in April and November respectively. Smt Vasundhara Raje, Minister of State for External Affairs visited Laos from 17-20 January 1999 to co-chair the second Meeting of the India-Laos Joint Commission (JCM) held in Vientiane in January 1999. An Agreement for US $ 2 million soft credit to Laos and a Protocol to renew the Cultural Exchange Programme for another three years (1999-2001) were signed during the visit.

India and Vietnam continued to work towards further strengthening and diversifying the existing traditionally close and friendly relations. The fourth session of the

India-Vietnam Joint Working Group Meeting (JWG) was held at Hanoi from 25-27 April. Smt Vasundhara Raje, Minister of State for External Affairs paid a visit to Hanoi on 18 and 19 June. Shri Dilip Ray, Minister of State for Coal paid a visit to Vietnam from 4-7 November to discuss programme of cooperation in the field of coal trade.

The cultural exchange programme between India and Vietnam for the years 1998-2000 was signed at Hanoi on 14 December 1998. H. E. Mr Nguyen Manh Cam, Deputy Prime Minister for Foreign Affairs visited India from 30 January 1999 to co-chair the 9th meeting of the India-Vietnam Joint Commission held in New Delhi. An agreement for extending soft credit of Rs 47 crore to Vietnam and a Work Plan for 1999-2000 in the area of agriculture were signed during the visit. The two sides agreed to setting up a Working Group on coal for cooperation in the sector.

Bilateral relations between India and Indonesia, which have been traditionally close and cordial, continued to progress satisfactorily. Relations with Brunei Darussalam remained friendly and cordial. Secretary (ER), Ministry of External Affairs, visited Brunei in early July for bilateral consultations on matters of mutual interest as part of the ongoing process. An Indian cultural week, first of its kind, was held in Brunei in June, as a part of celebrations of the 50th Anniversary of India's Independence.

Relations between India and the Philippines saw further growth during the year. Minister of State (MOS) for External Affairs visited Manila from 17 and 18 June 1998. The third India-Philippines Foreign Office Consultations were held on 23 and 24 April 1998 with the Indian delegation led by Secretary (ER). The Indo-Philippine Agreement on Promotion and Reciprocal

Protection of Investment was signed in Manila in April 1998. Three Indian naval ships-INS Delhi, INS Khanjar and INS Jyoti-visited Philippines from 24-27 October 1998. Close relations between India and Singapore have been underpinned by a steady growth in as East Asian economic potentialities shrunk. A large number of high-level visits have been exchanged to demonstrate the political commitment of both governments to further India-Singapore relations.

India continued to maintain warm and friendly relations with Thailand. Bilateral cooperation continued in all fields. There were several high-level visits to Thailand. Commerce Minister led a delegation in April 1998, to attend the 54th Annual Session of ESCAP. Indian Minister of Parliamentary Affairs and Tourism visited Thailand in September 1998, as the head of a Parliamentary delegation. A number of important visits took place from India to Malaysia during this period. Dr Murli Manohar Joshi, Minister of Science and Technology and Human Resource Development, led a delegation for the Commonwealth Games held in Kaula Lumpur from 11-21 September 1998. Relations between India and Australia were cordial and friendly before India's nuclear tests.

Bilateral cooperation had been in full swing and was slated to grow in diverse fields but suddenly hit a lull, after India's nuclear tests of 11-13 May 1998. Government of Australia reacted strongly to nuclear tests. It recalled temporarily it's High Commissioner for consultations. Other measures directed against India were, suspension of bilateral defence relations with India, recall of Australian defence adviser and of Australian defence personnel currently training in India and Indian defence personnel undergoing training at Defence College in Australia, cancellation of ship and aircraft visits, suspension of non-humanitarian aid, and suspension of Ministerial and Senior Official Visits.

India too conveyed its displeasure by responding similarly to Australian Government's actions. Australia in December 1998, however, decided to relax the suspension on Ministerial and senior officials' visits, but the other restrictions remained in place. Australia has recently been trying to start official contacts at high level. New Zealand Government reacted strongly to India's nuclear tests. It announced a temporary recall of its High Commissioner from New Delhi for consultations. Its Foreign Ministry summoned the Indian High Commissioner S. Kipgen twice to its Foreign Office to lodge New Zealand's protest against India even before High Commissioner had presented his credentials. New Zealand also declined to accept the accreditation of Defence Attache from Canberra.

Since the Pokhran tests bilateral relations have been somewhat lukewarm. But efforts are being made by the New Zealand Government to improve trade relations with India. New Zealand's Minister for International Trade Dr. Lockwood Smith visited India (10-15 October) to attend the eighth JBC Meeting in New Delhi on 12 October. A 30-member delegation comprising MPs and Speakers of State Legislatures led by Lok Sabha Speaker G.M.C. Balayogi attended the 44th Commonwealth Parliamentary Conference in Wellington, New Zealand (17-23 October). Bilateral relations between India and Papua New Guinea (PNG) have been friendly and cordial since the opening of resident Mission in April 1996 in Port Moresby. PNG deplored India's nuclear tests of May 1998 but it was more or less, a proforma protest, as they had earlier also condemned similar tests by France and China. The leadership showed understanding and India's security concerns.

India and Fiji enjoyed close, cordial relations in the past. The new constitution of Fiji came into effect from 27 July 1998. Trade relations between two countries resumed with the lifting of trade embargo by the Ministry of Commerce. Indian High Commission in Suva (Fiji) was reopened. A three member delegation from Ministry of External Affairs visited Fiji (1-3 November). Joint Secretary (South) also visited Fiji (11-14 November) to meet various important dignitaries/government officials. This was the first high-level official visit to Suva after the closure of Indian Mission nearly a decade ago.

Bilateral relations with Pacific-Islands have been cordial and friendly though there have been minimal contacts. The Pacific Islands mildly condemned nuclear tests. President of Nauru, HE Mr Kinza Godfrey Cloduman, visited India to attend the Global Environment Facility (GEF) assembly (1-3 April 1998).

India seeks good relations with all its neighbours including China. India believes that the Five Principals of Peaceful Co-existence, jointly enunciated by India and China, are of continuing relevance to the development of relations. India seeks a relationship in which both sides are responsive to each other's concerns. India remains committed to the process of dialogue to resolve outstanding differences and to the development of friendly, cooperative, good neighbourly and mutually beneficial relationship with China. The India-China border has remained generally peaceful. The Vice-Chairman of China's National People's Congress (NPC) met the Indian Speaker during the International Parliamentary Union (IPU) Conference in Moscow on 11 September 1998. A delegation of Parliamentarians visited China in October to participate in the sixth General Assembly of the Asiapacific Parliamentarians' Conference on Environment and Development. India-China trade relations have continued to grow.

India remains committed to friendly co-operative, mutually beneficial relations with Japan with whom it has shared cultural links and values of human freedoms, commitment to peace, stability and economic development of the people in Asia and the world. In the immediate aftermath of nuclear tests in May 1998, Japan took several measures including a freeze on Yen loans and grant assistance for new projects and calling off a series of scheduled meetings and visits.

Bilateral dialogue, encompassing issues covering multifaceted relationship, resumed in January 1999. This includes Foreign Secretary level talks, Trade Talks and MEA-MITI dialogue. Relations with the Republic of Korea (ROK) continue to be marked with cordiality and understanding. Smt Vasundhara Raje, MOS (EA) visited Seoul (21-24 January) for bilateral consultations. The ROK PM, Mr Kim Jong Pil, visited India (10-11 February). Alongwith the Vice-President he inaugurated the CII sponsored India Engineering Trade Fair (IETF '99) where ROK participated as a Partner Country. Buddhist leaders and scholars from ROK participated in the Buddha Mahotsava (November 1998). Exchanges of cultural delegations, students and research scholars continued. The Government of ROK opened an Honorary Consulate General in Calcutta in November 1998.

India's relations with the Democratic People's Republic of Korea (DPRK) continue to be friendly and cordial. Consultations between the Foreign Offices of the two countries were held in Pyongyang (14-18 February 1998) when a protocol of co-operation between the Foreign Ministries was also signed. Shri Mukhtar Abbas Naqvi, Union Minister of State for Information and Broadcasting visited Pyongyang (22-26 September 1998) to participate in the Sixth Pyongyang Film Festival for Non-Aligned and Developing countries. As India sent 50-metric tonnes of baby food and 1,000 metric tonnes of rice to DPRK during the year.

Relations with Central Asia

Both bonds of history and geo-strategic location of the Central Asian States (CAS) in an extended neighbourhood make India's relations with them a matter of priority. The region has profound strategic and economic importance for these countries made to strengthen and diversify relations and to bring a contemporary focus to age-old ties. Initiatives to develop all India which has round bilateral relations with Azerbaijan were continued. It has been decided to open a resident mission in Baku. Indo-Kazakh relations progressed smoothly. The second session of the Indo-Kazakh Joint Science and Technology Committee was held in Almaty in October 1998. A Kazakh parliamentary delegation visited in the first quarter of 1999.

Indian Airlines and Air Kazakhstan signed a code sharing agreement in September 1998 and the latter is in the process of starting their flights to India in the near future. India participated in the seventh Asia Pacific International Trade Fair (ASPAT'98) in Almaty in October 1998. Punjab National Bank opened its representative office in Almaty in October 1998.

Traditional relations with Kyrgyzstan progressed well. Foreign Office consultations were held in July 1998. India gifted a 'mini dairy plant' to Kyrgyzstan under the ITEC programme. Days of Kyrgyz Culture in India were held from 6-14 March 1999. Kyrgyz Defence Minister visited India from 20-27 February. Official-level consultations with Tajikistan on bilateral matters as well as situation in Afghanistan were held in Dushanbe in August 1998. Two consignments of humanitarian assistance were sent. India-Turkey relations witnessed significant forward movement with high level political exchanges and important initiatives in the commercial, economic and cultural fields. The high point of the year was the state visit of President Shri K.R. Narayanan in September 1998, followed by the visit of Vice-President Shri Krishan Kant in October 1998 to participate in the 75th Anniversary of founding of the Turkish Republic.

During President's visit, Agreements on Prevention of Traffic in Narcotic Drugs, and Bilateral Investment Promotion and Protection, besides an MOU on scientific and technological cooperation and a Protocol on exchange of trade information were signed. India participated in the Izmir International Trade Fair in August 1998. The third meeting of the Indo-Turkish Joint Business Council was held on that occasion. On the cultural and educational front, an Indian food festival was organised in Izmir in August 1998 when an ICCR sponsored cultural troupe visited Turkey. An Indian scientific delegation representing Central Electronics Limited (CEL) and Council for Scientific and Industrial Research (CSIR) visited Turkmenistan in June 1998 to study the possibilities of cooperation in the solar energy sector. A delegation from Indian Oil Corporation (IOC) also visited Turkmenistan.

Relations with Uzbekistan remained active. Two rounds of Foreign Office consultations were held in May 1998 when Secretary (East) visited Tashkent and in December 1998. The fourth Session of the Indo-Uzbek Joint Commission was held in New Delhi from 17-20 February 1999.

Relations with The Gulf

Dating back to historical times, India's ties with all countries of the Gulf have been cordial, substantial and mutually beneficial. Given India's geographical proximity, cultural affinity and economic complementarities with the Gulf countries, India's multifaceted relations with the countries of this region have continued to flourish. The warm, cordial and friendly relations between India and Bahrain received a fresh impetus with the meeting of the joint Committee on Technical and Economic Cooperation in New Delhi on 12-13 November 1998 after nearly seven years. Both sides expressed keenness to enhance industrial and technical cooperation for setting up joint ventures in the small and medium-scale sectors, as well as cooperation in fields of health, education, agriculture, youth and sports and information and culture. They also agreed to expedite finalisation of the pending bilateral agreements. India's relations with Iraq, which have traditionally been close, received a boost with the revival of the India-Iraq joint Commission for Economic and Technical Cooperation attended by H.E. Mr Amir Mohammed Rashid, Minister of Oil, from 31 August to 2 September 1998. An MOU on cooperation in the field of oil and a Cultural Exchange Programme for the period 1998-2001 were signed. India continued to reiterate its position calling for compliance by Iraq with the UN Security Council Resolutions on Iraq while reiterating that use of force against Iraq would serve no useful purpose but would only aggravate the sufferings of the Iraqi people. Friendly relations with Kuwait were strengthened by high-level visits between both countries. Two Indian naval ships paid a goodwill visit to Kuwait on 1-4 June 1998.

Following the Government's approval to the setting up of the Orissa Oil Refinery, an Indo-Kuwait joint venture, Indian Oil Corporation opened a Representative office in Kuwait in June. Relations between India and Oman have scaled new heights with the visit of the Prime Minister, Shri A.B. Vajpayee, accompanied by a high-level delegation which included Shri K. Ramamurthy, Minister of Petroleum and Natural Gas and Shri S.S. Barnala, Minister of Chemicals and Fertilisers to Salalah on 29-30 August 1998. The Omani Minister of Commerce and Industry, Mr Maqbool Bin Ali bin Sultan, visited India from 30 April to 2 May 1998 in connection with 'Oman week', which was inaugurated by the Vice-President on 1 May 1998. BHEL commissioned a 30-MW Gas turbinebased power plant turnkey project at a cost of Rs 560 million. A flotilla of three naval ships paid a goodwill visit to Oman from 30 May to 4 June 1998 and undertook joint exercises with the Royal Oman Navy. The formalities for setting up two multi-million dollar joint venture projects, namely the India-Oman Fertiliser Project and the Bharat-Oman Fertiliser Project and the Bharat-Oman Refinery Project, proceeded satisfactorily. An Indian Ocean (IOR) Exhibition was organised by FICCI at Muscat from 10-14 October 1998, in which 56 Indian organisations participated.

India's traditionally warm and friendly relations with Qatar continued to grow during the year. A Bilateral Investment Promotion and Protection Agreement (BIPPA) was initialled between India and Qatar in Doha on 30 November 1998. The meeting of the India-Qatar Joint Commission took place in New Delhi on 8-9 March 1999. H. E. Mr Yousef Hussain Kamal, Minister of Finance, Economy and Commerce of the State of Qatar, visited India in December 1998 in connection with the purchase of 7.5 million tonnes of natural gas per year by India from Qatar on long-term basis. India's traditional relations with the Kingdom of Saudi Arabia are marked by cordiality and friendship. The bilateral trade between India and Saudi Arabia amounts to about US $ 3.5 billion. The defence cooperation stepped up during the year. The battle ships-INS Rajput and INS Varuna-called at the Jubail Port on 6 June 1998 on a goodwill visit, the first time in ten years that Indian Naval ships have made a friendly port call in the Kingdom. A total of 95,119 Indian pilgrims performed Haj in March 1998, of whom 63,583 pilgrims had gone through the Haj Committee, Mumbai, and the rest through Private Tour Operators (PTOs) or privately on international passports.

The age-old multidimensional relations between India and the United Arab Emirates (UAE) were further strengthened and diversified during the year. With a view to promoting investment, the Bilateral Investment Protection and Promotion Agreement between the two countries was initialled in June 1998. The UAE-based Non-Resident Indians (NRIs) contributed US $ 1.26 billion to the Resurgent Indian Bonds (RIBs) which was around 30 per cent of the total global collection of the RIBs. The Vice-President of India, Shri Krishan Kant, made a stopover in Dubai en route to India. The UAE Minister for Petroleum and Mineral Resources, Mr Obeid bin Saif Al-Nasiri, visited India on 22-24 February 1999 to discuss cooperation in the energy sector. Indo-Yemen relations are characterised by mutual goodwill, cordiality and friendship. The annual Foreign Office Consultation was held in New Delhi during February 1999. Steps have been taken for making institutional arrangements with Yemen for close coopearation in curbing the menace of drug trafficking, combat terrorism and organised crimes; negotiations are under way for concluding these agreements, including extradition treaty.

Relations with West Asia and North Africa

India's multifaceted relations with the countries of West Asia and North Africa were further strengthened through exchanges of visits. Leading among them was the Prime Minister's visit to Morocco. There were ministerial and official level contacts with several other countries and a number of agreements were signed. India's gesture of humanitarian assistance to Sudan and the human resource development under the ITEC programme were manifestation of India's commitment to South-South Cooperation.

Relations with Middle East

India maintained its steadfast support for the Palestine cause and shared the widespread concern with lack of progress in the Middle East peace process. India welcomed the Wye River memorandum and supported its unconditional implementation. Relations with Algeria continued to be marked by warmth and closeness. On the heels of the G-15 Summit held in Cairo in May 1998, Vice-President Shri Krishan Kant met President Mr Liamine Zeroual of Algeria. Bilateral ties of friendship, mutual understanding and co-operation with Egypt were strengthened. Vice-President Shri Krishan Kant led the Indian delegation to the G-15 Summit in Cairo from 11-13 May 1998. An MOU for Co-operation in the Development of Small Scale Enterprises Sector in Egypt was signed in Cairo on 9 May 1998. President of the Court of Cassation in Egypt Justice Mehdat El-Maraghi visited India from 11-18 April 1998.

The first exclusive "Made in India" Exhibition held in Cairo from 15-19 April 1998, was inaugurated by Prime Minister of Egypt Dr Kamal el Ganzouri. A Round Table Conference on Indo-Egyptian Relations was held in New Delhi on 16 December 1998. The Minister of State for Health and Family Welfare, Shri Dalit Ezhilmalai, Minister of Environment, Shri Suresh P. Prabhu and Minister of Textiles, Shri Kashi Ram Rana also visited Egypt during the year. Cooperation with Israel in the areas of trade and agriculture continued to develop satisfactorily. The Deputy Director General in Israel's Foreign Office Mr Yitzhak Shelev visited India for the Fourth round of Foreign Office Consultations held in New Delhi on 21 January 1999. The Second Meeting of Indo-Israeli Joint Trade and Economic Committee was held in New Delhi on 27 October 1998. Minister of Urban Affairs and Employment Shri Ram Jethmalani visited Israel from 7-11 September 1998. Agreement on Cooperation in the field of Telecommunications and Posts between India and Israel, signed on 29 November 1994, was ratified by India on 24 September 1998.

Bilateral relations with Jordan retained their positive trends of increasing understanding and co-operation. Vice-President Shri Krishan Kant represented India at the funeral of King Hussein in Amman on 8 February 1999.

Both Houses of Parliament adopted an Obituary Reference to King Hussein on the opening day of the Budget Session of Parliament. At the request of the United Nations, India sent an Indian Army contingent as part of the UN Interim Force in Lebanon (UNIFIL). Secretary (East) in the Ministry of External Affairs visited Lebanon from 15-17 July 1998 for Foreign Office consultations. India's relations with Libya continued to be marked by understanding and co-operation. India has consistently believed and worked for a just and equitable solution to the Lockerbie issue.

Relations with Morocco witnessed qualitative enhancement. Prime Minister Shri Atal Bihari Vajpayee visited Morocco on 13-14 February 1999. During Prime Minister's visit, Bilateral Investment Protection Agreement, Tourism Co-operation Agreement and Agreement between Press Trust of India (PTI) and Maghreb Arab Presse (MAP) for mutual professional cooperation were signed. Foreign Minister of Morocco Abdellatif Filali called on Prime Minister Shri Atal Bihari Vajpayee on the margins of the NAM Summit in Durban in August 1998 and Minister of External Affairs (then Deputy Chairman of Planning Commission) Shri Jaswant Singh met Morocco's Prime Minister Abderrahmane El Youssoufi in New York on the sidelines of the Special Session of the UN on Narcotics and Drugs held in New York from 8-10 June 1998. Minister of State for External Affairs visited Morocco from 25-27 June 1998 and signed a MOU on Foreign Office Consultations.

Speaker of Lok Sabha led a Parliamentary delegation to Morocco in October 1998 and it was decided to establish an Indo-Moroccan Parliamentary Friendship Group. Minister of State for Finance (RB & I) Shri K.M.R. Janardhanan visited Morocco from 28-30 October 1998 to sign the Convention on Avoidance of Double Taxation between India and Morocco. Ambassador of the King of Morocco Mr Hassan Abouyoub visited India from 6-7 November 1998. India continued to extend political, material and technical support to Palestine. India's traditional friendly relations with Palestine were enhanced by several exchanges. Additional Secretary (UN) and Joint Secretary (WANA) visited Palestine Authority territory in August 1998 for pre-NAM consultations. Two MOUs and Agreed Minutes for the implementation of two Indian-aided projects, namely, construction of a Library at Al Azhar University and construction of a Library-cum-Activity Centre at Palestinian Technical College at Deir El Balah were signed during in June 1998.

India offered more than 50 training slots to the Palestinian personnel for specialised training courses during the financial year 1998-99. At the International Donors Conference held in Washington DC on 30 November 1998 to help the Palestinian people, India pledged an amount of US $ 1 million. The utilisation of this amount will be decided on consultation with the Palestinian authorities. Relations with Sudan were strengthened through expansion and diversification of bilateral economic co-operation. India reiterated its support for Sudan's territorial integrity and sovereignty. A 3-member Sudanese Parliamentary delegation led by the Deputy Chairman, Federal Relations Committee, Sudanese National Assembly Dr Salah Eldin Mirghani M A Gaili visited India in the first week of October 1998 to get acquainted with the functioning of the federal system in India. The Government of India sent relief supplies consisting of baby milk powder and medicines to Sudan to help the flood victims.

Bonds of understanding and co-operation with Syria were strengthened. Chief of Army Staff Gen V.P. Malik visited Syria from 10-14 December 1998. Secretary (East) in the External Affairs Ministry visited Syria in July 1998 for Foreign Office Consultations. Bilateral relations with Tunisia continued to develop satisfactorily. Tunisia's Minister for Environment and Land Use Planning visited India from 1-3 April 1998 to attend the meeting of Global Environment Facility in New Delhi. India maintained cordial relations and co-operation with the regional organisations, namely, League of Arab States (LAS) and Union of Arab Maghreb.

Relations with African Continent

As in the past, the year saw continuation of the high-level of interaction with the countries of the African continent. The special priority attached to the region, with whom ties have been both longstanding and timetested, was underlined by the visit of the Prime Minister to Namibia, South Africa and Mauritius in August-September 1998. This visit to Africa was the first foreign visit by the Prime Minister outside the sub-continent. A significant element of India's relationship with sub-Saharan Africa was the growing level of economic interaction. The overall volume of trade with the region exceeded Rs 10,000 crore. The relations between India and Mauritius continued to grow during the period. During Prime Minister's visit to Mauritius, a Protocol on Cooperation in the field of Meteorology and a Bilateral Investment Promotion and Protection Agreement was signed. Prime Minister Dr Navinchandra Ramgoolam paid a state visit to India in October 1998. The Vice-President of Mauritius Mr A.V. Chettiar visited India in December 1998- January 1999. During the visit of Mauritian Youth and Sports Minister in January 1999, a Protocol each on Cooperation in the field of Sports and Youth Affairs were signed.

Shri Suresh P. Prabhu, Minister for Environment and Forests visited Kenya to attend the Special Session of the Governing Council of the United Nations and Environment Programme at Nairobi in May 1998. General DRC Tonje, Chief of General Staff, Kenyan Armed Forces visited India on 20-28 March 1998. General V.P. Malik, Chief of Army Staff of India visited Kenya in July 1998. The High Commission of India organised a seminar on 'India-Kenya Relations : Vision - 2000' in Nairobi on 14 July 1998. India's growing relations with Uganda were further strengthened during the period under review. Ugandan President Mr Y. Museveni made a transit halt at Mumbai in April 1998. The Indo-Ugandan Joint Committee met in Kampala on 23-24 November 1998 and identified several areas of mutually beneficial cooperation. The Minister of Education of Rwanda visited India from 18-21 May 1998 and an Agreement between the Ministry of Education of Rwanda and Educational Consultants India Limited was signed.

During the year, several delegations from Ethiopia visited India seeking to gain from India's development strategy and experience. In May 1998, a Bilateral Cultural Exchange Programme (1998-2000) was signed with Ethiopia. India and Seychelles signed a Bilateral Trade Agreement at Mahe on 18 September 1998. The ties of friendship and cooperation between India and Madagascar continued to expand further. The President Mr Didier Ratsiraka met Prime Minister Shri A.B. Vajpayee, at Durban on the margins of the NAM Summit. After a gap of nearly 20 years, India participated at the Dar-es-Salaam International Trade Fair in Tanzania and won the first prize in the foreign participation category. The traditionally close and friendly relations between India and South Africa were sustained through exchanges of visits and bilateral consultations at all levels. General the Chief of Army Staff of India visited South Africa in July 1998. The Deputy Minister in the South African Deputy President's Office, Dr Essop Pahad, visited India on 2-10 October 1998. The third meeting of the Indo-South Africa Joint Commission took place in Pretoria on 4-5 December 1998. The Joint Commission reviewed the progress of cooperation in the entire gamut of bilateral relations and identified areas where progress could be accelerated. An Agreement on Air Services was also signed during the meeting.

The relations between India and Namibia were marked by the traditional sense of closeness and understanding. Prime Minister Shri Atal Bihari Vajpayee paid an official visit to Namibia on 30-31 August 1998. Four important bilateral agreements in the areas of Technical Cooperation, Agricultural Research, Technology Demonstration and Foreign Office Consultations were signed. An Agreement facilitating exchange of information between Press Trust of India and Namibia Press Agency was also exchanged. The relations between India and Zimbabwe continued to be warm and friendly. The first Indo-Zimbabwean Joint Trade Committee meeting was held in Harare from 17-19 August 1998. The India-Zambia Joint Trade Committee meeting was held in Lusaka on 6-7 January 1999. The Deputy Commander of the Botswana Defence Force, Major General T.H.C. Masire visited India from 24-30 January 1999.

The relations between India and the countries in West Africa continued to expand in all fields. Nigeria is an important trading partner of India in Africa with the volume of bilateral trade reaching Rs 3,000 crore in 1998-99. India gifted indelible ink worth Rs 74.65 lakh for use during the Nigerian elections.

Relations with Central Europe

India's traditionally warm, friendly and cooperative relations with the Russian Federation and the countries of East and Central Europe continued to develop steadily during the year. Close and friendly ties between India and Russia, based on continuity, trust and mutual understanding, constitute an important foreign policy priority for both countries. Prime Minister Mr Y. M. Primakov visited India in December 1998. Defence Secretary visited Russia in June 1998 and an Inter-Governmental Agreement on the Long- Term Programme of Military and Technical Cooperation for the period up to the year 2010 was initialled. Russian Minister for Atomic Energy visited India in June 1998 and signed a Supplement to the 1998 Indo-Soviet Inter-Governmental Agreement on the construction of a 2x1000 MW Nuclear Power Station in Kudankulam, Tamil Nadu. Foreign Secretary visited Moscow on 11 September 1998 for Foreign Office consultations. Lok Sabha speaker led the Indian Parliamentary delegation to IPU conference in Moscow in September 1998.

India's relations with other countries of the CIS-Armenia, Belarus, Georgia, Moldova, Ukraine—continued to develop satisfactorily. Smt Vasundhara Raje, Minister of State for External Affairs met Mr Ivan Antonovich, the Foreign Minister of Belarus in New York on 29 September 1998 during the 53rd Session of UNGA. Belarusian Foreign Minister, paid an official visit to India from 13-17 October 1998 and signed an Indo-Belarus ITEC Agreement. Industry Minister, Shri Sikander Bakht, led the Indian delegation to Minsk from 25-28 October 1998 at the first session of the Indo-Belarus Inter-Governmental Commission. Minister of State for Coal, Shri Dilip Ray visited Minsk from 10-12 January 1999. High-level visits were exchanged with several of these countries during the year, which confirmed the importance and priority that these countries attach to their relations with India. Bulgarian Deputy Minister of Trade and Tourism, Mr Hristo Mihailovski visited India from 27-30 April 1998. The 12th Session of Indo-Bulgarian Joint Commission was held in Sofia from 22-25 September 1998. President Petar Stoyanov paid a state visit to India from 25-28 October 1998. The Indo-Bulgarian BIPA, an agreement on mutual cooperation between ITPO and the International Fair Inc. Plovdiv, an MOU between the National Centre for Trade Information (NCTI) and the Bulgarian Export Promotion Centre, and an MOU between the CII and the Bulgarian Industrial Association were signed. The tenth meeting of the Indo-Bulgarian Joint Business Council was convened in New Delhi on 27 October 1998.

Indian Minister of State for Coal visited Prague in May 1998. The Indo-Czech Agreement on Avoidance of Double Taxation was signed in Prague on 1 October 1998 by the Indian Ambassador and Czech Finance Minister. The third session of the Joint Committee and second meeting of Indo-Czech Joint Business Council took place in Prague on 5 and 6 October 1998. The President of the Republic of Estonia, Mr Lennart Mery, paid a State visit to India from 3-10 February 1999. An agreement on co-operation in the field of Science and Technology and an MOU on co-operation between FICCI and the Estonian Chamber of Commerce was signed during this visit. Dr Murli Manohar Joshi, Minister for Human Resource Development, visited Hungary on 26-28 November 1998 in connection with the Golden Jubilee of the establishment of diplomatic relations between India and Hungary. He inaugurated a symposium on 'Hungary, India and the

European Union' on 26 November 1998. The Cultural Exchange Programme for 1999-2000 was signed during the visit. Latvian Under Secretary of State Mr Janis Karklins, visited India from 7-12 December 1998. He held discussions at MEA, besides visiting the five Latvian pilots detained in Calcutta in connection with the Purulia Arms Dropping Case. The text of the Agreement on the establishment of an Indo-Latvian Joint Commission was also initialed.

The Chief of General Staff of the Polish Armed Forces Lt Gen H. Szumski visited India on 30 March - 3 April 1998. Indo-Polish Working Consultations on Trade and Economic Related Issues were held in Warsaw on 22 and 23 June 1998. The Indo-Polish Working Group on Coal under the Indo-Polish Joint Commission for Economic, Trade, Scientific and Technical Cooperation met in Warsaw on 14 October 1998. The 13th session of the Indo-Romanian Joint Commission was held on 15-16 December 1998. A Protocol was signed between the two governments on Economic, Scientific and Technical cooperation. Shri Suresh Prabhu, Minister of Environment and Forests, visited the Slovak Republic from 3-6 May 1998 to attend the Ministerial Round Table of the fourth Meeting of the Conference of Parties to the Convention of Biological Diversity. The third session of Indo-Slovak Joint Committee took place on 7-8 October 1998 at Bratislava. Dr Ernest Petric, State Secretary, Ministry of Foreign Affairs of Slovenia, visited New Delhi on 2-6 February 1999 for the fourth round of Indo-Slovene Foreign Office consultations.

Relations with Europe

West Europe is a region of considerable political and economic significance to India. The European Union (EU), of which 15 countries of the region are members, is India's largest trading partner and the second largest source of approved foreign investment. A number of high level visits have been exchanged with West Europe. The President visited Germany, Portugal and Luxembourg, in September 1998. The Prime Minister visited France in September-October 1998. India also received the visits of the President of Switzerland, and the Crown Prince of Belgium and the Prime Minister of Luxembourg. The 11th Round of the India-EU Troika Ministerial Meeting was held in New Delhi on 13 November 1998. There has also been an exchange of several other Ministerial visits with various other countries. High level official consultations have been conducted with France, the UK and Germany.

India's trade with the countries of the region has grown and there has been a further strengthening of the investment and technology cooperation ties between India and Europe. The diversification and deepening of the economic linkages and continuing political dialogue between the two sides reflects a shared desire to pursue a closer relationship for mutual benefit. While most of the countries in West Europe and the EU expressed concern at the nuclear tests conducted by India in May 1998, the specific reactions by different countries were far from uniform. A few countries like the Netherlands, Switzerland, Norway, Sweden and Denmark imposed unilateral economic measures (primarily curtailing development assistance and banning arms sales) with the others being opposed to such action. Austria held the Presidency of the EU during the second half of 1998.

The Nordic countries were critical of India's nuclear tests. While Sweden, Norway and Denmark stopped their development assistance programmes to India, Finland and Ireland did not impose any economic measures. India's relations with Portugal received an impetus with a series of high level visits. The President visited Portugal from 10-14 September 1998. A Double Taxation Avoidance Agreement was signed during this visit. A nine member parliamentary delegation from Portugal visited India from 15-22 December 1998. This was the first visit to India by a parliamentary delegation from Portugal to India. The Third Session of the Indo-Portuguese joint Business Council was held in New Delhi on 5 and 6 January 1999. Normal interaction continued with Spain. Bilateral Foreign Office Consultations were held in Madrid on 3 and 4 December 1998. The Indo-Spanish Joint Commission and joint Business Council was held in Delhi from 15-16 February 1999.

Relations with North America

Relations with the United States during the year can be seen broadly in two phases. In the early part of the year, there was continuation of a broad based dialogue which both countries had agreed upon. In that context, US Permanent Representative to UN, Bill Richardson headed a delegation to India from 14-15 April 1998. The Indian and the US side had useful exchanges of views on a number of important international, bilateral and regional issues. Following India's nuclear tests, the US reaction was extremely critical and negative. The United States saw the tests as a challenge to the nonproliferation regime which the United States and other nuclear-weapon states have sought to put in place to preserve their monopoly of nuclear weapons.

The US took the initiative in meetings of the P-5 and G-8 to orchestrate condemnation of the nuclear tests. Since then, the reaction has toned down and, to some extent, moderated. Articles and statements from eminent US political personalities and strategic analysts reflect a better understanding of India's security concerns. There has also been considerable debate in the United States regarding the effectiveness of the coercive economic measures called "sanctions". After the nuclear tests and the apprehensions expressed in several countries, it was decided to have a more intensive dialogue with the United States. Shri Jaswant Singh, then Deputy Chairman, Planning Commission and Mr Strobe Talbott, Deputy Secretary of State have been designated as Representatives to conduct this dialogue.

The talks are being conducted on the basis of the comprehensive proposals that India has put forward on disarmament and non-proliferation matters, its unilateral moratorium on explosive nuclear tests, willingness to discuss converting this moratorium into a de jure obligation, its offer to enter into constructive negotiations on the FMCT and reaffirming its policies on stringent control on export of sensitive technologies. After six rounds of discussions the talks have narrowed down four issues. These are the CTBT, the FMCT, Export Controls and Defence Posture. The US has recently announced a partial lifting of the restrictive measures imposed against India. These relate to EXIM, OPIC, TDA Financing and Military Training. The US has stated that these measures are being lifted in recognition of the progress made in the bilateral dialogue. It is, however, noted that non-basic human needs financing from multilateral financial institutions are still subject to US restrictions. India regards these coercive and restrictive measures as unjustified and counterproductive which should be lifted. The US has also issued a list of Indian Government Organisations, Research

Institutions, PSUs and Private Companies, which will be subject to export restrictions. This step is with clearly punitive intent. India has made it clear to the US that such measures will be regarded as adverse developments in its relations and will not be conducive to the ongoing dialogue.

The Governor General of Canada, Romeo LeBlanc and Mrs LeBlanc, accompanied by Canadian Revenue Minister, Herb Dhaliwal, paid a State visit to India from 26 March to 1 April 1998. Canada reacted very adversely to India's nuclear tests in May 1998, and unilaterally restricted government contact. The Canadian position contained a number of elements which were totally unacceptable to India. Canada also placed restrictions on assistance under CIDA. Subsequently, Canada informed that all ongoing projects would continue to receive funding and that new projects of a basic needs nature could be taken up.

Trade between India and Canada continued to flourish. Last year, Indian exports to Canada registered an increase of nearly 23 per cent . This year, during the period January-July, the Indian exports have reached C$ 536.569 from C$ 424.532 during the same period last year marking a growth of 26.38 per cent. On the other hand. Indian imports from Canada during this period have declined to C$ 182.614 from C$ 287.695 showing a decrease of 36.52 per cent. India's relations with the countries of the Caribbean, Central America and South America have been traditionally warm and friendly. Interaction with the countries of the region is conducted through bilateral consultative mechanisms. In the economic field a concerted effort has been made to diversify and enhance bilateral cooperation. India has trade and economic agreements with seven countries of the region and set up Joint Business Councils with some other countries. In continuation of the FOCUS LAC Programme, exclusive Indian exhibitions have helped the dissemination of information on the opportunities available for mutual beneficial economic interaction. The trade between India and the LAC region in 1997-98 has grown to over US $ 1.3 billion.

Relations with Latin America and Caribbean

In the field of culture, India enjoys considerable goodwill in the LAC region. Some of the countries like Guyana, Suriname and Trinidad and Tobago have a substantial percentage of people of Indian origin and have more than 500 institutions, schools, libraries and streets named after the Indian leaders. India also has been able to establish institutional relations with the regional organisations like the Organisation of American States (OAS), Association of Caribbean States (ACS) and the Andean Community where India has Observer Status. After the nuclear tests on 11 and 13 May 1998, Brazil cancelled the Agreement with India on Cooperation in Peaceful Uses of Nuclear Energy. The OAS General Assembly held in Caracas, 1-3 June 1998 through a resolution condemned Indian and Pakistani nuclear tests and urged them to refrain from further testing, missile deployment and weaponisation. The President of India Shri K.R. Narayanan paid a State visit to Peru from 29 April-3 May 1998. Two bilateral documents:

i) MoU on Cooperation in Space Technology between ISRO of India and its counterpart Peruvian agency CONIDA and

ii) A Work Plan for Cooperation in the field of Agriculture—were signed during the visit. Peru is the first country in Latin America with which India has signed a MoU for cooperation in space.

The President also paid a State visit to Brazil from 3-8 May 1998. An Implementing Arrangement for cooperation in the field of Health and Medicine under the Agreement on Cooperation in Science and Technology was signed. A MoU on Cooperation between Foreign Service Institute of India and the Rio Branco Institute of Brazil was also signed during the visit. A Festival of India was held in Brazil on the occasion of the President's visit. The Minister of State for External Affairs Smt Vasundhara Raje led the Indian delegation to the Ministerial Meeting of the NAM Coordinating Bureau in Cartagena, Colombia 18-20 May 1998. Utilising the opportunity provided at the 53rd Session of the UNGA, Prime Minister had a meeting with the President of Honduras and Minister of State for External Affairs met the Foreign Minister of Uruguay.

India actively participated in the Open Ended Working Group of the UN General Assembly on the question of Equitable Representation and an increase in the membership of the Security Council and other matters related to the Security Council which continued its consideration of a variety of complex issues during the year. After protracted consultations instituted by the President of UN General Assembly, a compromise resolution was arrived at, which stated that the General Assembly would not adopt any decision on the question of expansion of the Security Council without the affirmative vote of at least two thirds of UN membership. The Prime Minister, in his address to the 53rd UNGA on 24 September 1998 called for the Security Council to be made more representative, reflecting the interests of the developing world. He further reiterated that India was qualified, had the ability, and was prepared to accept the responsibilities of permanent membership.

Peace-Keeping in South Asia: Role of International Bodies

United Nations

In keeping with its commitments to the maintenance of international peace and security and at the request of the United Nations, India decided to provide a military contingent for participation in the UN Peace-Keeping Operation in Lebanon—UNIFIL (United Nations Interim Force in Lebanon). With the induction of an Indian infantry battalion in southern Lebanon in November, India has emerged as the second largest troop contributor to UN Peace-Keeping Operation. Indian troops, military observers and civilian police personnel are currently serving in Peace Keeping Operations in Angola (MONUA) and Western Sahara (MINURSO), Kuwait (UNICOM) and Lebanon (UNIFIL), Bosnia and Herzegovina (IPTF), and Haiti (MIPUNOH). The statute of the international criminal court was adopted on 17 July 1998 at Rome. India abstained, along with 20 other countries. The US, China, Russia and Israel voted against the statute. The statute provides for automatic jurisdiction of the international criminal court over genocide and crimes against humanity.

India's fundamental objections to the statute were the provisions of powers to the UN Security Council, inter alia, to bind even those states who are not signatories to the ICC statute; the deliberate exclusion of the use of weapons of mass-destruction, including nuclear weapons, from the list of war crimes and, similarly, the exclusion of terrorism as a crime against humanity. Developments in the regional and global security environment continued to engage serious consideration. A balanced assessment of the trend over recent years led the Government to undertake a limited series of nuclear test explosions and announce that India is a nuclear-weapon possessing state. In the aftermath, India elaborated its nuclear doctrine based on maintaining a minimum credible deterrent and, a commitment to no-first-use of nuclear weapons. This has been set out clearly in Prime Minister's statement at the UNGA in September 1998 and subsequently in Parliament in December 1998.

Diplomatic efforts were undertaken to project India's rationale for decision to the international community. High-level dialogues in this regard have been undertaken with the USA, France, UK and Russian Federation. We have also shared perceptions regularly with the non-nuclear weapon states, in the non-aligned community and elsewhere. We have made clear that India's nuclear capability is purely defensive, does not in any way reflect a threatening, aggressive posture, and will contribute to strengthening stability both in Asia and in the global context. We have also taken initiatives for proposing confidence building measures with countries in neighbourhood, with a view to enhancing trust and expanding the scope for mutually beneficial bilateral relations, and creating a peaceful and stable regional environment. The initiatives have yielded positive results.

India's stand in multilateral disarmament fora reflects the continuity of its long-standing commitment to global nuclear disarmament. India's unilateral declaration of a moratorium on nuclear explosive testing was welcomed as were subsequent statements relating to CTBT. Currently, we are actively engaged in multilateral negotiations in the

CD at Geneva for the conclusion of a Fissile Material Cut Off Treaty. This treaty will prohibit future production of fissile materials for nuclear weapons or other nuclear explosive devices. We have also drawn attention to exemplary record of nonproliferation and the rigour of export control system, indicating readiness to make it even more stringent. There has been appreciation of these clarifications and steps by interlocutors. India also continued its efforts to generate support in the international community for making use of the opportunity created by the end of the Cold War, for reducing the salience of nuclear weapons and moving towards a nuclear weapon free world. A new initiative taken by India in this regard in the UN General Assembly generated wide support.

India was successful in reviving its proposal on a comprehensive international convention against terrorism which had been circulated by it at the 51st UN General Assembly in 1996. A resolution on "Measures to eliminate international terrorism" was adopted by consensus in the sixth committee, deciding that an adhoc committee could consider, on a priority basis, the elaboration of such a comprehensive convention. India participated actively in the discussions on human rights issues in sessions of the UN Commission on Human Rights, the Economic and Social Council and the General Assembly. India called for a constructive, balanced and cooperative approach to human rights issues, emphasizing the universality, indivisibility and inter-relatedness of all rights and inter-dependence of democracy, human rights, development and international cooperation. The 54th Session of the Commission on Human Rights was held in Geneva from 16 March to 24 April 1998, in which India actively participated.

International Labour Organisation

During the International Labour Conference in June 1998, a declaration on Fundamental Principles and Rights at Work was adopted by the International Labour Organisation (ILO). The Indian delegation contributed extensively to the drafting of the declaration, ensuring thereby its promotional character and incorporating safeguards precluding its misuse for trade and protectionist purposes. During the year, India also participated actively in the work of the Asia-Pacific Group of the ILO related to redefining the role of organisation in the new millennium.

UNESCO

Close interaction between India and UNESCO in the fields of education, culture, science and communication has been mutually beneficial and enriching. India actively participated in the two international conferences organised by UNESCO during 1998 - the inter-governmental conference on cultural policies for development held in Stockholm and the world conference on higher education held in Paris. Director General of UNESCO during his visit to India in January 1998 agreed to set up four more UNESCO chairs in Indian universities.

The 12th Summit of Non-Aligned Movement (NAM) was held in Durban, South Africa on 2-3 September 1998. The Indian delegation for the summit was led by the Prime Minister. The Prime Minister underlined that disarmament continued to their corner stone of India's foreign policy and that India had undertaken several initiatives to establish a nuclear-weaponfree and non-violent world order. The summit adopted the final document containing formal position taken by NAM on global issues, analysis of the international situation, economic and social issues. The Durban declaration reiterates the continued relevance and importance of NAM in the post-cold war world and focuses on the concerns of the developing world in a more consolidated manner. References to disarmament, terrorism, UN reforms and UNSC restructuring and expansion, were of considerable significance.

Commonwealth

India, the largest member of the Commonwealth, is represented in all its important controlling bodies of the secretariat and organisations. It is the fourth largest contributor, a major source of expert assistance provided to other commonwealth countries and a major destination for commonwealth trainees. India's High Commissioner to UK, led the Indian delegation which participated in the commonwealth senior officials meeting (CSOM) in London during 9-11 November 1998. CSOM reviewed the developments and progress in implementation of decisions of the 1997 commonwealth heads of governments meeting.

International Law Commissison which was reviewed at the 52nd session of the UNGA resulted in the Commission adopting its first reading a set of draft articles on the Principle of Prevention of Trans-Boundary Harm arising from hazardous activities. The 53rd session of UNGA at its sixth Committee(Legal) considered subject matters such as status of the protocols Additional to the Geneva conventions of 1949 and relating to the protection of artmed conflicts, consideration of effective measures to enhance the protection, security and safety of diplomatic missions and representatives; convention on jurisdictional immunities of states and their property; draft guiding principles for international negotiations; report of the International Law Commission on the work of its 50th session; report of the UN Commission on international trade law; report of the Committee on relations with the host country; establishment of international criminal court; report of the special committee on the charter of the UN and on the strengthening of the role of the organization; and measures to eliminate international terrorism. India participated in the 31st annual session of the UN Commission on international trade law (UNCITRAL) and in the Preparatory Committee negotiations on the establishment of ICC. India hosted the 37th Annual Session of the Asian African Legal Consultative Committee.

Multilateral Economic Relations

The world found itself in a difficult and uncertain economic environment during the year. One country after another experienced a sharp downturn in its stock market and a depreciation of its currency owing to a decline of confidence in the viability of its banks and financial institutions. Although largely protected from similar capital outflows, the Indian economy suffered on account of declining demand for its goods and services in South-East and East Asia, Russia and in recession-struck Japan. But despite the uncertain market conditions, Indian exports sustained their growth in the US and other select developed markets. Driven by globalisation, rapid diffusion of new technologies, and multilateral harmonisation of international economic activity, there are changes continuously taking place in global trade and investment, with both government and business having to respond.

In the light of these parameters, India has pursued promotion of its relations with international multilateral economic organisations and regional, sub-regional and supra-regional economic and trade groupings. India's Dialogue Partnership with ASEAN saw many positive developments this year. The Second Meeting of the ASEAN-India Joint Cooperation Committee (AIJCC) was held at Singapore on 28-29 April 1998. India reaffirmed its solidarity with ASEAN in the wake of the financial crisis plaguing the region. Measures outlined by India in this context included Government-to-Government Credit, Exim Bank credit for trade finance, facilities for counter trade, EXIM Bank credit finance for outward and inward investment to and from South-East Asia, feasibility study and consultancy financing by EXIM Bank for infrastructure projects, guarantees and counter guarantees for trade finance, and enhancement of Indian Technical and Economic Cooperation Programmes for ASEAN countries.

Bibliography

Ashis Nandy, "The Uncolonized Mind: A Post-Colonial View of India and the West" In The Intimate Enemy, Delhi: Oxford University Press, 1983, pp. Ix-xx, 64-113.

Ashutosh Varshney, "Ethnic Conflict and Civic Life", New Haven: Yale University Press, 2002.

Ayesha Jalal, "Democracy and Authoritarianism in South Asia: A Comparative and Historical Perspective", Cambridge University Press, 1995, Chapter 1, pp. 9-28.

____________, Democracy and Authoritarianism in South Asia, Cambridge University Press, 1995. Chapters 4-7.

Chandra, Kanchan, "India as a Patronage Democracy" In Why Ethnic Parties Succeed: Patronage and Ethnic Headcounts in India. (Manuscript) Week Four (February 27): Social Structure Hardgrave and Kochanek, 13-25.

Chandra, Kanchan, "Post-Congress Politics in Uttar Pradesh: The Ethnification of the Party System and its Consequences" in Indian Politics and the 1998 Election: Regionalism, Hindutva and State Politics. New Delhi: Sage Publications, 1999.

Kenneth W. Jones, "Religious Identity and the Indian Census" in N. Gerald Barrier, ed., *The Census in British India*, New Delhi : Manohar, 1981. Pp. 72-101.

Paul Brass, "Language Problems" in The Politics of India Since Independence,Cambridge University Press, Chapter 5, 151-191, 1990.

Robert L. Hardgrave and Stanley A. Kochanek, "India: Government and Politics in a Developing Nation", Forth Worth: Harcourt Brace Jovanovich, 1999.

Samina Ahmad, "Pakistan and the Bomb: Public Opinion and Nuclear Options", Notre Dame: University of Notre Dame Press, 1998, Chapter 3, pp. 47-68.

Scott Sagan, "The Perils of Proliferation in South Asia," Asian Survey, November/December 2001.

Shelby Tucker, "Burma: The Curse of Independence", London: Pluto Press, 2001.

Sumit Ganguly, "Explaining the Kashmir Insurgency – Political Mobilization and Institutional Decay," *International Security* 21: (2) Fall 1996, 76-107.

Index